THE REMINISCENCES OF

Captain Daniel Webb Tomlinson IV
U.S. Naval Reserve (Retired)

INTERVIEWED BY

Barrett Tillman
and
Paul Stillwell

U.S. Naval Institute • Annapolis, Maryland

Copyright © 1995

Preface

This is an exciting oral history because Captain Tomlinson was a true pioneer in the aviation history of the United States. He developed a life-long love of flying when he was a boy, served as a Navy pilot in the 1920s, had a successful career in commercial aviation in the 1930s, and then returned to active duty for service in World War II and afterward. Along the way he blazed a trail with such achievements as the founding of the Navy's first formation acrobatics team, the Three Seahawks; did early work on instrument flying; had an influential role in the development of the Douglas DC-1 and its illustrious successors; and showed the Navy how to run its air transport service like a commercial airline.

Throughout all of this, Tommy Tomlinson was his own man. He flew a personal Curtiss Jenny as a barnstormer when he was in the crew of the battleship <u>Oklahoma</u>. He kept a plane at the Naval Academy in the 1920s when no one else could. He humiliated the Army Air Corps in mock combat. He resigned from the Navy because he wasn't allowed to attend the funeral of a close friend and mentor. He flew in all kinds of weather because he knew when he could take chances and when he couldn't. He refused to kowtow to authority when he was convinced he was right. Remarkably, he survived all of this and lived to tell the stories in this colorful oral memoir done when he was nearly 90 years old.

I am grateful to Barrett Tillman for doing most of the interviewing connected with this oral history. He is an aviation historian and author and certainly well qualified to conduct the questioning. Dr. Richard K. Smith, another historian and author, provided the impetus by recommending Tomlinson for an oral history after meeting him and hearing some of his stories. It was my pleasure to meet Captain Tomlinson and his wife Peg when they were in Annapolis in 1987 for the 70th anniversary of his Naval Academy graduation. He was outfitted in a blue jump suit and wore miniature naval aviator's wings on his lapel. He was knowledgeable and feisty, an enjoyable person to meet. I am grateful to Tomlinson for doing a good deal of followup work in making numerous handwritten additions and corrections to the original transcript to get it to this form. Mrs. Tomlinson has also been most helpful as the project moved along toward completion. Historians and other readers are the beneficiaries of their efforts.

                                                Paul Stillwell
                                                Director, History Division
                                                U.S. Naval Institute
                                                May 1995

CAPTAIN DANIEL WEBB TOMLINSON IV
U.S. NAVAL RESERVE (RETIRED)

Daniel Webb Tomlinson IV, born in Batavia, New York, 28 April 1897, was appointed to the U.S. Naval Academy from his native state in 1914. Graduated and commissioned ensign in June 1917, with the class of 1918, he served with the U.S. Navy until his resignation, in the rank of lieutenant, on 28 February 1929, to enter commercial aviation. Transferred to the U.S. Naval Reserve in the rank of lieutenant in April 1929, he subsequently was promoted to captain, 11 September 1942.

After graduation from the Naval Academy, Tomlinson was assigned duty in the minelayer Dubuque (PG-17), which was engaged in convoy duty in the Atlantic and was also used as an instruction ship at Annapolis. During the summer of 1918, when German U-boats were operating off the Virginia Capes, Tomlinson, who had been placed in charge of the aviation mechanics' school at Hampton Roads, Virginia, made many patrol flights as observer and second pilot in HS-2L and H-12 flying boats. Twice in the course of these patrols he was forced down at sea by engine failure, but in each instance a Navy patrol boat located the flying boat and towed it back to its base.

Tomlinson was ordered to duty aboard the battleship Georgia (BB-15) in July 1919 and served as her assistant chief engineer until she was decommissioned the following year, when he was ordered to Destroyer Engineers' School, San Diego, California. After completion of instruction there, he became chief engineer of the destroyer Breese (DD-122) in which he served for a month before reporting to the Naval Air Station, Pensacola, Florida, for flight training. He was a member of the second class of regular Navy officers to be trained after World War I. Due to previous experience gained on aviation patrol duty during the war, he soloed in three hours and was designated Naval Aviator #2923 on 11 August 1921.

Upon completion of his training at Pensacola, Tomlinson was assigned duty at the Naval Air Station, San Diego, California, where he served for a year. In June 1922, ordered to duty in the battleship Oklahoma (BB-37), he bought his first JN from the Army. During weekends ashore, or whenever he could, he barnstormed the Pacific Northwest. Between 1923 and 1925 he was an instructor in the department of marine engineering and naval construction at the Naval Academy. During this period he completely overhauled his second Jenny in the pattern shop of his department. The interest engendered in the midshipmen in the process of rebuilding this plane resulted in the incorporation of a course in aeronautics in the curriculum of the academy. He also carried on a series of experimental flights. Ordered to sea duty in 1925, he was retained at the academy through the summer to assist in the inauguration of the first course of instruction in aeronautics.

In September 1925, Tomlinson obtained 30 days' leave, at the end of which time he was to report to Commander Aircraft Squadrons Battle Fleet, at San Diego, for duty. He was granted this leave in order to fly his rebuilt Jenny across the continent to San Diego. This type of plane had never been flown across the Continental Divide, and there was considerable doubt it could be done. He accomplished the flight from his home, Batavia, New York, to San Diego, in 7 days, 49 hours, and 45 minutes of elapsed flying time.

From October 1925 to September 1926 he served with Fighting Squadron Six, the Navy squadron that first developed dive bombing. He first was flight officer of this squadron, later was executive officer, and was commanding officer when it was redesignated Fighting Squadron Two. As commanding officer he led the famous Three Seahawks, a Navy aerobatic group that carried off top honors at the National Air Races at Mines Field, California, in 1928. The other two members of the team were Lieutenant Aaron P. Storrs III and Lieutenant William V. Davis, Jr. In addition to the performance by the Three Seahawks, the entire squadron demonstrated tactical maneuvers and group aerobatics, winning for their performance the personal acclaim of Rear Admiral Joseph M. Reeves, then Commander Aircraft Battle Fleet, and Assistant Secretary of the Navy Edward P. Warner.

After the races, Tomlinson once more flew his Jenny across the continent to report for duty with the Test Section, Naval Air Station, Anacostia, D.C. During approximately three months of duty at Anacostia he successfully beached the Navy's largest seaplane, the PN-11, after one engine caught fire during a test flight. He also safely landed an experimental Vought Corsair after its stabilizer had failed in a terminal velocity dive. On 28 February 1929 he resigned from the Navy to enter commercial aviation.

During the period between his resignation and his return to active duty with the U.S. Naval Reserve in 1941, Tomlinson was a recognized figure in commercial aviation. From February to September 1929 he was vice president in charge of operations for Maddux Airlines. When Maddux merged with Transcontinental Air Transport, he became manager of operations for the Western Division of the combined companies. In 1930 TAT merged with Western Air Express, resulting in the organization of Transcontinental and Western Air, Incorporated. For six months Tomlinson became the superintendent of the Western Division of the enlarged organization and had headquarters in Los Angeles. In 1931 he went east as assistant to the president of TWA and was a member of the mechanical committee that helped with the specifications for future transport airplanes. With the cancellation of airmail contracts in 1934 he chose to go back on the line. As a pilot for nearly a year he flew the single-engine night mail across the Alleghenies between Newark, New Jersey, and Columbus, Ohio. In the spring of 1935 he was called by Jack Frye, then president of TWA, to become his assistant at the airline's headquarters in Kansas City, Missouri.

During 1935 and 1936 Tomlinson carried on engineering and flight research for TWA. One of his first assignments was to fly the Douglas DC-1 across the continent nonstop. On this flight he set a new record for transport planes of 11 hours and 5 minutes, making the flight almost exactly ten years after his first transcontinental trip in the old Jenny. This time he reversed the direction, flying from Burbank, California, to Newark, New Jersey. He later established 18 other speed and endurance records with the same DC-1. During 1936 he also carried on stratospheric research that involved more than 30 hours of flying above the 30,000-foot level and cruising for more than five hours at 35,000 feet. Out of these experiments came the plans for the Boeing Stratoliners to fly passengers safely and comfortably above the weather.

On loan from TWA to North American Aviation during the latter part of 1936 and early part of 1937, Tomlinson demonstrated military aircraft to the Army at its experimental and test station at Wright Field, Dayton, Ohio. Among the planes he demonstrated early in 1937 was North American's first twin-engine bomber, prototype of the B-25, and the company's first basic combat trainer, thousands of which were later built for advanced trainer use by the Army, Navy, and flying services of various Allied nations. He also undertook to test for the Curtiss-

Wright Company the first Allison-engine pursuit plane to be flown, the forerunner of the famous P-40. On his third flight the plane caught fire, but Tomlinson stayed with it and successfully landed it rather than bail out and set back the important research program through complete loss of the plane. He also demonstrated the SBC-3 dive bomber to the Navy at Dahlgren, Virginia. After this period of test flying, he returned to piloting passengers for TWA between Kansas City and New York. In June 1939, having completed a year of this airline flying, he became chief engineer for TWA. Early in 1940 he spent several months in Seattle, Washington, taking part in demonstration tests of the new Boeing Stratoliner, which his previous experiments had made possible. In June 1940 he became vice president in charge of engineering for TWA, and at this time was actively engaged in development work of the Lockheed Constellation.

In June 1941 Tomlinson requested orders to active duty from the Bureau of Aeronautics. In the rank of commander, U.S. Naval Reserve, he was assigned duty as commanding officer of the Naval Reserve Aviation Base at Fairfax Airport, Kansas City, Kansas. He had been instrumental in having this base established in 1935 and was active in the reserve aviation squadron based there. That squadron won the Noel Davis Trophy for efficiency in 1936, 1937, and 1938. In 1942 Tomlinson was made commander of the Naval Reserve Aviation Base in Gardner, Kansas, and later that year returned to Fairfax to become chief of staff to Rear Admiral Elliott Buckmaster when the Naval Air Primary Training Command was formally established at Fairfax. After serving in that assignment for a year, Tomlinson reported for duty 27 September 1943 with the Naval Air Transport Service as Commander Air Transport Squadron Pacific. On 31 March 1945 he was designated Commander Naval Air Transport Service, Pacific Wing. For his services in that assignment he was awarded the Legion of Merit with the following citation:

> For exceptionally meritorious conduct in the performance of outstanding services as Commander, Naval Air Transport Service, Pacific Wing from 2 October 1943 to the present time. Through his inspiring leadership, organizing ability, energy, and devotion to duty he organized and operated his Command during a time of constant expansion, developing safe, scheduled air transport operations with increasing efficiency both in safety and utilization of aircraft and personnel. His outstanding services and performance of duty contributed materially to the

success of operations against the enemy in the Pacific theater of operations and was at all times in keeping with the highest traditions of the United States Naval Service.

In August 1945 Captain Tomlinson was ordered to the Twelfth Naval District for demobilization. He left active service in 1946 and then was recalled to active duty in 1948. He served as deputy commander of the Berlin Airlift, then closed his service career with an assignment as deputy commander, Continental Division, Military Air Transport Service. He retired officially on 1 August 1951.

Authorization

The U.S. Naval Institute is hereby authorized to make available to individuals, libraries, and other repositories of its choosing the transcripts of four oral history interviews concerning the life and career of the undersigned. The interviews were recorded on 9, 10, and 11 September 1985, in collaboration with Barrett Tillman for the U.S. Naval Institute, and on 18 September 1987 in collaboration with Paul Stillwell for the U.S. Naval Institute.

The undersigned does hereby release and assign to the U.S. Naval Institute all right, title, restrictions, and interest in the interviews. The copyright in both the oral and transcribed versions shall be the sole property of the U.S. Naval Institute. The tape recordings of the interviews are and will remain the property of the U.S. Naval Institute.

Signed and sealed this 22 day of Nov. 1994.

D. W. Tomlinson
Captain Daniel W. Tomlinson IV, USNR (Ret.)
by Margaret F. Tomlinson P.O.A. for

Interview Number 1 with Captain Daniel W. Tomlinson IV,
U.S. Naval Reserve (Retired)

Place: Captain Tomlinson's home in Silverton, Oregon

Date: Monday, 9 September 1985

Interviewer: Barrett Tillman

Q: We'd like to start by learning something about your family's background and your parents, where they came from and where they settled.

Captain Tomlinson: Henry Tomlinson came over in the mid-1600s and settled in Connecticut. The story in the genealogy book that I have on him is he was run out of England for non-payment of his wine taxes. My great-great grandfather was a sheriff in Vergennes, Vermont, and a farmer during the War of 1812.

Q: My great-grandfather grew up in Vergennes, in that area. About all we know about him is that when he was about 18 years old, he took off on his own and went to Mobile, Alabama, with a letter of introduction to someone. According to family history, he didn't use it. He got himself a job with a produce company, loading watermelons on a barge. Sometime in the 1820s or 1830s he cornered the

Daniel W. Tomlinson #1 - 2

market on resin or something of that sort which was a major business in that area and hit the jackpot.

The next record we have of him, he set himself up as a banker in New York, where he appeared with $50,000 in gold. We don't know the details of his next move. He took over the mortgage of a man by the name of Remson, who had built a beautiful stone house in western New York, near Alexander, an area which was then in its early development. There were still a few Indians around. He established a local bank. He married Susan Everett; we do not know too much about her background, other than that she was from the old Revolutionary family with roots on Long Island.

Soon after that, in the 1830s or 1840s, the New York Central Railroad was organized. He saw the future in that, and he and several others invested heavily in it. Alexander was in the northern foothills of the Alleghenies. Naturally, the railroad came up north along the Hudson River, west up Mohawk Valley, and then jumped a divide into the Genessee River Valley and west to Buffalo. Its route lay about seven or eight miles north of Alexander. He moved his bank to Batavia, New York, where the railroad ran through the center of the town. During the Civil War, due to his connections in Mobile, Alabama, he was accused of being a "Copperhead."* In 1870 the bank building was

---
*"Copperhead" was a nickname for a person in the northern states who sympathized with the South during the Civil War.

being expanded. He climbed up on scaffolding to inspect the work, fell, hit his head, and died of concussion, age 55.

My grandfather was then in the coal and lumber business in Batavia. Being the only son, he became president of the bank, which was owned by him and four sisters. My father was born in '72. He went to Cornell College two years, then went to the bank in Batavia as a teller. He wasn't inclined toward banking; he had the mechanical trend.

My mother was Marion Gould. Her brother, C. A. Gould, at that time was a millionaire. He had the exclusive patent rights on the car coupler that the railroads used--Gould Coupler and Battery Company. He made the batteries used in the early railroad cars. Since he had had trouble with his treasurer, he then got my father out of the bank to be his treasurer and paymaster. My mother died when I was a month old. She was apparently a very energetic woman, because she got on her bicycle in Batavia and rode at least a mile and a half from my father's home to my grandfather's home in East Main Street. When she came back on the bicycle, she walked into the house and dropped dead. What happened was that the exercise broke loose some blood clot, probably as the result of my birth. When it hit her heart, she was gone instantly. My grandfather and grandmother raised me until I was nine years old.

Daniel W. Tomlinson #1 - 4

My grandfather was president of the bank. The bank had loaned Batavia Baker Gun and Forging Company a lot of money--maybe $50,000 or more. Grandfather was worried about the future of this company, so he enticed my father to leave Gould Coupler. C. A. Gould had tried to get him to go to main headquarters in New York with him, but he didn't like New York any more than I did later. He moved to Batavia. At the end of World War I, he paid the loan off, and he and a woman who was secretary-treasurer of the old Baker Gun and Forging Company owned the company.

Q: Obviously he had a large influence on you with your later interest in mechanical things.

Captain Tomlinson: That's right. In 1916, on leave from the Naval Academy, I bought a one-cylinder Indian motorcycle. My father said, "Young man, you had better learn how to take care of the engine and the whole machine. I will show you, and then you will take care of it yourself." Of course, it was only a one-cylinder Indian engine, but the principles of the internal-combustion engine were all there. Later at the Naval Academy, when the time came for me to study internal-combustion engines, I knew more about them than the lieutenant who was trying to instruct. I would take over and explain them.

I obviously inherited my father's mechanical bent.

Daniel W. Tomlinson #1 - 5

It's significant in respect to my development that I was taken to see the first hot-air balloon ascension that came to Batavia. It was one of those early hot-air balloons where they built a big bonfire, and through a conduit finally the bag filled up and took into the air with the balloonist hanging onto a trapeze. When the bag was filled full of hot air and smoke, it would go up maybe 1,000-1,500 feet. When he sensed the time was right, he just cut loose and came down with a parachute. Then the balloon turned over, belched smoke out into the sky, and fell.

Then the next thing that impressed me greatly was the Curtiss exhibition flier who was paid to come and put on a flight from the half-mile track west of town. At that time I was in high school. Before that, I had become enamored of kite flying--anything that went up in the air. There was an older boy who lived across the street. He was really good at building and flying kites, and he taught me how to build all kinds of kites. I built one big enough so that I had to use a clothesline to hold it. I rigged in the line a little trapeze, and I was going to send a little kid, about five years old, up with it. I said, "I'll give you a ride. Here, you sit on this bar." Fortunately, when the kid was only about six or seven feet in the air, my stepmother came out and stopped that monkey business.

When the Curtiss flier was going to make this flight, I just skipped school. I could run the half-mile in those days; I was on the track team. I went to the fairgrounds and was out on the racetrack. The pilot was going to take off in front of the grandstands. He took off toward north. Beyond the stands there were several horse barns off to the west side. There was a definite crosswind from the west. The wind was blanked by the stands, which were high. They had no brakes in those days; he had to have people hold the plane as he ran up the engine. I was there hanging on when he nodded his head and everybody let go. He got off the ground, and when he was just about at the end of the grandstand, he suddenly hit a downdraft and crashed into a fence at the edge of the track. I was the first one to reach the wrecked plane. He had one leg broken, tangled up in the wires. He was smoking a cigar and cursing a blue streak. I decided then, "I'm going to be an aviator!"

The next airplane pilot I saw was Cal Rodgers.* He was related to John Rodgers in the Navy. He flew across the country, and he wanted $500.00 to fly over towns on his route. The Batavia tightwads wouldn't pay the $500.00, but we figured he'd circle close enough so we could see him. They were just finishing the new Episcopal church steeple at that time. My grandfather and uncle took me up in this tower to watch the plane. We could see him coming from

---

*Calbraith P. Rodgers, a civilian, made the first coast-to-coast airplane flight. Flying an open-cockpit biplane, it took him 49 days and 69 stops from Long Island, New York, to Pasadena, California, in 1911. He was a cousin of John Rodgers, who was designated naval aviator number 2.

Buffalo. He was flying 200 or 300 feet over the New York Central tracks, which went right through the center of town. When he came to the west edge of the town, he turned and went around the south side. I watched him.

I'll never forget my very dignified old grandfather; he had his walking stick, which I now have. As the plane went by, he started jabbing the walking stick on the floor and said, "Damn fool! Damn fool!" I have often wished that the old gentleman had lived long enough to see what happened to the grandson at his side. He died in 1917, just before I graduated from the Naval Academy. Naturally, when I went into the Navy, aviation was my goal.

Q: What prompted you to Annapolis, as opposed to West Point?

Captain Tomlinson: I had a great-uncle by marriage, Charles Train, who married my great-aunt Grace.* He became a rear admiral and was in command of the Asiatic Squadron when he died. He visited my grandfather a number of times. There was a lot of talk about Europe and Russia. At the appropriate time, I was taken by my father down to the Brooklyn Navy Yard and taken through some ships to excite my interest.

---

*Charles Jackson Train, Naval Academy class of 1865, married Grace Tomlinson in June 1871. He died on 4 August 1906 while on duty in Chefoo, China. He served as Commander U.S. Asiatic Fleet from March 1905 to his death.

I might as well take the skeleton out of the closet and shake it. I was a little bit of a problem in high school--nothing really vicious, but you could say it was nasty; I had fun anyway. Finally, about 1912 a friend of mine and I were left out of the Christmas exercises for having committed some minor indiscretion. This irritated us no end. My friend was a farm boy. All the farm kids at that time trapped skunks, muskrats, or what have you, and sold the furs. So we put our heads together. They called me Dan in those days. He said, "Dan, I've got a couple of skunks at the farm."

I said, "Let's take the glands out, and we'll fix the Christmas exercise," which is exactly what we did. We operated on the skunks and got the necessary glands out. The school was built back in the 1850s or so, a three-story brick building that used the old-fashioned steam radiators in the big assembly hall where the exercises were going to be held. My pal and I and a couple of others always knew how to get into that high school. We got in there early in the cold morning with these glands, and we rubbed the skunk oil on the radiators before the steam heat came on. Unfortunately, we got some scent on ourselves. There were no Christmas exercises that morning. Unhappily, my father was on the school board, and this embarrassed him no end. So it was decided in the family that the next year, 1913, I'd better be sent elsewhere.

So, true to form, I was sent to a very nice military school at Bordentown, New Jersey. Everything sailed along for a couple of months, but as usual in many of those schools, the kids came from rather wealthy, snooty, stodgy families. They were the petty officers and tried to lord it over the new kids. One of these characters took after me, and I just beat the hell out of him, which wasn't exactly according to military ethics. So my father had to come down to get that straightened out.

My grandfather and family were well connected in western New York and knew the congressman. The first thing I knew, I'd been given a principal appointment for the Naval Academy.

Q: And you hadn't even applied?

Captain Tomlinson: No. So I was shipped out of Bordentown. I have to laugh about this. I was a pretty good rifle shot on the rifle team. The Bordentown Academy paid my expenses to return over a weekend to participate in a team shoot against another school.

I went over to Shadman's preparatory school in Washington. The school was a mile or more away, easy walking distance from my Aunt Grace's home; she was the widow of Admiral Train. Of course, she'd been designated to keep an eye on Daniel. I had no trouble at Shadman's. I decided, "This looks pretty good. I'll go for it."

I took my entrance examinations at the post office in Rochester, New York, in April 1914. I had no trouble at all. I entered the Naval Academy in June of 1914. This is true. After I got in there, I discovered I was being paid $60.00 a month and getting my education. It was kind of rigorous, but I decided, "This is all right." I had no serious trouble at the Naval Academy. I could have probably stood better scholastically than I did, but, again, I was deeply interested in aviation. I spent a lot of time building model airplanes, flying them with rubber bands in the armory. I knew a lot about models, how they flew, basic aerodynamics.

Q: This was well before there was an aviation corps, wasn't it?

Captain Tomlinson: They had an aviation detachment. I don't really know what you would call it. At that time it was across from Annapolis at the old engineering station located on the east side of the Severn River. Then they moved it to Pensacola. It was a small unit; I think there were never more than half a dozen naval aviators at that time.

Daniel W. Tomlinson #1 - 11

In 1915 I went to the West Coast on the youngster cruise as a midshipman and watched Art Smith fly at the San Francisco Exposition.* Art Smith was good; he was my hero. He did loops and spins and everything with his pusher.** I thought, "That's for me."

Then 1916 came along, and Glenn Curtiss set up in Buffalo a school to train people to go to England as instructors.*** No fee--he'd train you, but then you had to go to England as an instructor. I applied, without consulting my family. I was accepted. But to get out of the Naval Academy honorably--I discovered to my horror--I'd have to have my father's permission. Of course, he wouldn't give it. I was broken-hearted, because I didn't care about anything except flying. I stuck it out, hoping that when I graduated I'd be able to get into the aviation branch of the Navy.

In 1917 the war was on, and we were graduated a year ahead of time because there was a shortage of junior officers. I applied for aviation--period! All my class had to go to sea, because we'd studied steam engineering,

---
*The Panama-Pacific International Exposition was held at San Francisco from 20 February through 4 December 1915 and drew an attendance of more than 18 million people. The Panama Canal had first opened for traffic 15 August 1914.
**In the terminology of the era, a "pusher" was an aircraft that had the engines facing aft, pushing the plane. The type with engines facing forward was known as a "tractor." That is, the engines were pulling the plane.
***Glenn H. Curtiss (1878-1930) was the founder of the Curtiss Aeroplane and Motor Company of Hammondsport, New York. He built the first U.S. Navy aircraft, the A-1 Triad, and trained many of the Navy's early aviators.

navigation, regulations, etc. Then to crown the misery of the matter, they assigned people alphabetically. The people in the class starting with A, B, C, and so forth got the battleships, cruisers, and destroyers. When they got down to the T's and V's, we drew what was left--the junk.

Harry Von Hasseln, Guy Duker Townsend, and D. W. Tomlinson were assigned to the USS Dubuque.* It had been a gunboat; then they turned it into a minelayer. It was moored to a dock in New London, Connecticut, when I reported. German submarines were operating off the East Coast. The fleet was anchoring in Long Island Sound. The Navy wanted to put an antisubmarine net across the entrance to the Sound. This became a nightmare. The crew of the Dubuque and other personnel there had to build these nets. They put them on a barge and towed them to the entrance. They lasted about a week. When the kelp would get to them, the nets would disappear. That went on for the summer.

Then the Dubuque was ordered to Annapolis to be used by first classmen for training in spotting, as it was called in those days--observing the point of fall of shot relative to being over or under the target.

---
*Ensign Harry W. von Hasseln, USN; Ensign Guy Duker Townsend, USN; the USS Dubuque (gunboat number 17) was commissioned 3 June 1905. She had a standard displacement of 1,084 tons, was 200 feet long, and 35 feet in the beam. Her top speed was 13 knots. She was fitted out as a mine training ship in 1915.

Q: For gunnery.

Captain Tomlinson: Yes. The _Dubuque_ had some six-pounders; these they could fire in the Chesapeake Bay safely. The ship spent the winter there: October, November, and December. Then we froze in. That was the winter that the Severn River's ice was a foot thick. I put on my skates aboard the ship and stumbled down the gangway. I went skating up the Severn River, right off the Santee Dock in Annapolis.

Ships were needed for convoy duty between New York and Halifax. The ships used were those that could not make the transatlantic round trip without refueling. No way the _Dubuque_ could do that. An icebreaker was sent from Baltimore to get us into the Chesapeake Bay so we could proceed to Norfolk. We were to have either 4- or 5-inch guns installed, two forward and two aft. This gave us all great concern, because the _Dubuque_ wasn't built for that sort of duty. It was a composite ship; the hull was steel, but from about a foot above the waterline down, the skin was oak, copper-sheathed. We could just see the guns tearing loose if they were put on the weak deck.

Anyway, we started down the Chesapeake Bay. It was miserable. The bay was so full of ice, I'll never forget it. I was officer of the deck, and when we were passing Wolf Island Light, we ran into an ice field. There was whooping and hollering down below: "We're flooding." We hit the ice, and it caved in the wooden bow. Fortunately, we were able to control it, because the major break was just in the paint locker, which we were able to seal off. We reached Norfolk at slow speed, and the guns were installed.

The <u>Dubuque</u> returned to New York. I was getting disgusted with the Navy on this convoy duty. My good classmate, Guy Duker Townsend, was the engineer officer. I was assistant navigator. I forget what Harry Von Hasseln was. We started on a convoy. The convoy was supposed to make--let me say 14 knots; that may be a little high. Probably the <u>Dubuque</u> in its prime, when it was first built, might have made 14, but I doubt it.

About that time we lost our regular Navy skipper and inherited a passed-over lieutenant commander. I think he graduated back in the 1890s. He was half-Hawaiian. he was a sundowner if there ever was one, just a miserable SOB.* For anything that displeased him, he'd cuss you out. He made life miserable for all hands.

Generally, we'd sally from New York and start around Cape Cod, then head up north, and night would come on. As we steamed at darkened ship, we would be struggling along and couldn't make the convoy speed. The <u>Dubuque</u> had two

---

*"Sundowner" is a Navy term for an officer who is extremely strict, even sadistic, in enforcing rules--a martinet. It comes from an old regulation that officers and men of a ship in commission had to be back on board by sundown.

small triple-expansion steam engines, two Scotch boilers, and two cigarette-like stacks sticking up high. We would begin to lose the convoy, and the skipper would literally jump up and down. He was screaming down the voice tube to the engine room; that's all we had to communicate with in those days. He would holler down this voice tube; it's a wonder the thing didn't melt.

What he was calling poor Guy Townsend down there was a fright. Guy could pat his firemen on the back, and they'd start shoveling coal into these Scotch boilers. Then, all of a sudden, the stacks would torch. That meant that they were getting too much coal, and the rich gases that weren't burning in the firebox were going up the stack. When they hit the air, they had more oxygen, and WHOOEY!--flames 50 to 100 feet in the air.

Q: Like a volcano.

Captain Tomlinson: Just like a volcano in each stack. That's when that voice tube would practically melt from the skipper's cursing. Poor Guy Townsend down below was doing his best; his situation was hopeless.

This went on for a couple of months, and I was thoroughly disgusted. I won't go into any horrible details, but I saw to it that when we got back into New

York from one of these trips, there were orders for me to report to the naval training station in Hampton Roads for shore duty.

Another thing related to that I could see no answer to. We'd been tipped off that the Cyclops had disappeared.* After the next convoy trip, the Dubuque was to go search for the Cyclops. It was a farce, the Dubuque trying to act as convoy.

Q: The Cyclops was down in the Caribbean, wasn't it?

Captain Tomlinson: Yes. They were going to send this madhouse ship, which was commanded by an SOB skipper, down into the Caribbean. I learned after World War I that when the Dubuque returned from searching without result for the Cyclops, nearly half the crew deserted when she made her first port in the U.S.

My orders to Norfolk were a lucky break. I'll never forget it. I reported to Captain Crose, an old-timer.** He was a fine old gentleman of the prewar Navy. I stood in

---

*The USS Cyclops was a collier that had been put in service as part of the Navy Auxiliary Service in 1910. She was commissioned in the regular Navy in May 1917 and in 1918 assigned to the Naval Overseas Transportation Service. On 4 March 1918 she put to sea from Barbados and disappeared without a trace.
**Captain William M. Crose, USN, commanding officer Naval Training Station, Naval Operating Base, Hampton Roads.

front of his desk, and I was all "finned out."* He said, "Young man, do you know anything about airplanes?" I told him all about my airplane model building and flying them at the Naval Academy.

Oh, boy, did I take that bait.

He said, "I've got a job for you. We've got to set up here a school for aviation quartermasters as mechanics." Apparently at that time they had taken enlisted people into aviation as aviation quartermasters. This was to be the main training school. At that time I was a senior lieutenant.

The school started. The naval air station was across from a big parade ground which was used as a landing field; it was on the shore of Chesapeake Bay. They didn't have too many land planes. That was the air station where I learned to fly--at least the basics.

At that time, in the summer of 1918, the German submarines were operating off the Virginia Capes. I discovered right away that the air station needed aviators to ride as copilots, to act as navigators and observers and gunners on the antisubmarine patrols they were sending out. They had a miscellaneous lot of seaplanes. A couple of these were old prewar Curtiss R's with pontoons, with 200-horsepower V-2 Curtiss engines. Also the HS-2L, which

---

*"Fin out," a term no longer used in the Navy, referred to the practice of standing at rigid attention with one's hands firmly against the seams of his trousers.

Daniel W. Tomlinson #1 - 18

was the single-engine Liberty boat that would fly pretty well.* Then they had one H-12, which was the first twin-engine Liberty boat, flat-bottomed and no balance on the controls.** They had an H-16, which was another experimental job, a twin-engine Liberty boat. Then they had one F-5L, which became an accepted seaplane after World War I.***

These patrols would go out for four or five hours. As a graduate of the Naval Academy, I knew navigation and seamanship, so I became a stopgap copilot. Whenever I could get away from my duties over at the school, I'd go out on patrol flights. It was only natural for the pilots to teach me to fly, and it came naturally for me. They'd start off flying a straight course, then gentle turns, climbs, and glides. Then a couple of them decided, "What if something happens to me? I'd better teach that baboon to land this kite." Mainly in the HS-2Ls, I got instructions in landing and takeoffs.

---
*The HS series comprised the standard Navy flying boat used for coastal patrol during World War I. The HS-2L was the final refinement in the series. It had a wing span of 74 feet and length of 39 feet. Gross weight was 6,432 pounds and maximum speed 82.5 miles per hour at sea level.
**The H-12 and H-16 flying boats were predecessors of the HS series. Each had two engines, compared with one engine in the HS types. The H-16 had a wing span of 95 feet, length of 46 feet, gross weight of 10,900 pounds, and maximum speed of 95 miles per hour at sea level.
***The F-5L flying boat, built by Curtiss, was a refinement of the earlier H-boats. The two-engine F-5L had a wing span of 104 feet, length of 49 feet, and maximum speed of 90 miles per hour at sea level.

Daniel W. Tomlinson #1 - 19

Q: Who were some of the pilots who instructed you?

Captain Tomlinson: Dick Depew was the operations officer. One who later became a Golden Eagle and was a director of TWA was Roland Palmedo.* Also Luis Baron, who was head of the experimental pier.

Q: I was going through a roster of the class of 1918 and was surprised at the number of future aviators. I see Forrest Sherman, who was number two in the class, and both Tommy and Clifton Sprague from the CVEs.**

Captain Tomlinson: Tommy and Clifton Sprague went through Pensacola with me in 1920, when I finally received formal training. We had the same instructor.

Q: What about Miles Browning? Was he there at that time?

Captain Tomlinson: No. Thank God, I had no contact with Miles Browning.***

---

*Ensign G. G. Depew, USNRF; Ensign Roland Palmedo, USNRF. TWA--Trans World Airlines.
**Forrest P. Sherman eventually reached the rank of four-star admiral and served as Chief of Naval Operations from 1949 until his death in 1951. Thomas L. Sprague and Clifton A. F. Sprague were both flag officers in World War II and commanded escort carrier (CVE) divisions.
***Miles R. Browning was a brilliant but often difficult officer who reached the rank of captain in World War II and served as chief of staff to Admiral William F. Halsey Jr. Because of his demanding, sometimes erratic behavior he was not selected for flag rank.

Q: I understand he was an irascible character.

Captain Tomlinson: Very.

Q: Did you have much dealing with Jocko Clark?*

Captain Tomlinson: No. Jocko went through Pensacola later, I think, and we were never together on duty.

Q: You did very well at Annapolis--39th out of a class of 199. That's why it surprised me when you talked about assigning graduates on the basis of the alphabet instead of their qualifications.

Captain Tomlinson: Apparently they paid no attention whatever to individual preferences. It was a rather stupid policy.

Q: After a year or so of experience as a line officer, how did you regard Annapolis's preparation for fleet service? Was it good, bad, or indifferent?

---

*Joseph J. Clark was a carrier commanding officer and carrier task group commander during World War II. As a vice admiral, he served as Commander Seventh Fleet during the Korean War.

Daniel W. Tomlinson #1 - 21

Captain Tomlinson: It was a good background for anybody who wanted to get into aviation. I never took any advanced courses at MIT or anything of that kind, but with books I understood a lot of it right from the start.* Of course, later on, when I was chief engineer and vice president of TWA, I could talk to these people.

Q: How would you regard the leadership aspects of Annapolis training?

Captain Tomlinson: I never gave it much thought. I didn't stand very high in that, because I didn't take complacently to the hazing business. I laughed at some of that stuff. Unless you stood in with the upper classmen, they were the ones who largely marked you. I passed, I think. I was never concerned. I never even bothered to look at my fitness reports in Washington.

Q: Obviously you took to flying training very well. Do you remember how many hours you had when you soloed?

Captain Tomlinson: I took six hours of instruction. In my flying as a copilot, I put in at least 60-70 hours on patrol flights.

---
*MIT--Massachusetts Institute of Technology.

Daniel W. Tomlinson #1 - 22

To give you an idea of how anxious I was to fly, one day I saw an obviously fresh-caught new ensign reporting aboard at Norfolk Naval Air Station. He had nice, bright gold lace and a new uniform. I collared him and said, "You're just reporting on board?"

"Yes, yes."

I said, "Would you like to fly an HS-2L?"

He said, "Sure, I would."

"There's one down on the beach ready to fly. I know Dick Depew, and I think I can fix us up." So I did. I introduced him to Dick after he had already checked in and was attached to the station.

"Sure, you can take the HS-2L. Go down to the beach and take it." Everything was very easy in those days--no flight plans or anything of that sort. So we went down, and the plane captain was there. I knew how to start the engine. I taxied out. I can't even remember this pilot's name. He said, "You can fly one of these things. You fly it."

So I got over on the left-hand side and started the engine. I taxied out under the old archway that was left from the exposition; it's gone now.* I've got pictures of it. I took it off easily, made a big circle, flew

---
*The Hampton Roads area was the site of the Jamestown Exposition, which lasted from May through December 1907 and commemorated the 300th anniversary of the establishment of the successful Jamestown colony in 1607. The exposition included a large naval review.

around over Chesapeake Bay, came down, and made a pretty decent landing. Then the new naval aviator moved over to the left side, took it up, flew it around, and made two or three landings. Then we taxied back through the arch. When we got on the beach, I thought he was acting kind of funny. I said, "How much time you got in these planes?"

He answered, "Oh, I was never in one before." So I sort of considered that my first solo.

I didn't get to Pensacola until October of 1920. I was on board the old battleship Georgia.* We were tied up at Mare Island, waiting to go out of commission in the winter of 1919.** It was along in November-December of 1919 when a call came out for volunteers for aviation, which F. B. Connell, A. S. Marley, a classmate, and I applied for.*** F. B. Connell got it; Marley and I didn't. We put the Georgia out of commission in the spring of 1920, and I went to San Diego to take a course in destroyer engineering. I wound up as engineer officer on the USS Breese, an old four-stacker of World War I.

In the fall of 1920 another call came in for volunteers for aviation, and I put in. The executive officer of the destroyer, Lieutenant Twining, class of

---
*The USS Georgia (BB-15) had been commissioned in 1906. As a pre-dreadnought type battleship, she was essentially obsolete following World War I and was decommissioned on 15 July 1920.
**Mare Island Navy Yard, Vallejo, California.
***Lieutenant Francis B. Connell, USN; Lieutenant Albert S. Marley, Jr., USN.

1916, and I got it.* It was required that we take a preliminary physical examination in San Diego, and, if passed, proceed to Pensacola for a further physical examination and training. So Twining and I got out a Navy directory to locate a doctor to examine us. There was one close aboard on a sub tender in the harbor. We called away the dory to take us to the tender. The doctor looked at my orders and said, "You want to get into aviation? Are you crazy?" He had our orders, and he grabbed me first. He put a stethoscope on me and listened. I knew from the time I was at the Naval Academy--because they made a note of it--I had what is called a regular irregularity, which the doctors said was no problem. This medic said, "Huh. You're out." Just like that.

I looked at Twining, who was standing close. We could tell that this old so-and-so wasn't going to do us any good. So before he could make a move, we walked over to his desk, picked up our orders, and ran for the dory. We got off of that ship fast!

We went back and checked the directory again and found out that down in the lower bay there was another mother ship with a lieutenant (j.g.) doctor. We could tell from his number that he was fresh-caught. So away we went in the dory again. He started on me. I told him, "I know this irregularity exists, and that there's never been any

_____
*Lieutenant Robert B. Twining, USN.

Daniel W. Tomlinson #1 - 25

question raised about it."

He said, "Oh, yes, it's all right." So we got cleared.

Now, I've still got a hurdle to get over. I knew that with my right eye I could see only 17/20, and you were supposed to see 20/20 each eye. But I was determined to make a stab at it. So we went on to Pensacola, and my knees were shaking; I was scared. We went into the big examining room, and the door to the head was across the room from where I was. Alongside the door to the head was the eye chart. Tomlinson developed a very weak bladder. By the time I'd gone to the head four or five times, I had the chart memorized. That was the only way I got into naval aviation. I proved that I could fly. Later I used to laugh at some medics. I would say, "Look, big boy, there are a lot of people out there pushing daisies because what they saw didn't mean anything to them. It's not how much you see; it's how much what you do see means to you." In later years my vision acuity was never questioned. On annual medical exam reports, on the aviation part would be the notation "waived."

Q: What you know about it.

Captain Tomlinson: Yes. Anyway, I never had any further trouble after that.

Daniel W. Tomlinson #1 - 26

This is interesting too. Tommy Sprague, Ziggy Sprague, Twining, and I were assigned to Doc Cook, who was a bow-legged Georgia cracker, an ensign who was reputed to be the best instructor at Pensacola.* He would take each student out for an indoctrination flight. I can't say positively, but I think I was probably the only one in the class who had even been off the ground in an airplane. Doc Cook took me off, and we got squared away at about 1,000 feet. He shook the controls, the signal for me to fly. Pretty soon he pointed down, so I throttled back and landed on Pensacola Bay, no problem at all. Then he pointed up, and I took off. Doc indicated by hand signals that I circle around and land in front of the N-9 beach.** Then he had me taxi in, which I did. After we got out, we walked back toward the office. He didn't say anything. Then he stopped before we got to the office, and he said, "Where did you learn to fly?"

I gave him a very brief rundown of my experience.

He said, "I could probably pass you for solo, but I don't think it would be the thing to do."

I looked him in the eye and said, "Doc, you're 100% right. I want you to teach me how to control that airplane

---
*Ensign Mark R. Cook, USNRF.
**The Curtiss N-9 was the standard Navy primary and advanced seaplane trainer of World War I. It had a wing span of 53 feet, length of 31 feet. gross weight of 2,765 pounds, and maximum speed of 80 miles per hour. The N-9 remained in service until 1926.

in any conceivable position that it can get into in the air." He did not live to know how well he taught me.

Q: The training curriculum had evolved from World War I to 1919, and the fundamentals of flying obviously haven't changed. How much do you think had been learned, say, from the start of World War I up to the point you started flight instruction?

Captain Tomlinson: The very early airplanes obviously were extremely critical with respect to the safety factor, strength, and controllability in marginal positions or in spins. With the coming of the World War I airplanes, there was a major step forward from the old bamboo struts and that kind of construction. You now had an airplane with better control, improved strength factors, controllability in unusual positions, and inherent stability.

Q: The fundamentals had been absorbed then.

Captain Tomlinson: The basics of flight remained the same, but the capabilities had improved.

Q: Do you think flight instruction had improved comparably during that time?

Captain Tomlinson: I wouldn't know, because I had no previous background or experience in the very early airplanes.

Q: You were designated a naval aviator in August of 1921, one of the first 3,000 naval aviators--number 2,923.

Captain Tomlinson: Yes.

Q: So that obviously established a baseline for people you dealt with throughout your career.

Captain Tomlinson: Another thing took place. As a result of this extra instruction from Doc Cook, and my determination to know all about controllability and technique of flying, at noon hours, instead of going to the regular mess hall, I arranged so I could go down to the beach. I'd get a quart of milk, and that would be my lunch. I'd get an N-9 that had a good motor in it, with power, and I'd take it up to the stunt field area and twist the plane every way I could think of. As a result, before I got my wings, outside spins didn't mean anything to me. I'd get up a couple of thousand feet and lay the plane over on its back, do an inverted spiral down to about 500 feet, roll it right side up, and land. This kind of flying didn't endear me to the higher-ups. I had approximately 30 hours of acrobatics that none of the other people had. They simply did what was required of them; that was all.

Q: How many pilots were in your class?

Captain Tomlinson: About 40. I've forgotten. I've got a picture of them.

Q: I was wondering what the completion rate would have been.

Captain Tomlinson: We only lost four or five of the original group; a few just couldn't handle it. I was very sorry Mouche Twining, with whom I roomed in Pensacola, failed. I don't know why. Some people just can't; they become aerial menaces.

Q: Were there very many who discovered flying wasn't what they thought it would be and they changed their minds? Or was it just failure to make the grade?

Captain Tomlinson: That voluntarily quit?

Q: Yes.

Captain Tomlinson: This is not positive, but I think there

were a few who did. Of course, one of the things that annoyed me, particularly in the past--it's changed now--but in my early years after I became a naval aviator, there were too many who only did the flying that was required and no more. I knew that these aviators flew, but they were scared all the time they were up there. Unhappily, as time went on, some of the senior officers in the vital commands were in that position. Navy policy brought top people in, who after leaving Pensacola, never flew or earned their flight pay except when there was a safety pilot with them. That didn't sit well with me.

Q: I've heard numerous aviators comment on the differences between, say, Mitscher and men such as Halsey and King, those people who were put through Pensacola in the mid-Thirties simply because their rank was needed in aviation assignments.*

Captain Tomlinson: That's right. Of course, a lot of the younger ones in my time chose aviation, not only because they loved to fly, as I did, but because they felt the

---

*Vice Marc A. Mitscher, USN, commander of the fast carrier task force in the Pacific in World War II, graduated from the Naval Academy in 1910 and qualified as a naval aviator in 1916. Admiral Ernest J. King, USN, World War II Chief of Naval Operations, graduated from the Naval Academy in 1901 and qualified as an aviator in 1927. Admiral William F. Halsey, Commander Third Fleet in World War II, graduated in 1904 and qualified as an aviator in 1935.

Daniel W. Tomlinson #1 - 31

aviation branch offered better possibilities of promotion and better duty and increased pay.

Q: Career enhancement.

Captain Tomlinson: Yes.

Q: Were there any of the pilots in your class who seemed to enjoy flying as much as you did?

Captain Tomlinson: Yes, George Cuddihy was one, for sure.* There may have been others.

Q: So you would have to wait until you got out into a fleet squadron before you could really enjoy it.

Captain Tomlinson: At Pensacola I learned this too. For instance, it was taboo in those days to fly into a cloud. Of course, any acrobatics below 1,500 feet, that was a court-martial offense, practically. It occurred to me at Pensacola that the future for aviation was very limited if you couldn't fly through a cloud. I've never been able to find anyone else who was as interested in flying through clouds and weather as I was. When I bought my first

---

*Lieutenant George T. Cuddihy, USN, who was also a Naval Academy classmate of Tomlinson. He was later killed in an airplane crash in 1929 at Naval Air Station Anacostia.

airplane, after I was kicked out of naval aviation, I learned how to fly through clouds. It was very tricky and dangerous, but I could fly up through as much as 5,000 feet to get to the top. Always, when confronted by weather, my goal was to get "on top" or at least reach an altitude well above any nearby mountain peaks.

Q: Sure, where you can see what you're doing.

Captain Tomlinson: I did that before the gyro instruments came along. Then, in 1925, a friend of mine got me one of the first needle-ball gyro instruments that I could install in the Jenny.* I immediately taught myself to use it. I got the instructions, read them, fixed myself up a hood, and practiced using it. I think that I was the first naval aviator to really teach himself to fly instruments. I never knew of any others who even attempted to use the so-called needle-ball bank.

Q: Was this while you were out at San Diego?

Captain Tomlinson: Yes. I flew my first JN from Mexico to Canada in April 1923 and my second JN from Annapolis to San

---

*Jenny was the nickname drawn from the Navy designation JN for a Curtiss-built plane. Following World War I many were sold as surplus to private owners and were widely used for barnstorming. The JN-4H model of the Jenny had wingspan of 44 feet, length of 27 feet, gross weight of 2,017 pounds, and maximum speed of 93 miles per hour.

Diego in September 1925. I kept it in VF-2B engineering hangar until September 1928.* I could fly it at any time in any weather when off duty.

Q: I never knew the full story about landing in Coronado.

Captain Tomlinson: When I reported to duty at San Diego, George Murray was the executive officer.** He said, "I'd like to see your log book." So I showed him my log book. He immediately opened it up, and the yeoman who took care of these log books had entered my extra flying that I'd done as stunts. This was about 30 hours. He looked at me and said, "You're a stunt boy? We'll have to watch you."

Q: For Pete's sake.

Captain Tomlinson: Right off the bat, my rank entitled me to be operations officer at the station. Murray put me under a reserve who got out later on. I was at the bottom of his list. I was "that dangerous stunt pilot." Well, that burned me up. I said to myself, "All right, since I'm a stunt pilot, I'll show them."

---

*VF-2B was the abbreviation for Fighting Squadron Two, in which Tomlinson served in the late 1920s.
**Lieutenant Commander George D. Murray, USN. During World War II Murray was commanding officer of the carrier Enterprise (CV-6) and later promoted to flag rank.

At that time in the Navy, to spin an HS-2L was considered absolutely deadly. Take the twin-engine flying boats; the old F-5Ls were pretty comfortable. "Oh, don't stall. Oh, no. You must never stall. Don't get near a stall." Hell, I took a couple of HS-2Ls out. I took them up there, and I did the falling leaf. I never spun an F-5L. I reneged on that. But I'd stall it and do a halfway falling leaf with it, lumbering around, and bring it out.

I did something that a lot of other pilots didn't bother with. Any new airplane that I flew, I spent quite a little time flying it right on the edge of a stall, making all kinds of turns. Later on, when we went into retractable gear and flaps, I'd fly it under various configurations, so I knew exactly what that airplane would do. In an emergency, should I have to fly or land at minimum speed, it was no problem.

Q: Low-speed controllability.

Captain Tomlinson: Yes. Controllability under marginal conditions, which, if you're familiar with them, you can cope with them. Otherwise, that's what killed a lot of pilots. Pilots would get into these unusual marginal conditions, which they had never experienced or trained themselves to handle. They would do the wrong thing and not recover. My flying didn't endear me to many around North Island, particularly the people up in the fleet detachment, which was separate from the air station.

I wanted to learn to fly land planes. They had a couple of 150-horsepower Hispano Jennies at the air station, so I contacted a pilot who could fly them.* He took me around the island one afternoon. I made a landing, no problem. He said, "Tomorrow morning you take this plane and spend a couple of hours flying around. Get used to it."

So the next morning I took off. I didn't have to go just around the island this time. He said I could take a couple of hours. So I went out a little farther, circled around over Coronado, and looked down at my house.** I was up about 1,500 feet. I looked around and thought, "There's my house down there." All of a sudden, the motor quit. I was scared fartless. The bay and the ocean were in sight. If you've got wheels under you, it is different. There was Olive Avenue in Coronado right below me. At least I could get the plane on the ground on Olive Avenue, and I did. I had to dive under some telephone wires. The street was a bit too narrow and took off each upper wing

---
*The power plant in the JN was a Wright-Hispano engine.
**The naval air station was (and still is) on North Island, Coronado, California.

overhang on the trees. When I came to an intersection, there came a milk truck. Fortunately, there weren't any wires across this intersection. I was going pretty fast, really charging down Olive Avenue. I just hopped over the milk truck and landed on the other side. I had no brakes. I made a perfectly good landing, but I couldn't control the plane directionally, and the plane ground-looped over the curb between trees. The airplane wasn't too badly damaged. Actually, the station repaired it, and it was flying in about a week or ten days later.

The stuff hit the fan after that: "That crazy Tomlinson landing on Olive Avenue in Coronado." I forget the name of the captain who was in command of the air station. He said, "Young man, you've created an awful uproar over there. I'm going to have to put you under hack for five days." There was no question about the engine quitting, because what had happened was a common fault with this model Hispano. On the left bank, there was an air pump which was operated by one of the valve cams. There was a leather washer in the air pump. When that washer would dry up, the pump failed. You had to have air pressure on the gas tank to force the gas up to the carburetor, which was between the V in this Hispano motor. No question--the motor quit on me.

I went under hack for five days. A couple of weeks later, orders came from Washington to try me by general court-martial for failing to maintain altitude in accordance with Navy regulations. I had to laugh. As my counsel I got a smart sea lawyer. He also was one of the famous drunks at that time but sharp as a whip when he was sober. We had no trouble convincing the court that even Jesus Christ couldn't make it; this motor quit. He might have been able to walk on water, but I doubt if even He could fly without power. So I was acquitted. That took care of that, and I went back to duty.

By October I could fly pretty well. I could fly anything available. Art Gavin was assembly and repair at the air station, and he used me to test new airplanes that he'd assembled.* He'd put one on the field, call me to fly it or check it for stability, controllability, and balance in order to see that it was okay. I took out a new VE-7 fighter.** It was a nice-flying airplane and handled beautifully, very much like an S.E.5.***

Q: Built by Vought.

---
*Lieutenant Arthur Gavin, USN.
**The VE-7, built by the Lewis and Vought Corporation, was one of the Navy's earliest carrier-based fighter planes. It had a wing span of 34 feet, length of 25 feet, gross weight of 2,100 pounds, and maximum speed of 117 miles per hour at sea level.
***The S.E.5 was a British-built fighter acquired by the U.S. Navy in France during World War I. It had a wing span of 27 feet, length of 21 feet, gross weight of 2,058 pounds, and maximum speed of 123 miles per hour at sea level.

Daniel W. Tomlinson #1 - 38

Captain Tomlinson: Yes. I was flying around in this plane, and I'd put it through acrobatics--the loops and rolls--to make sure the wires and everything were all tight. I looked to my left, and there was a line formation. There were four Voughts similar to the one I was flying; they were from a fleet air squadron. I'd never seen a line-abreast formation before, so I flew closer to watch. I wanted to see what they'd do next, because at Pensacola all we'd ever flown was the old V formation.

I was off to the right of the leader and back, to give me a good vision of the formation. I thought, "Okay, they're over there; I'm over here. I can watch this maneuver." I saw the leader zoom a little. I recognized that as a signal, and I noticed the wingmen on the left side started to drop back. All number two had to do was drop back a little bit, and he was in position. Then number three had to drop back and go clear over on the right side of the leader.

Q: To form an echelon.

Captain Tomlinson: To form a V. Apparently that was the signal to go back to V. I wasn't close to the formation. I was off on the right side; to this day I don't know exactly how far. But I was accused of attempting to join the formation. I was well away, witnesses said. I don't know for sure, but I felt I was a safe distance away. I saw the pilot who was flying in number-three position move over. He went right through the slipstream of pilot number two. I saw him wobble and drop back. Then he was still moving to the right on the same level at which the leader was flying. He hit the leader's slipstream, and I saw him wobble again. Then I lost sight of him.

The next thing I knew, I had no tail and my left wing was gone. He apparently swung wide over there, because about five feet of his left lower wing broke my fuselage off in back of the cockpit. His propeller just chewed off both upper and lower left wings. Later I found witnesses from North Island; a man on Point Loma; another by Dutch Flats, where they had flying fields; and another in San Diego. I had four witnesses who saw the whole thing. They testified that I was flying along by myself.

I wasn't out completely. I realized it was a helpless situation. We didn't have parachutes in those days. I took the seat cushion out from under my seat and held it in front of my face. That's the last thing I remember. When the place crashed, the thing that saved me--and I've got a picture of it--was that upper and lower right wings were still firmly attached to the stub of the fuselage, including the cockpit and engine section. The plane went into auto-rotation and fell like a spinning leaf, much slower than it would have in a dive or a vertical sideslip.

Q: A vertical descent.

Captain Tomlinson: Practically a vertical descent but quite flat, auto-rotating due to the balance of the wreckage with the right wings firmly attached. There was an empty gas tank under my seat. The plane hit the filled-in ground out in front of the Marine barracks. The motor was four feet in the soft fill.

This other pilot's plane spiralled. He came out of the spiral, leveled off partially, and hit the ground at an angle of about 15 degrees. Unhappily, his head snapped forward when he hit. The control stick hit him in the forehead and killed him.

Q: Otherwise he would have survived?

Captain Tomlinson: He should have, except for the control stick hitting his forehead. I've got a picture of it. All his controls were functional, even though his left lower aileron was damaged due to the wing tip striking my fuselage.

That really touched things off. I was unconscious for

four or five days. Then a court of inquiry was held at the naval hospital a few days after I regained consciousness-- before I had any opportunity to locate witnesses. They alleged I was attempting to join the formation and was an overtaking airplane and was responsible for the accident. The next thing I knew, here came orders from Washington again. They were not from a local command but from the Navy Department. They charged me with manslaughter and unlawfully trying to join this formation by being an overtaking aircraft.

Another strange thing was that there were four planes in the formation, and none of the other three people saw the collision.

I think the trial was in January, as soon as I was out of the hospital. My family, of course, was scared stiff, and so was I. I got in touch with the son of my great-uncle, Rear Admiral Train.* By that time his son, Russell Train, was a captain in the Navy, on duty in the Navy Department. He recommended as my counsel a commander who was on duty at San Diego at that time. He had been on the Adjutant General's legal staff in Washington.

By that time, I was able to get around and pass the word. I needed witnesses who saw the actual collision. Today I can't tell you just how I made contact with these

---

*Captain Charles Russell Train, USN.

witnesses who saw the accident.

Q: The four witnesses.

Captain Tomlinson: There were four. Anybody with any sense, just looking at the pictures of the wreckage, should have been able to see that to accuse me of being an overtaking plane was absurd. I was acquitted.

I might as well put this in now. Five or six years later, at a cocktail party in San Diego, one of the officers who was a member of the court came up to me. He said, "I want to tell you something. You know, except for one vote, you would have received a full and honorable acquittal," which apparently takes a unanimous vote. It was the senior medical officer on the court-martial; he at that time was a full commander. He was the one who tried to turn me down medically in San Diego in 1920, and he still hated aviators!

I was restored to duty after the acquittal. The air station set up a school for land planes. Most of the students were lieutenants and lieutenant commanders; there might have been one or two commanders. There were about three or four instructors. They were a wonderful group, and practically all of them made rear admiral during World War II. Because of experience, I was selected to be the one who led the cross-country flights in addition to

Daniel W. Tomlinson #1 - 43

regular land-plane instruction. We'd go from North Island to Los Angeles or wherever, and I'd pick out the fields to land in. I thought everything was going fine, January through June.

Then came orders from the Navy Department, revoking my designation as a naval aviator and ordering me to duty aboard the battleship Oklahoma.* They couldn't convict me by general court-martial, so they were going to punish me one way or another. Then on top of that I heard, "He's too dangerous to be allowed to fly naval aircraft." This never came through in writing, but I was tipped off it was the talk in Washington.

I said, "That added insult to injury."

I joined the Oklahoma. Very soon after, we took off on the summer cruise and went to San Francisco, Seattle, and through Puget Sound. In October we got back from that summer cruise to our home port at San Pedro. As soon as we returned, I borrowed $250.00 from Annapolis Banking and Trust Company--bless them--and bought a Curtiss Jenny from the Army Air Corps at Rockwell Field, North Island.**

---
*The USS Oklahoma (BB-37) was commissioned 2 May 1916. She had a standard displacement of 27,500 tons, was 583 feet long, and 95 feet in the beam. Her top speed was 20.5 knots. Her main battery comprised ten 14-inch guns. She later capsized at her berth during the Japanese attack on Pearl Harbor in December 1941.
**Throughout this oral history, Captain Tomlinson frequently uses the term "Army Air Corps." From 4 June 1920 through 2 July 1926 it was known officially as the U.S. Army Air Service; from 2 July 1926 through 20 June 1941 it was the U.S. Army Air Corps.

Daniel W. Tomlinson #1 - 44

I was determined to fly and prove certain senior officers were not infallible. I had two very good friends: George Cuddihy and Lambert Hewitt.* Lambert Hewitt was chief pilot at Pensacola when I was there. I knew about the sale of these Jennies, so I sent a check for $250.00. They bought the JN and assembled it for me. I had met Earl Daugherty, who was the number-one pilot around Los Angeles and Long Beach. He learned to fly in 1911--an early bird-- and he had a field at Long Beach. Earl was a great character, wonderful pilot, and a lot of fun. I arranged with Earl to use his field. He said, "Sure, bring your airplane up here. Tie it down beyond the hangar and make yourself at home."

When I got word from George Cuddihy that my Jenny awaited me, I got away from the Oklahoma on a Friday night and got down to North Island the next morning. They had my JN all set up for me to fly. I flew it around the island. It was a used JN, and that's where I pulled a boner. I should have gone into debt for $400.00 and gotten a brand-new one out of the original crate. However, this JN was perfectly flyable, and the engine was all right. That was something to start with, anyway. After all in those days $250.00 was a piece of dough in my situation.

So I took off for Long Beach. I thought I was sitting

---

*In 1920 Lieutenant (junior grade) Lambert Hewitt, USNRF, was stationed at Pensacola, later left the service.

on top of the world. I headed for Earl Daugherty's field on Saturday afternoon. I was just having a ball and heading for La Jolla. I didn't waste any time. I was flying offshore past Del Mar. Then I was off Encinitas, about a mile offshore. I was flying at about 1,000 feet. Suddenly the engine quit cold--no warning.

Q: No warning at all?

Captain Tomlinson: Just like that. I looked over toward the beach. What was I going to do with this airplane of mine? I'd heard stories about landing on a beach. It was the only chance I had. It was low tide. I didn't want to land up in the sand; I'd nose up if I did that. You've got to put your wheels down on the wet sand. So I came in and made a perfectly good landing there. As the plane slowed down, I kicked the rudder and just eased her up on the sand above the high-water line. People came running and helped me pull the plane up onto the beach.

Well, there I was. I didn't know beans about an OX-5 engine.* Fortunately, I had a friend by the name of McDaniel, a wonderful old Navy chief. So I scurried around and contacted him by phone that evening. He said, "I'll be out tomorrow morning. I'll fix you up."

---

*The 90-horsepower Curtiss OX-5 engine was used in some models of the Jenny.

Sure enough, here came McDaniel with his little old four-door rat trap. At that time everybody was in church. he said, "Tommy, how did it quit?"

I said, "Mac, it just quit, like I'd cut the switch." So he got up on the engine and yanked the cover off the breaker points of the magneto. Then he removed the magneto and took it apart. The breaker spring had broken.

"Got to find a watchmaker," he said. We finally got one out of church.

Q: A Sunday morning.

Captain Tomlinson: Sunday morning, we got this character out of church. He was a little bit annoyed. Old Mac took the little platinum point out of the broken spring, took a watch spring this fellow had, cut it off to the right length, put in the platinum point, then put the magneto back in. The OX-5 ran fine.

I had to be back for quarters aboard the <u>Oklahoma</u> the next morning. I needed to reach Long Beach before midnight. The tide was not clear out, but I looked at it. By the time the plane was ready to fly, it was getting toward noon. I thought I'd try it. Stupid. I <u>learned</u>. You learn a lot of things fast at times! I was just about ready to take off, and here came an extra high wave that caught my wing tip. The JNs had wing skids that hung down about 18 inches. I was about to take off. I closed the throttle right away. Then I saw the next wave coming. So I gave the OX-5 full throttle and put on full right rudder. The plane turned toward the beach, tail up above the oncoming wave. As the plane neared the high-water mark, I eased back on the throttle and pulled back on the stick to get the tail down.

When the tail came down, it broke the tail skeg off. Old McDaniel was still standing on the beach, bless his heart. He said, "Oh, we'll fix that." We got hold of someone who had the needed tools: a saw, drill, and a few other items. We found an oak fence post that looked about right. It took until about 4:00 or 5:00 o'clock to make a new tail skeg and install it. By that time, the tide was going out. I wasn't going to attempt any more takeoffs at high tide. It was dusk before I figured the tide was out far enough so that I could get off safely. I finally got off about 1900.

The engine purred, and the flight up the coast to Long Beach was no problem. I'd done some night flying in land planes, but I had never landed a land plane at night. I knew Earl Daugherty was experienced, and he told me how to do it. His trick was to put three oil lanterns in a line on the field, 200 feet apart. That's all you needed. You lined those lights up and came in and touched down just as you passed the first one. I had been around Earl's field, as I had spent several Sundays out there with him. He would come out and put out the lanterns if he heard a plane circling the field at low altitude.

When I arrived, the night was blacker than the inside of a cow. No lights in the airplane; I didn't have a flashlight--nothing. I arrived over Long Beach at about 3,000 feet, and Earl's field was north on American Avenue. I knew about where to go, but suddenly the engine RPM dropped from about 1,250 to 1,100 RPM. (I found out later that the problem was a strainer in the bottom of the gas tank that had corroded and partially blocked the gas supply to the carburetor.) At least I had 3,000 feet to maneuver. What in the hell was I going to do? I thought, "Here's the end of Tomlinson's venture." I could have made Earl's field, but with 1,100 RPM, I couldn't hold altitude. I could glide a long way with 1,100. But it would be fatal to get out there if he weren't home. So I looked down, and there was the beach again. There was a line of lights on the boulevard along the beach. I circled. Another thing that I observed, as I looked down, was the phosphorescence of the surf. It was visible, and I could tell right where those waves were breaking. Although I couldn't see exactly, I could estimate where to set the plane down between the waterline and the high-tide line.

Landing the airplane on the beach there at night caused a big whoop and holler. Earl's father owned an apartment house, maybe a block or so from where I landed, and Earl was there. So Earl came rushing out. This was about 9:00 o'clock at night. I had to get back to that ship. Earl was a wonderful character. He said, "Tommy, just forget about it. I'll take care of it. You get the hell out of here and get back to the ship. I'll have the airplane at the field when you get ashore the next time." So I did.

Q: What was your duty on the ship?

Captain Tomlinson: When I reported aboard, the executive officer said, "You're senior watch officer." I'd never been on the bridge of a battleship. Senior watch officer!

We had orders to proceed north to San Francisco. The *Texas*, a coal-burning battleship, was the flagship, and we were to follow the *Texas*. The OOD watch officers laughed and said, "You're going to have fun up there following the *Texas* with those coal-burning boilers. She goes by spurts and stops." So I thought I'd be smart and put myself on the midwatch, hoping the captain and everybody else would be in their bunks, and they were. Nobody else saw it. But I want to tell you, that first four-hour watch was a nightmare. You were supposed to keep 500 yards astern of the ship ahead. Here I had been used to keeping formation with an airplane throttle. But with a battleship the procedure was, "Reduce five turns. Add five turns." Once, when I fell back too much, I rang for ten turns of the propellers. You talk about a nightmare! But I got away with it and learned to survive. I had to!

Q: Did your time on the Oklahoma last throughout 1922?

Captain Tomlinson: Yes. I went south on the Oklahoma with the Pacific Fleet. That was when I broke my ankle down in Panama.

Q: How did that happen?

Captain Tomlinson: A group of very nasty aviators--Bimbo McReavy, Hooks Marley, Rhea Taylor, Dick Allen, and Tomlinson--were relaxing in Annie Kelly's saloon.* Over at another table we saw an equal number of blackshoe Navy officers.** Don't ask me why, but we decided to throw them out. A barroom battle started. I was wearing low shoes with rubber soles. In the course of the fight, I pivoted on my right foot to take a roundhouse swing at one of the contestants. The next thing I knew, I was on the

---
*Lieutenant Clarence J. McReavy, USN; Lieutenant Albert S. Marley, Jr., USN; Ensign Rhea Taylor, USN.
**In the early days of naval aviation, the aviators wore brown shoes with their khaki uniforms and green uniforms. They thus acquired the nickname "brown shoes" to distinguish them from the traditional surface ship officers, who were known as "black shoes."

floor with my foot and ankle twisted about 90 degrees. I returned north aboard the Mercy.*

Before I left on the cruise, I had been flying the Jenny in the latter part of October, November, December, and early January. I'd been carrying wing-walkers and plane changers and looping around telephone wires with the rest of the crazy pilots.

Q: Barnstorming.

Captain Tomlinson: Yes. We all did a lot of show-off stunts to attract a crowd. I flew the plane to North Island to leave with George Cuddihy and Lambert Hewitt until I came back from the cruise to Panama. I said, "Take your girls for a ride in it." Cuddihy and Hewitt did just that.

When I came back on the Mercy, I was walking around with a cane. The cast was off, but I could walk all right. I went down and recovered the airplane. Several people said, "Did you know old Lambert Hewitt won a horse race with it down in Agua Caliente?" He'd taken some girl there to chase the horses around the racetrack. Luckily, he didn't land in Mexico. That's the way things went in those days.

I had a month's leave due me plus sick leave. The

---

*The USS Mercy (AH-4) was a hospital ship.

Daniel W. Tomlinson #1 - 52

<u>Oklahoma</u> was due to go to Bremerton Navy Yard for overhaul.* The year before, when we were up there, we spent the Fourth of July at Port Townsend. I was married, although not very happily. I met a very charming debutante girl at a garden party in Port Townsend, Washington, and invited her to the ship for the dinner and dance we were having on the Fourth of July 1922.** I wanted to see her again.

Q: In Port Townsend?

Captain Tomlinson: Yes. A charming girl. I realized what an awful mistake I had made. I wanted to take her for a flight. I figured I'd fly up to Seattle and join the ship at Bremerton. I'll show you a picture of it as I took off from Earl Daugherty's field. A spare propeller was tied on the right wing. My suitcase, a spare wheel, a spare cylinder, and valve overhead parts were in the front seat.

It was quite a trip. I had inquired of pilots around Los Angeles who had flown north, because there were no directories of landing fields, maps, or any information. You made your own landing field. It helped if you'd been tipped off to some pasture of likely places to land in advance.

---
*Puget Sound Navy Yard, Bremerton, Washington.
**The girl was Francel Hill, whom Tomlinson married many years later.

Q: No aeronautical charts at that time.

Captain Tomlinson: Nothing. You'd go to a stationery store and get a Rand-McNally state map, which was not much good. I found automobile maps for north of San Francisco and used a Rand-McNally to Frisco. I couldn't find anybody around Los Angeles who had flown north of Frisco. By that time, Earl Daugherty had put me up for membership in the Professional Pilots Association of Los Angeles. It was a fairly select group, only people who were recognized as competent, safe pilots. There were about 50 or 60 members; I don't remember exactly. You'd go to one of their monthly meetings and inquire, "You flew up that way?" I couldn't find any information.

Someone said, "You land at Crissy Field. You'll find someone who's flown forest patrol up north, and they can tell you."

So I took off from Earl's field. It was a foggy morning. I got to Newhall Pass, at the north end of the San Fernando Valley, and it was socked in tight. I had a ceiling over the San Fernando Valley of maybe 400 or 500 feet. No way I could get through Newhall Pass. You had to get through the pass before you could climb up over the grapevine highway to Bakersfield. I saw a nice green field below big enough to land. The oats looked a little high, but there wasn't anything else. I went in for a pretty good landing, except that the oats chewed the copper tipping off my prop. Fortunately, when I left Long Beach I had that spare prop tied on the right wing. That's the way you did it in those days.

So here I was hobbling with a cane. That prop had chewed the oats up, and the airplane was the worst mess you ever saw. Wings, wires, struts, one bay out on each side plastered with green oat glue. A lot of kids came out. I had some small change, and I paid them to scrape this goop off. I went to work and changed the prop, and then I sat waiting. I knew the fog would lift by noon.

Finally, it lifted, and I took off. I had been advised, "Just go northwest of Bakersfield, and you'll see the landing strip." So I was sailing off to Bakersfield. I cleared the hump by about 50 feet over the road. There was a right turn there, then the Teton Pass to Lake Lebec, then downhill. I held about 3,000 feet going into Bakersfield, not knowing exactly where to find the strip. I was over the west edge of Bakersfield when the OX-5 sputtered and slowed down. Again I had spasmodic RPM--800, maybe 900--little spurts of power. So I looked around. Bakersfield was just over to my right, but some fields were right under me. I saw something that looked pretty good, so I went down and made a good landing in a Japanese truck garden.

I removed the carburetor and took it apart. A little copper safety wire secured the shaft on which the float chamber was balanced. It had deteriorated, and the pin had come out. This caused the mixture to become too rich. So I put in a new safety wire and reassembled the carburetor, replaced it, and away I went. By that time, it was getting late, so I by-passed Bakersfield and landed along the highway into the next town north. I spent the night in a nearby motel--no problem.

I took off the next morning. Someone had told me that in Fresno, on the north side of town, there was a graveyard, and you could land right alongside it. I arrived over Fresno. I guess I must have been stupid, but, anyway, I couldn't see the graveyard. There was a suburban development with a leveled-off street, so I just landed on the street east of Fresno. I took off and landed alongside the graveyard to get gas. It was a small strip. There were a couple of Jennies around Modesto, so I flew there and got gas. Then I headed for Frisco and had no problem finding Crissy Field. I got together with the Army Air Corps reserve unit, and they said, "There are some pilots here who have flown forest patrol up north."

I found a flying sergeant who had flown to Seattle.

He said, "Go to Mather Field. They'll gas you up. Then to Red Bluff. Land alongside the highway. You can see where they've cleared off the sagebrush. There's a hotel nearby."

So I fueled at Red Bluff. Next day I took off early, because now I was facing the mountains. I got by Shasta okay; I was about 100 feet in the air over the hump. I followed the highway; it wasn't paved in those days. I was told at Crissy, "You can land around Yreka." There's a couple of places that are okay." Yreka is close to 3,000 feet. At this point the OX-5 didn't have the sap that it should have had; the valves were not seating. Beyond Yreka, the sergeant told me, "Just follow the railroad up over the Siskiyus." When you get to Medford, land inside the racetrack." I passed Yreka.

I'd better go back a ways. With this Jenny I had decided that when the conditions were right, I had to learn to fly up through fog. When I had a ceiling of at least 1,000 feet, I'd pull up into the fog and would try to fly blind. I had no gyro instrument then.

Q: Spin out?

Captain Tomlinson: Many times.

I thought, "There's got to be some way." So I

suddenly hit on an idea. The Jenny had floorboards under the rudder bars. I had rubber heels on my shoes. I decided, "I'm going to stabilize this plane directionally before I start to climb up through the clouds. I am going to get my rudder all set for the torque and lock it by jamming my rubber heels against the floor boards. When I go into the clouds, I'm going to fly just using ailerons to steer." I had found that trying to use the rudder, I over-controlled and tried to correct the compass error too rapidly. Once you got into a spin from over-controlling and then recovered, you would go into an opposite spin. What could you do about it?

I thought, "Maybe I can do this: I'll let that compass swing slowly. It's inevitable. Once it shows 15 degrees error, I'll start easing it back on course slowly." I had no airspeed indicator, but there was a tachometer on a Jenny. A change of five RPM would tell me whether I was descending or climbing. I had a bubble to indicate sideslip either way. I don't know how many hours I spent, but I finally worked it out so that I could climb up 2,000-3,000 feet through clouds and come out the top close to my course. I always knew that if the plane got away from me, it was "Katy bar the doors," unless I had a ceiling underneath.

Here I was, north of Yreka and flying along okay and

following the railroad track. The mountains were getting higher, and I could see that railroad track climbing higher with mountains on each side. I was watching that railroad track. I was a little over 3,500 feet altitude. All of a sudden, the tracks went into a tunnel. I flipped that plane on edge and reversed course. I thought, "That damn sergeant."

I did not have enough gas to go back to Red Bluff. I was afraid to land near Yreka for fear I'd never get off and would have to do a top overhaul on the OX-5 engine. So I decided, "I'm going up into this." It began to snow heavily. There were 8,000-foot peaks scattered around. I finally got the plane up to 7,000 feet, trying to get on top of the clouds. I figured out before I went into the snowstorm a course to Medford that would get across the hump of the Siskiyus. (I had a good compass; I'd had it remagnetized, so it was as good as you could get.) When I got to 7,000 feet, I steadied on course to Ashland. My sine curve averaged the course pretty close. I allowed 15 minutes at 7,000 feet on this course. If I didn't see something, I had to turn back. I was scared. It was snowing so hard I could barely see the wing tips. I was glued to that compass, altimeter, and tachometer.

I think I had less than a minute to go when I sneaked a quick look over the side. I had just a glimpse down there through a hole in the clouds. I could see a highway and was sure it had to be the road to Ashland. I threw the JN into a tight, diving spiral. I didn't want to spin. I just put her in a flipper spiral under control. I didn't want to drift to either side, as I knew I had mountains for a few miles either way. I came out underneath the cloud and was probably about four or five miles south of Ashland. The ceiling was about 500 feet and visibility two miles.

Q: That was just meant to happen.

Captain Tomlinson: I got into Medford with no problem and fueled. I figured I could make it into Eugene. The sergeant had told me there was a forest fire patrol field, a pasture, on the south side of Eugene. So I followed the road; that's all you could do through those mountains in that area at that time. I was still getting light snow, but I made it through a couple of passes. I was not over 100 feet above the road. I was probably 50 feet under the overcast. As soon as I got through each pass, I'd ease down a little lower.

Finally, I figured, "This has got to be the last hump to clear into Eugene." It was socked in tight. I could see clouds lying on the critical ridge off to the west, so I turned west toward Yoncolla. I figured I'd sneak along the ridge, and if the ceiling lifted just a bit, I'd get into the Eugene valley. About the time I got to Yoncolla, I ran into a hailstorm. There I was, sitting in that cockpit. I didn't mind my face, but I was worried about the copper tipping on my wood prop. The hail lasted a couple of minutes.

Q: What about the fabric?

Captain Tomlinson: It didn't bother the fabric. No. The hail was pea-sized, buckshot-sized. When I came out of the hail, I saw just a light spot over the ridge. I figured, "I've got to chance it." I headed for the ridge, and when I was right close, I was on top of the trees. Near the crest I pulled up again into the cloud. I figured I'd count to five and then ease down on the other side. I flew blind, and when I came down, I was just on the other side; I probably had a couple hundred feet over the treetops. then I went into Eugene.

It had been raining in Eugene for days, and I landed on the field slimy with mud. I had to put water in the radiator as well as take on fuel. When I got up on the radiator, I slipped and fell off and landed on my bad ankle, the one I'd broken. That didn't help it a bit. I was still able to hobble with my cane. I got the prop fixed. The hail had not bothered the copper tipping, but there were several nicks below the copper tipping; the wood was chewed. I got some sandpaper and smoothed the surface; it wasn't too bad.

Next morning, I headed for Portland. I'd been tipped off to land on the parade ground at the Vancouver barracks. I landed and found an Army Air Corps captain I had met in the course of my flying. We had a fine time together. I needed a part for an overhead rocker arm on the OX-5.

The next morning I flew west down the Columbia River to a small landing strip and picked up the part. Then I headed for Camp Lewis. Lieutenant Harry Hoffman, who was number one turret officer on the Oklahoma, junior to me, a Naval Academy classmate of mine, was at Camp Lewis in charge of the ship's rifle range party.* I had written Harry I'd stop and take him for a ride.

Q: This is at Tacoma?

Captain Tomlinson: Yes. The previous summer I had gone there and borrowed a Hisso Jenny from another Air Corps friend of mine, and I'd flown back over to Seattle to chase people off the quarterdeck of the Oklahoma. So I knew where to land at Camp Lewis.

---
*Lieutenant Harry D. Hoffman, USN.

I landed and saw somebody waving. There was a nice glade of widely spaced trees, so I taxied in there. That was Colonel Gatley's front yard.* This old-timer came out. He was just tickled to death. He said, "Fine. Harry and a couple of others are coming over to play poker tonight. This is just great luck." So there I was with my airplane sitting in Colonel Gatley's front yard, and he told me to spend the night with him. It was a panic. I never had more fun in my life. This old colonel had charged up San Juan Hill with Teddy Roosevelt. He was one of the real old Army characters. I'll never forget that poker party. Once we both had to go the toilet, so we were both in there. He said, "You and me, and Teddy Roosevelt and I used to pee in the same pot."**

The poker party went on until daylight. Harry Hoffman was in the group. I wanted to get started for Seattle. The party finally broke up. This old character had three strikers, he called them. They did little other than brew beer for him. We'd been sitting there drinking beer and eating Limburger cheese on rye bread. That was a poker party!

I said, "Harry, I'll take you for a ride." So we went out to the JN. I took all my gear--my suitcase and my

---
*Colonel George G. Gatley, USA.
**Colonel Theodore Roosevelt, who served with the Rough Riders in Cuba during the Spanish-American War, was later President from 1901 to 1909.

spare parts--out of the front seat. I knew the motor was getting kind of puny, but I thought I could get the plane off. There was a three-mile run. So I put Harry in the front seat, and I got off the ground all right. But I was up not quite level with the top of the trees, and I was not climbing at all. So I throttled back and settled down. I said, "Harry, I've got to give you a rain check." So I taxied back, put Harry off, and put my stuff back in. Harry weighed about 170, and I imagine my gear in the front seat didn't weigh over 40 or 50 pounds. It made enough difference so that I got off clear of the trees and headed for Sand Point.

Lake Union was my landmark. When you pass Lake Union on your left and Lake Washington on your right, you'll see the narrow strip through the trees at Sand Point, which was not much in those days.* When I was about at the center of Seattle, one cylinder quit. I was flying on seven cylinders. I had all the altitude I could get, because I knew it was going to be marginal. As I approached Sand Point, another cylinder quit. I got over Lake Union. I was on six barrels, and that wasn't enough. The plane was shaking due to the uneven engine operation. I knew the OX-5 needed a top overhaul and hoped I could get some help.

---
*Sand Point later became a naval air station.

The plane staggered into Sand Point. The only Army Air Corps officer on duty there at that time was Major Muhlenberg.* He lived in an old farmhouse. He and his wife lived there, and he had one technical sergeant whom I'll never forget. He told Mulenburg, "You should have seen that plane come in. He just missed the stake fence. He had an angel under each wing and St. Peter held up his tail." I'll never forget it either. Anyway, I was there.

I spent the next week as the guest of Major Muhlenburg. He and his wife were wonderful. I removed the cylinders of the OX-5, but they didn't have any shop there; they didn't even have any work benches. I carried enough tools. Sitting on the floor of that hangar, I ground those valves and put the OX-5 back together. My idea was to fly it over to Bremerton Navy Yard. I thought there might be someplace where I could land there and remove the engine. I wanted to take it to the machine shop aboard the "Okie" and do a real overhaul job on it.

While I was working on the engine, I took the ferry to Bremerton. The Oklahoma was in dry dock by that time. I looked around the Navy yard, and the only place I could find to land was a small Marine parade ground. I knew it was going to be very close, but I could get in. I cleared the matter with the colonel. Almost in the Navy yard industrial area there was a ballpark under a cliff. The

*Major Henry K. Muhlenberg, USA.

commandant's quarters were on higher ground back of the cliff. (The location is hard to describe. The area is all changed now.) I figured I could just fly out of the ballpark.

When I got the plane going at Sand Point, I landed on the colonel's parade ground. When I came in, I cut the switch and my prop stopped at a 45-degree angle. I slipped in, then fishtailed and held my breath.

Q: Working the rudder back and forth.

Captain Tomlinson: Yes. When I stopped, my prop was six feet from the colonel's stoop.

Q: That's tight.

Captain Tomlinson: That was the shortest landing I ever made. I took the wings off and hauled it by truck to alongside the Oklahoma. The engine was taken aboard to the ship's machine shop, where a real valve job was done, and then reassembled. I hauled the plane back to the ballpark. and tied it down. Someone told me, "You better not take it out of there without the commandant's permission." Then I found trouble. I called on the rear admiral who was commandant. He was one of the crusty old characters with a long beard and mustache. The bull surgeon on his staff was the one who had tried to stop me from going to Pensacola and who had voted against me on the general court, which prevented me from getting a full and honorable acquittal.

Q: This guy was a plague for you.

Captain Tomlinson: That's a gross understatement. He had filled this old admiral full of "This horrible Tomlinson."

The admiral said, "I don't know what we're going to do about this. I have to study the matter." I was thereby grounded.

Then I found there was no way I could stand a deck watch on the Oklahoma with my bad ankle. I had broken another small bone at Eugene when I fell off the radiator. I was detached and sent to the hospital. They treated me there for a week or ten days. They said, "There isn't anything further we can really do for you here. We're going to put you on outpatient status." That was perfect. I found a suite in the Butler Hotel in Seattle, which in those days was quite a place with a popular night club in the basement.

I could get out close to Sand Point by streetcar. I went out there and met a man who owned a Curtiss Seagull. He had hired a pilot to fly it for him. I did not know the pilot's background. The pilot was out on the lake trying to take if off, and it wouldn't fly. I stood on the beach with the owner, whose name was King Baird. He was an automobile dealer. I said, "Mr. Baird, I think that engine is out of time. He'll never get the plane off."

Baird said, "Do you think you can fix it?"

I said, "If you have a manual on it so that I can learn how to set the gears properly, yes." He had no information. He stopped the pilot, who wasn't getting anywhere. I said, "Do you know anybody in the area who has a similar motor?"

"Yes, over near the Lake Washington ferry, a pilot had a couple of boats there."

"Let's go over there," I said.

We took the valve cover off another six-cylinder Curtiss Kirkham. The spark plugs were on top of the cylinders. We took the spark plug out of number-one cylinder, and I got a length of stiff wire and had somebody turn the prop over. I very carefully marked on the wire where the piston was when the exhaust and intake valves opened and closed. Then I was able to go back to Sand Point and retime the valve setting of the others. The gears were one tooth off the correct setting. As soon as I fixed that and got the engine going, I took it off and flew King Baird around the lake. He said, "How would you like to fly this for me?"

I said, "Sure." We worked out a 50-50 split at that

Daniel W. Tomlinson #1 - 68

time. The pilot deducted actual expenses and got 50% of the rest. I carried two passengers at a time and did charter work. I did all right.

Virtually in the city of Bremerton was an inlet of Puget Sound which bordered a public park. It was adequate for takeoff and landing. There was a little beach where I could taxi up, fuel, and load passengers. I'd fly over there noons and carry some of the passengers. I thought maybe the word would get around that I was not as dangerous as some thought. This info must have reached the Navy yard commandant. I decided to try him again and told him my situation. He said, "Young man, Sunday morning you can fly that airplane out before 7:00 o'clock and don't you dare come back."

So I was over there Saturday night to fly my plane in the morning. I obtained a can of medical ether. It was about a pint. I had a five-gallon auxiliary gas tank in the upper wing center section, standard on the Hisso Jennies. I'd gotten one and put it in my plane, because it was handy and fitted right inside the center section over the front cockpit, gravity feed.

Then I took everything possible out of that airplane and put five gallons in this reserve tank, plus the medical ether, which really put "oomph" in the gas and gave me an extra five RPM on takeoff. I had to fly out diagonally. There was a street with lampposts I had to cross. I figured it very carefully. I had about five feet on each side. I knew I would just be airborne at that critical point, and I was. I made it, just! I climbed and headed across the Sound for Sand Point, but the outer Sound was fogged in tight. With five gallons of gas, I didn't dare go over the top and look for a hole over Lake Washington. If there was no hole, I'd be in a bad fix with so little fuel. So I figured, "Well, I've done it before."

I got right down on the water--wheels maybe five or ten feet off the surface--on a compass course heading for Seattle. Any time I was close to the ground I always kept plenty of speed. Suddenly there was Alki Point dead ahead. Whew! I couldn't turn back since I might hook a wing, so I just pulled up in a wingover, blind. I made a 180-degree turn, praying I could see the water quickly enough to recover, and I did with probably 15-20 feet to spare.

After I drew a couple of deep breaths, I steadied on a course back toward Bremerton because coming over I'd seen a golf course on the end of Bainbridge Island--just before hitting the fog. I got back there and landed. I got gasoline out of a tractor. By noon the fog burned off, and I flew to Sand Point.

Q: How long did you spend in that area altogether?

Captain Tomlinson: I spent the whole summer. It was a

riot. After I recovered the Jenny, I flew up to Port Townsend to see this young lady and took her for her first airplane ride. I spent the night at her home and told her in no way could I get a divorce. She would have married me. She had been engaged to an Army man at Fort Casey before I entered the picture. Then he had gone to Honolulu. She said, "I'll go to Honolulu."

I said, "My dear, there's nothing I can do," and wished her good-bye. That was in 1923.

Q: Did you ever hear from her again?

Captain Tomlinson: Yes, in 1973, 50 years later, I was free. I found her in Seattle, a widow for 20 years, and she had three grown sons. We were quickly married and had seven wonderful years together. Then she died of cancer.

As for the flying, I had that duty done. I flew around the Puget Sound area. On the Fourth of July, they were having a big parade in Seattle. I forget the name of the main street; the city was quite different then. I had already been propositioned by Major Muhlenburg to fly an Air Corps D.VII.*

Q: Oh, boy.

---

*The Fokker D.VII was the best German airplane of World War I, making its appearance over the western front in the spring of 1918. After the war ended, the United States received 142 D.VII fighters as part of the war reparations.

Daniel W. Tomlinson #1 - 71

Captain Tomlinson: The American Legion was having a picnic, and he asked me to put on an acrobatic flight with the Fokker D.VII over the park. I took my Jenny, with some gal I knew, and flew over Seattle. They were having a parade. I did a couple of loops below the tops of the buildings over the main street as the parade was in progress. That raised a bit of an uproar. After this foray, I took the Fokker D.VII out and put the show on.

Q: How did you like that?

Captain Tomlinson: The Fokker D.VII was a beautiful airplane to fly, but the engine was tricky. The engine was a high-compression one with two positions on the throttle, which nobody told me about. The first time I took it up, I used full throttle. I was just starting the turn-around and blew a plug. Full throttle was not supposed to be used below 3,000 feet.

Q: Was this a Mercedes or BMW engine?

Captain Tomlinson: BMW. I had no trouble coming back in. They put a plug in, and it worked okay after that.

There was a man at Sand Point by the name of Ed Mooney. He had seen me stunting the JN. He became enamored of it. He offered me $500.00 for it, twice what I paid for it, so I sold it.

I spent the rest of the summer, until September, in the Puget Sound area. I was riding high by this time. I had the Seagull, and I was making $25.00 to 30.00 a day several days a week in addition to my Navy pay. I had a suite of rooms in the Butler Hotel, always a case of good Scotch under the bed. In fact, it was funny. I never did fly any liquor, never did any bootlegging. But I used to be out flying at night, and I'd fly into Lake Washington over Seattle. This was a place near Medroma Ferry, which was easier to get to from the hotel than Sand Point. There was a fixed light on the ferry building, and I'd simply come in at maybe 11:00, 12:00 o'clock, whenever, and I'd fly past that light level with my top wing and let the plane settle down. Then my friend would be on the beach with the headlights of the Chevrolet pointing over the lake. I'd look for these two eyes to guide me to the ramp. However, my night fly-in over Seattle aroused curiosity, and an article appeared in The Seattle Times that it was suspected a bootlegger was flying in booze from Canada.

In early September a doctor at the hospital told me, "This weekly treatment isn't doing you any good. I think we'll put you up for physical survey." So I received orders to Washington for survey. They gave me the choice: I could either retire physically with 75% base pay, which wasn't much at senior lieutenant's pay, or I could go to the Naval Academy as an instructor, shore duty only, so I took the latter.

Q: That lasted until 1925?

Captain Tomlinson: I reported there in September of 1923, assigned to the Department of Steam Engineering and Naval Construction. There was an ex-Army Air Corps pilot who was flying a Jenny for the owner, someone in Baltimore. The field was off the street nearby from where my house was located, out on West Street. I made contact with this pilot. When he wasn't available, I began flying the Jenny, carrying passengers, $5.00 for a straight flight and $10.00 for acrobatics.

In 1924, when September leave came around, I conceived the idea of renting this airplane and taking it up to western New York and barnstorming the county fairs. I contacted the owner and offered him $500.00 for the use of the Jenny for a month; he agreed. I sent my family, my wife and two kids, up to my father-in-law's place in East Pembroke, New York. I flew up there and barnstormed. I made over $1,500 on a good Sunday. I would have a roll of bills and many "yellow backs" amounting to several hundred dollars. Usually, they were tens and twenties. I always liked those gold-backed bills. I paid him, and he gave me

Daniel W. Tomlinson #1 - 74

a receipt stating I returned the plane in better condition than when I had received it.

After I turned the plane back to him in Baltimore, then this Air Corps lieutenant got it again and flew it back to Annapolis. He never tied it down, just left it on the field. I always tied the airplane down. A thunderstorm came along, picked it up, took it about 50 feet, knocked the landing gear off, broke the prop, and broke both lower front spars. So I bought it from the owner for $175.00. I then put in a request to the head of the steam department pattern shop, where I could rebuild it in my off-time.

My request was approved. I had plenty of space to work on the wings, et al. I spent the winter of 1924-25 rebuilding the plane. I did a nice job. I sold the old 90-horsepower OX-5 engine and replaced it with a new 100-horsepower Navy OX-6 engine with dual ignition, an important safety feature. The engine had sat in a chicken house for five years, and I gave it a thorough check. I replaced one cylinder. One day the head of the steam department watched me and said, "Do you really think that thing will run?"

I said, "I'll bet you $5.00 it will run the first time I pull the prop through to start it." When the time came, it did, and he paid on the spot!

Q: Did you have any help on that?

Captain Tomlinson: Yes, and that's interesting too. There were about six midshipmen who came in to help me.

Q: So you got them hooked on aviation?

Captain Tomlinson: Jim Russell was one of them; he retired as a four-star admiral.* Others were George Dufek, a rear admiral who did the antarctic experiment, and David McDonald, a four-star admiral and CNO.** I lost track of the others; I don't know what happened to them. Jim Russell has told me that it was the interest aroused by my airplane at the Naval Academy that caused more candidates for aviation from the classes who were there during my tour of duty, when I was doing this flying, than from any other classes. I especially attracted their interest in the summer of 1925, when I had permission to base my JN on the parade ground, Farragut Field.

Q: I think the first so-called aviation class was 1926, wasn't it, where they had flight indoctrination at Annapolis?

---
*Midshipman James S. Rusell, USN, Naval Academy class of 1926. His oral history is in the Naval Institute collection.
**Midshipman George J. Dufek, USN, class of 1925. Midshipman David L. McDonald, class of 1928, later Chief of Naval Operations from 1963 to 1967. McDonald's oral history is in the Naval Institute collection.

Captain Tomlinson: Yes. These midshipmen who helped me--part of the deal was for them to bring their girls out during June Week, and I'd take them for a ride, which I did.* I wish I had my log books; it's all there with the names. I carried quite a few passengers besides.

Then I ran into trouble at this field, because the kids would climb over the plane at night. One put his foot through the wings. Again, I decided to beard the lion in his den. This had never happened before. I wrote a letter to the superintendent of the Naval Academy, explaining my situation and requesting permission to base my airplane on Farragut Field, the big parade ground where the midshipmen drilled on the south side of Bancroft Hall.

It came back approved, with the proviso that I could only take off or land either before breakfast call in the morning or while the midshipmen were at mess. I guess he was afraid I'd run over some of them. I've got pictures of the airplane in front of the old football stands on Farragut Field there. That was the only airplane that was ever so authorized, and I was an outcast from naval aviation.

One weekend during the summer, I heard an air show was to be held at Chester, Pennsylvania, so I took my wife and flew up there. I didn't like the looks of the field, but

---

*June Week was the time of graduation for each Naval Academy class.

you could get in and out. Then Pete Mitscher, Al Williams, and a couple others flew in from Anacostia.* One of them had a Vought, the other one had a DH, and there were two other planes. Pete Mitscher was in command of the fighter squadron at San Diego in 1921 when I had my troubles. He hated my guts, apparently. He never did forgive me. He blamed me. I never knew him, but I knew he was death on me. So I didn't like it when he showed up.

Both the slope of the field and the direction of the wind were wrong. A young man came up, finally, with $5.00. He wanted to fly. As a matter of pride, I had to take him up. It wouldn't look good if Tomlinson didn't take this passenger up. I had to take off downwind, downhill, into a long valley. I flew for two or three miles before I got above the tops of the trees. I managed to get back and land. I thought, "I don't want anybody else to show up." But, sure as hell, in about 15 minutes, here came another prospective passenger. I was standing there talking to these VIP naval aviators--Al Williams, Mitscher, et al. But the man had $5.00 and wanted to fly. Well, again, it was a matter of pride. I was on the spot.

The wind had picked up a little bit, so I decided to take a different approach. I figured if I got clear down to the bottom of the slope, I'd do better to take off into

---

*Lieutenant Commander Marc A. Mitscher, USN; Lieutenant (junior grade) Alford J. Williams, USN.

the wind, uphill. That way I'd be off the ground before I hit the steep part of the hill and be able to clear a row of trees. I tried it, and I was just about to clear the trees when I hit the downdraft. I had two choices. I could stack the plane in the trees; I felt we'd walk away from it. Or I could make what I called a "death turn" and deliberately stall in under semi-control as we hit the ground. There was a cornfield and a farmhouse to my left. I could reach the cornfield, and at least we'd be on the ground. I saw a Jenny taken out of trees once, and it was a complete wreck after being removed. That's why I chose the cornfield, and the impact knocked the landing gear off, broke the prop, and damaged the left wing. This passenger in the front seat didn't smell very good when he got out, so I gave him his $5.00 back and said, "Go into town and get yourself some clean drawers."

Q: Were you able to rebuild the airplane?

Captain Tomlinson: Yes. The old German farmer was a good-hearted soul. He had a cellar-ful of dandelion wine, which he dispensed freely. He helped me disassemble the plane, his wife helped me, and a couple of other people helped me. I hired a truck, took the plane apart, and put it in the truck. I was back unloading it at the Naval Academy steam department by 8:00 o'clock in the morning.

Fortunately, in those days College Park, Maryland, toward Baltimore from Washington, had a warehouse full of Jenny parts left over from World War I. I bought a new wing for $25.00, landing gear for $15.00, a toothpick prop for $3.00. I rebuilt it, was flying it again in a couple of weeks, and again parked it on the parade ground. I always got a big bang out of it. John Rodgers assembled one of the early pusher planes on Farragut Field and took off, but he never came back. He and I were the only aviators to fly off Farragut Field with official permission.

Al Williams, without any authority, tried to land on Farragut Field to attend a football game. He came in with a VE-7 but apparently knocked the landing gear off--a stupid thing. It annoyed him and others to know Tomlinson could use the field but they could not. No other airplanes were allowed to land after Williams's debacle. The superintendent wrote a letter to the Navy Department: "No more Navy airplanes on Farragut Field."

It was time for me to be detached. The interest aroused by my flying while I'd been there instructing was well known in the Navy Department. All knew my nefarious history. But at that propitious time for me, naval aviation finally got its foot in the door at the Naval Academy. The academy was sold on incorporating a course in naval aviation, and I had played a key part.

Daniel W. Tomlinson #1 - 80

I had orders back to naval aviation when that happened. Then after my misfortune with Mitscher watching at Chester, Pennsylvania, the Navy Department revoked my orders. I was sitting there with no orders. But I had a friend who was assistant detail officer, Lieutenant Ben Holcome.* He was from the Naval Academy class of 1916 with Raddy Radford and other good friends of mine.** I had taught him to fly at San Diego before he went to Pensacola, which put him way ahead. Because of the regulations, I couldn't allow him to solo, but he was all ready for solo when he reported to Pensacola. So, in desperation, I wrote to him. I said, "If they'll order me back into naval aviation, I will fly my Jenny across the continent to San Diego. And if I don't get there, I will never bother them again."

I got my orders, which didn't mention anything about redesignation as a naval aviator or duty involving flying. It was simply, "On detachment, you will proceed and report to the Commander Aircraft Squadrons Battle Fleet for assignment."

Q: That was presumably the first time a Jenny had made that trip, wasn't it?

---
*Lieutenant Benjamin R. Holcome, USN.
**Lieutenant Arthur W. Radford, USN, a naval aviator who later became a four-star admiral and served as Chairman of the Joint Chiefs of Staff from 1953 to 1957.

Captain Tomlinson: First time—yes, so far as I have been able to determine.

I had 30 days' leave. When that summer leave was over, I returned to western New York and barnstormed the county fairs. I picked up another wad of yellow-backed bills. I've got pictures of that barnstorming today. I gave the OX-6 engine a thorough top overhaul and headed west. Luckily, I had ideal fall weather and no delays. I crossed the Continental Divide over the railroad tracks at Benson, New Mexico, with 50 feet to spare. It took me 7 days, 49 hours, and 5 minutes.

When I reported the next morning to the chief of staff, he said, "We have dispatch orders redesignating you as a naval aviator and to duty involving flying. You better behave yourself."

Q: Had Radford had any influence in getting that?

Captain Tomlinson: No. I had a lot to do with Raddy later on. Raddy Radford, Jack Towers, Baldy Pownall—there were a couple of others who understood me and on whom I could depend for support.*

---

*Commander John H. Towers, USN; Lieutenant Commander Charles A. Pownall, USN. Both were flag officers in the Pacific during World War II. Pownall's oral history is in the Naval Institute collection.

Q: We're up to October of 1925.

Captain Tomlinson: I was assigned to Fighting Squadron Two.

Q: At North Island?

Captain Tomlinson: Yes. It is interesting, how I arrived at North Island. Everything had changed since I was there in 1921. All I could see were VE-7s lined up on the warm-up ramp, so I just taxied up into position at the end of that line. I cut the prop, and I was sitting there just relaxed. I made it! It was close. A couple of conditions were too close for comfort. I recognized Lieutenant Spig Wead, who was a squadron commander, and Spig hadn't been too friendly to me in 1921.* It made me a little concerned. He looked at me, and I was the damnedest-looking mess. I had been sitting in that plane with these goggles on in the bright sun, and all I wore for a helmet was a pulled-down handkerchief with four knots in the corners. My face was just black. The Jenny was all covered with desert dust. He walked up and looked at me and said, "Where in the hell did you come from?"

---
*Lieutenant Commander Frank W. Wead, USN, who later had to retire from the Navy for physical disability and became a successful Hollywood screenwriter.

I said, "From the East Coast." He turned and walked away. I thought. "I've had it. I'll probably be assigned to a torpedo plane squadron or a garbage barge or something." But when I reported the next morning to the chief of staff, the morning after he told me I'd better behave myself, he said, "Tomlinson, Spig Wead has asked for you to be assigned to his fighter squadron." This was the choice billet in the fleet air command!

Q: The best job in naval aviation at that time, I would imagine.

Captain Tomlinson: Yes.

Daniel W. Tomlinson #2 - 84

Interview Number 2 with Captain Daniel W. Tomlinson IV,
U.S. Naval Reserve (Retired)

Place: Captain Tomlinson's home in Silverton, Oregon

Date: Tuesday, 10 September 1985

Interviewer: Barrett Tillman

Q: We're up to October 1925, and you've joined Fighting Squadron Two at North island.

Captain Tomlinson: One of the first things that developed was important in naval aviation history. After I joined the squadron, Spig Wead had conceived the idea of glide bombing. We had VE-7s, which were nice airplanes, 200 horsepower, actually Hispano engines built under a license by Wright--a good-flying airplane. We fixed up the original experimental bomb racks under the wings to drop these little marker bombs. They had smoke shells in them. We started trying this style of attack at Ream Field. It was just a little Army Air Corps practice landing field in my time and had been abandoned. But the field was available as a place where we could place a marker. We started trying the idea.

Q: Did you have any kind of sight to do this?

Captain Tomlinson: I've forgotten exactly. We tried using our machine gun sight.

Q: A ring-and-bead affair?

Captain Tomlinson: Yes, very rudimentary. We found that we could come somewhere within a couple of hundred feet of the target. We couldn't dive the VE-7s steep enough to give accuracy. It was less than a month that we got the first Curtiss Hawks; that was a horse of a different color. The Hawks we could really dive, almost vertical. Accuracy became possible.* We could really hit the target.

Incidentally, as those things happen, the Navy was asked to send somebody up to demonstrate the capability of the Hawk at Clover Field for an Armistice Day celebration. Spig detailed me. The Navy was afraid to fly those planes cross country. Most pilots just made their approach too damn fast when they came in to land. Here I'd been flying passengers out of small pastures. I had to land within 10 or 15 feet of a mark every time I came in. On final approach I'd slow an airplane down within a couple miles per hour of stall speed. Of course, I tried it out in the air, like I explained to you before. I never had any

---

*The Curtiss F6C Hawk had a wing span of 38 feet, length of 22 feet, gross weight of 3,171 pounds, and a top speed of 155 miles per hour at sea level.

trouble making a slow, accurate, short landing. It had become a habit out of necessity.

We soon found out that with this one airplane, which could really dive, we could start hitting the target.

Q: You were making maybe 60- to 70-degree dives?

Captain Tomlinson: At least. Before long, we got an F6C-4 with a Wasp engine. It had a special landing gear for landing aboard the carrier. It had hooks on the axle to pick up the fore-and-aft wires; that was the only difference between the standard Army version, PW-8, that we first received.

Then, in a very short time, less than a month, we got two FB-2s.* They were what the Army called the PW-9; it was the Boeing answer to the Hawk. It had the same 12-cylinder Curtiss engine, known as the D-12. Their flight characteristics were very close to the Curtiss Hawk. It wasn't quite as nice handling or as maneuverable a plane as the Hawk was, but it was okay. We could dive them too. We were really going strong on dive-bombing.

Soon we transferred our practice dive-bombing operations from Ream Field to the old parade ground at Camp

---

*The Boeing FB-1, a predecessor of the FB-2, had a wing span of 32 feet, length of 23 feet, gross weight of 2,835 pounds, and top speed of 159 miles per hour.

Kearny, which today is NAS Miramar.* Then Spig put in official reports on what we were doing. We'd been doing this at first strictly on the cuff to find out if it was feasible. The Bureau of Ordnance set up annual dive-bombing exercises to be carried out and official records to be kept of each pilot's accuracy.

Q: At what altitude would you normally release?

Captain Tomlinson: I think we tried to release somewhere around 1,000-1,500 feet or under. We had to be careful, because sometimes we'd get too near terminal velocity as we got the newer airplanes and learned how to fly them. We'd approach in echelon at about 20,000 feet, the leader choosing the approach altitude, and fly over the target. We liked to make the dive into the wind if possible. You'd come downwind, and you'd look over the side until you figured you were above the target. Then you'd do a half-roll, and down you'd come. If you did it right, you'd be near vertical over that target at about 1,500 feet.

Q: How low would you recover then? It must have been almost on the ground.

Captain Tomlinson: In the average pullout, we'd probably
___
*NAS—naval air station.

get seven or eight G's. We never had any trouble. That was the start of dive-bombing. It's always irritated me that Spig Wead never received any credit for it. He got credit for a lot of things, but that was the greatest contribution that he made. After all, it was dive-bombing that won the Battle of Midway and other major battles. it was what sank the Jap carriers and major ships. I've talked to Walker down at the Naval Aviation Museum and others, and Wead has never been given any credit for it.*

Another interesting thing: after I had landed on North Island in October, I wondered what I was going to do with my airplane.

Q: The Jenny?

Captain Tomlinson: Yes. I looked around. VF-2 had two hangars, the operations hangar and the engineering hangar. One side of the engineering hangar might have one VE-7 in it. There was a lot of available space. I said, "Spig, I've got to do something with this Jenny. I can't just leave it sitting out here on the line. Would you approve if I parked it in the engineering hangar? I'll see if I can get permission from Captain Reeves."** He was

---
*Captain Grover Walker, USN (Ret.), then director of the Naval Aviatoin Museum.
**Captain Joseph M. Reeves, USN, who had a great deal to do with the advancement of carrier aviation in the fleet. His flagship was the USS Langley (CV-1), from which VF-2 operated when at sea.

Commander Aircraft Squadrons Pacific.

Spig said okay.

So I wrote an official letter to the captain. It came back approved. There I was, flight officer of the squadron, with my own private airplane, and special permission to keep it in the engineering hangar. Very handy. When the Navy hauled down the "balls"--signals on the mast on the balloon annex--it meant the weather was unfit to fly. I could then pull the Jenny out and would fly it to Long Beach to have a chat with Earl Dougherty or drop in and see Eddie Martin at Santa Ana. I flew at night, too, just to make people aware that night flying was no real problem.

I used it a lot for hunting in the fall. I'd come over before daylight and take off. I had a number of fields picked in the back country. I'd always drive over these in my Ford car before I landed there because of the gopher holes and ditches not easily seen from the air. I'd come back with my limit of dove or quail in time for quarters at 9:00 o'clock in the morning. That was a great life I had with that plane at my disposal any time. I don't know of anybody else in naval aviation who enjoyed that prerogative.

The squadron operations went on. We knew that the next airplane that we were going to get was the Boeing

FB-5, which was just a slightly larger model of the FB-2 with a 500-horsepower Packard engine in it. In January 1926 we made the cruise on the Langley.* We started training in December of 1925. In fact, I qualified in December of 1925, using VE-7s, aboard the Langley.

Q: Did you have an opportunity for field carrier practice?

Captain Tomlinson: I'm going to get to that. Lieutenant Commander Baugh was on the Langley.** He was to set up this practice landing field on the area of North Island which was Rockwell Field. It's all Navy now. Everybody was supposed to make 100 practice landings on this crazy training deck. I laughed. I went down and looked at the Langley and said to the flight deck officer, "This is easy. For three years I have been flying passengers off fields smaller than this. What's the mystery?"

Of course, they didn't like that at all, because the Langley was a real sacred cow, the first Navy carrier. Landing on it was supposed to be very difficult. Actually, the established landing procedure was what made the landing

---

*USS Langley (CV-1) was originally commissioned as the collier Jupiter (AC-3) in 1913 with Commander Joseph M. Reeves, USN, in command. She was later converted to the U.S. Navy's first aircraft carrier. She was commissioned as the Langley in 1922 with Commander Kenneth Whiting, USN, in command.
**Lieutenant Commander Harry V. Baugh, USN.

difficult. The approaching pilot was to fly his airplane searching for signals from a signal officer on a platform on the stern, just off the port side of the landing area; he had a flag in each hand. The pilot was **not** to use the landing deck in any way as a point of reference. The results, and there are ample movies to confirm my estimate of the picture, were from ludicrous to sad.

After I made two or three landings, then I started coming in doing a loop to a landing. I'd just come down, practically roll my wheels up and over, and land on the spot. By that time, Spig had broken his neck and was gone. Honus Wagner was the squadron commander.* He got a little irritated about that and said, "I don't think you need to make any more landings."

This is interesting too. Jake Gorton and a couple of other guys were signalmen.** The idea was that you were supposed to come in and watch the signalman.

Q: Yes, the early landing signal officers.

Captain Tomlinson: You're supposed to watch him and fly your airplane from what he's telling you with these flags. Then, when he does this, you're supposed to cut your throttle and fall on the deck.

---

*Lieutenant Commander Frank D. Wagner, USN.
**Lieutenant Adolphus W. Gorton, USN.

Q: When he runs the flag across his throat.

Captain Tomlinson: Yes. The number one signal officer, Jake Gorton, was a friend of mine. I told Jake what he could do with his flags when he knew I was coming in.

The regulation procedure was supposed to terminate in a full stall landing, minimum speed. They frequently did it with the result that the plane crashed into the barrier or on the deck with broken wheels or broken landing gear. I simply watched the rise and fall of the stern and kept a safe five miles per hour above stall speed. That gave me adequate control, and I made a wheel landing under control between the ramp and the first wire. True, I pulled the first wire out maybe ten feet farther than if my landing speed was full stall. As my hook caught, I would ease forward slightly on the stick--always a gentle, smooth landing. I made 61 landings and missed the first wire once. I got bawled out several times, but they finally gave up. It was impossible for certain senior people, real old-timers, to admit they were wrong.

I could lay the plane on the deck where I wanted it to go. The tail would probably be about six inches off the deck. These other people were coming in there falling onto the deck--a damn good landing if they didn't fall over two

Daniel W. Tomlinson #2 - 93

feet. Some of them would fall three or four feet, break the wheels, catch the third or fourth wire. Some of them would float over the gear; they'd wait too long. They would watch the signal man and fly into the barrier. It was a laugh. They got a little irate at me, but I just said, "Sorry, boys. *I'm* flying that airplane." Of course, that's what they're doing today. They're flying into the gear. There have been changes.

We checked out with the VE-7s, and then I checked out on the Curtiss Hawks and the FB-2s. No problem; I used my procedure. I went six or seven miles an hour faster, because it was a little heavier airplane and more tender near stall.

We made the trip south on the Langley with VE-7s. We had no problems. Everything was quiet. Nobody bothered me. I didn't bother any of them. Then the FB-5s came in; they were something else. They were really the dive-bombing babies. You'd go up 20,000 feet, and I'll tell you--those things would come down at terminal velocity. We became good at hitting the target with them.

Old Whiskers Reeves, as we called him, wanted to put on a demonstration of an attack on the flagship in the Pacific Fleet.

Q: This was Admiral Reeves? This Whiskers Reeves that you mention was a rear or a vice admiral at that time?

Captain Tomlinson: Reeves was a good admiral. He was only a rear admiral at that time.*

We went out and made this dive-bombing attack. I forget who commanded the fleet then; it really shook them up. When we got back from the exercise, we were laughing. We could look down and see these people ducking and lying down on the bridge. We came down a little bit low. Those things made the damndest roar you ever heard. They were something.

Coming to the end of 1926, the admiral figured that's what we'd take on the cruise to the Caribbean in 1927. The Langley was going to go through the canal to the Caribbean that year.

The FB-5 had one bad characteristic that I didn't like. It had this big, heavy Packard motor. When you were coming in the way these signal flag people were bringing people in, practically on the edge of a stall, it was very critical. You could just give it a little power to increase speed. The FB-5 fully stalled if you gave it too much power. The sudden torque of this 500-horsepower motor meant you were on your back in a flash. I could see pilots getting low on Langley approaches goosing that Packard a

---
*Reeves was promoted to rear admiral in the summer of 1927.

Daniel W. Tomlinson #2 - 95

mite too much, then on their backs 100 to 200 feet off the water. It took the FB-5 a good 500 feet to recover from an inverted stall position--deadly at low altitude. I did a lot of practice at altitude. I used to practice marginal conditions, get at top cloud level and fall into cloud layers. I didn't like that FB-5 characteristic a bit. In that squadron, I could practically put my finger on certain pilots and say that they were sure to go in.

I always wrote my father newsy letters about what was going on and what I thought about things. I never pulled any punches. I wrote a letter to him when we got the FB-5s. The admiral was joyous about what they did as dive-bombers, and he was all gung-ho to take them on the cruise on the Langley in early 1927. I said, "I'm afraid if we take those airplanes, we're going to lose two or three people in the squadron for sure." What I didn't know was that my father played baseball on the Cornell team with Jim Wadsworth, who at that time was a senator and chairman of the Military Affairs Committee.*

Without consulting me, he sent my letter to Senator Wadsworth, and Wadsworth took it up to the Navy Department.

Q: You heard about that right quick, I bet.

---

*James W. Wadsworth, Jr. (Republican-New York) served in the U.S. Senate from 1915 to 1927, later in the House.

Captain Tomlinson: It happened pretty fast, just before these planes were supposed to go on the Langley. That scared old Reeves, and, boy, he didn't dare take them. But he wrote me a letter, grounding me from flying fast airplanes because of my expressed fear of them. I was left behind to have the FB-5 all ready when the Langley returned. So I laughed. When the Langley finally took off with the VE-7s on the cruise, I took off in my JN as a good-bye gesture. They were out probably 10-15 miles off the shore. I dived right down alongside the bridge with the Jenny, did a loop, and thumbed my nose at them as I went by.

Q: Did they have anything to say about that when they got back?

Captain Tomlinson: Not a word was ever said about it. I can't remember just what happened.

Boeing had used excess World War I wheels on the FB-5s. These wheels used to collapse with the plane parked in the hangar. Only a few pilots qualified with them on the Langley. I had no trouble, but others attempting the standard stall landing broke many wheels.

By the time they came back from the cruise, I had the FB-5s all ready for big squadron operations for the summer of 1927. One of the things I was told by the squadron commander to do was to have an insignia fixed up on the side. Jack Tate was quite a character--"Drunk 'n' Dirty Tate," they called him.*

Q: He's the one who had the Russian daughter?**

Captain Tomlinson: Yes, that's the one. He was quite a character. He went over to the library and did some studying, and he came back with this design of a shield. On the bottom and across it were machine guns, then sort of scroll on top with "Fighting Two." Then there were four quadrants with a black bar across underneath, with the name of the plane captain on one, the name of the pilot on the other. In one of the quadrants were a couple of little airplanes dogfighting. I had the planes in the hangar, all beautifully painted up, waiting for the squadron to come back.

Here came a Rolls-Royce, and a dignified Englishman got out. He said, "Can I see your airplanes?"

I said, "Sure, gladly." I took him over through the hangar and proudly displayed these beautifully painted-up

---

*Lieutenant Jackson R. Tate, USN. For Tate's recollections of serving in the Langley in the 1920s, see his article, "We Rode the Covered Wagon," U.S. Naval Institute Proceedings, October 1978, pages 62-69.
**In the mid-1970s Tate received national publicity when his daughter, born to a Russian actress after Tate served as a naval attaché in Moscow in World War II, received special permission to visit the United States.

FB-5s standing there. He pointed to the insignia on them, and he said, "Are you familiar with heraldry?"

I said, "No, we left that to Lieutenant Tate."

He said, "Well, the way you have the black bars on the insignia, you are telling everybody that you are all bastards on both sides of your family."

So after that, when the crowd came back, I said, "You are my little bastards. If you have any complaints, speak to Jack Tate."

Q: I'm not sure, but I think this same insignia is still in use by Fighting Two on its F-14s.

Captain Tomlinson: I might have a picture somewhere that I can show you.

Soon, happily, the F2Bs came along, and we did away with the FB-5s. They were put in storage.*

This is a little skip, but about two years after I left the service and was with Maddux Airlines, a friend of mine wrote, "Tommy, you'll be interested in this. They got the FB-5s out of storage and gave them to a Marine squadron to operate off the Saratoga."** They figured the Saratoga

---

*The Boeing F2B fighter began reaching fleet squadrons in 1928. It had a wing span of 30 feet, length of 23 feet, gross weight of 2,805 pounds, and top speed of 158 miles per hour at sea level.
**The carrier Saratoga (CV-3), converted from a battle cruiser, was commissioned 16 November 1927.

would be big enough for the FB-5s. After two Marines spun in on the approach, just as I had predicted, that was the end of the FB-5s.

Q: How long after this did you go to the National Air Races?

Captain Tomlinson: In the summer of 1927. We were afraid--and the admiral was too--of what would happen if we had to land one of them in the water. With that big, heavy motor up in the nose, it would go down like a rock. So we got engineers from Boeing down, and they conceived the idea of putting inflatable balloons in the V of the shock struts on each side. If you went in, you could trip them, and then they would be flotation gear. We said we would have to test them coming out of terminal-velocity dives.

I was selected to go up to the Boeing factory to run these tests. I was up there about six weeks, and it was a circus. I'd take the plane and go into a terminal-velocity dive. These balloons would come out and inflate; for a minute or so, they would just go crazy. Of course, the balloons would tear off. They finally made an installation that would stay put. I climbed to 20,000 feet on full throttle, then dived until the airspeed stabilized at terminal velocity.

By that time, I had learned that they were going to

hold the 1927 National Air Races at Spokane. It just worked out perfectly. I wrote ComAircraft, Admiral Reeves, requesting permission to return the FB-5 via Spokane so I could observe the National Air Races. This came back approved. Without my knowledge, Admiral Reeves had designated three pilots; I knew only one of them. The one from our squadron had an F2B. Another one from an observation squadron had a UO used as an observation plane on a battleship. Then I think there was one torpedo plane. These three different types of planes were sent up to represent the Navy at the National Air Races.

I went over and stayed with a Naval Reserve aviation cadet who was then about to complete his training as a student. I think he had soloed. He came from a wealthy family and had a beautiful home in Spokane. I flew the FB-5 over there.

Jim Doolittle was there with his Three Musketeers, flying Curtiss Hawks.* He had his carburetors fixed so they he could fly at full power inverted. They did perfectly beautiful formation acrobatics, slow rolls off the ground, and they didn't have to worry about losing power inverted. They put on a beautiful show.

The Marines had a squadron, flying the same airplanes, except they didn't have their carburetors fixed. Tex

---

*James H. Doolittle, who gained fame for leading an Army Air Forces bombing raid on Tokyo in April 1942. His oral history is in the Naval Institute collection.

Daniel W. Tomlinson #2 - 101

Rogers was their leader; he was a Naval Academy man.* He had one pilot with him who misjudged. They came down at an angle to the spectator stands at about 45 degrees. Each one came down to about ten feet, and then each did a climbing slow roll on the pullout. This pilot rolled upside down, and his motor conked out. Instead of trying to complete the slow roll, he tried a half loop out. When he came down out of that half loop, he was turned at 45 degrees back toward the stand. He didn't quite make it. His wheels hit the ground. I was standing there and saw the whole thing. The wheels came up and broke the two front spars in each lower wing, and the wheels flew off. One wheel went into the stands but didn't hurt anybody too seriously. His propeller tips were curled back. You've never heard anything howl like that engine. Here was this half-wrecked airplane; he just cleared the stands and went over some wires, and he used his head. He had enough speed coming down out of this half loop, so he turned and made a belly landing out in the field. I never saw a pilot so scared in my life. That broke up the Marines' act.

I had known Jim Doolittle before. A friend of mine had roomed with Jim when they went to MIT together. I had flown with my friend to Roosevelt Field where Jim and Joe were on duty.** That's where I met him. We were getting

---
*Captain Ford O. Rogers, USMC.
**Roosevelt Field on Long Island was the takeoff point for Charles Lindbergh's transatlantic flight in 1927.

together at parties. Finally, at one big party both of us were pretty tight. I got Jim over to one side and said, "Goddamn you. What did you do to those carburetors to make them run upside down?"

He said, "Tommy, that's simple. Disconnect your gas line to your carburetor and fill it full of solder. Then drill the right size hole through that solder so that you've got one master jet. When you turn upside down, that master jet, regardless of the non-operation of your float, meters enough fuel for the engine to run at full throttle." Of course, there was one other little joker. You had a reserve pipe in the bottom of your gas tank that stuck up about six inches. So when you were going to do that act, you wanted to take off with a full tank and be using the reserve fuel valve. When you turned upside down, the stand pipe would be sticking up into the fuel, and you wouldn't lose suction. It worked. You can run at full power for 45 seconds inverted. You can do outside loops and all kinds of things that you can't do without that continuity of power in your inverted position. So I learned that important trick.

Some years later, this pilot Williams, who was leading the Musketeers, was killed when he tried to duplicate my inverted act at 50 feet. I figured I had 45 seconds that I could run without losing oil pressure. That was the critical thing.

Q: Yes, to avoid engine damage.

Captain Tomlinson: Yes. You lose oil pressure after 45 seconds inverted, but 45 seconds is long enough.

I always came in downwind. I'd roll inverted as I crossed the border of the field, and in 30-45 seconds I was past the main grandstands. I could roll out climbing with no problem. Williams tried to do it, but his motor quit on him, and he hooked a wing on the rollout.

That's how I got started on the formation acrobatics. These three pilots from the Navy with three different airplanes tried to fly formation, and it was absolutely ludicrous!

Q: Completely different types.

Captain Tomlinson: Yes. It was silly to even try.

Right then I decided that the Navy would have a top-notch team at the 1928 races. When we got back, the FB-5s, after all this expense of putting on the flotation gear, went into storage. Then we got the F2Bs, starting in the fall of 1927. I began selecting my wingmen. I picked out Bill Davis and Putt Storrs, both excellent acrobatic pilots.*

Q: How did you select them?

Captain Tomlinson: I simply watched the pilots in day-to-day operations. I watched them, then took them up to try them out. I said, "You're going to fly ten feet apart, and we'll do a loop in formation." I eliminated several right quick. I said, "All you've got to do is watch me. Just look at my airplane. Don't look at another thing. Just watch me for signals, look at my airplane, and fly close. There's nothing to it."

I made my selection and began training them. The ticklish part of it was that it was all contrary to flight regulations. Nothing had ever been done of that kind before. I had to train them to do this stuff off the ground so it would be impressive. They'd never done anything of that kind because they had followed regulations.

When I first started training them, I'd get them on top of an even overcast with a markedly level top. That's after we had been doing flipper turns and wingovers and easy maneuvers. You can do that and be seen with no kickback. Then we started doing loops up on top. Looping,

---

*Lieutenant (junior grade) William V. Davis, USN; Lieutenant (junior grade) Aaron P. Storrs III, USN.

Daniel W. Tomlinson #2 - 105

I just touched my wheels on top of the clouds, and I'd come out at least 100 feet higher. Then I started going back and doing it alongside of a mountain, and then finally level with the ground in the back country, around Ramona and Escondido, where we hoped not to be seen. I started doing it right off the ground. Bill and Putt learned fast. Then we graduated into slow rolls, squirrel-cage loops, and inverted flight.

Q: What sort of approval was necessary to do this?

Captain Tomlinson: There wasn't any approval. It was all on the "QT." Our necks were out--but good.

This is kind of funny. In 1928 I had them pretty well trained after a couple of months. They were doing well. You can't keep a thing like that absolutely quiet, but nobody had even seen anything and couldn't pin anything on us. But then we got up to San Francisco on the old Langley, on the cruise north to Hawaii in 1928. The fleet air was to put on a big parade over San Francisco. I was told by the chief of staff--not by the admiral, but by Gene Wilson, chief of staff--"At the end of the parade, Tommy, I want you and your section to put on a show."*

---
*Commander Eugene E. Wilson, USN. Wilson's autobiography Slipstream, third edition (Palm Beach: Literary Investment Guild, 1967), discusses Tomlinson and his flight demonstration team. See pages 126, 133-134, 150.

I said, "Okay." We did put on a show. The last thing we did, I flew inverted halfway down Market Street--below the tops of the buildings. I didn't trust Bill and Putt to be inverted under such conditions. They flew cocked up on each side. I was upside down, going right down the middle of Market Street.

Q: That must have gotten some comment.

Captain Tomlinson: We never heard a word. It was significant that Admiral Reeves included the three of us to attend a very fancy luncheon for the "brass."

After that, the fog moved in. Of course, the rest of the people all disappeared while we were doing this act over the city. I sneaked out--not to the Golden Gate, but I went out another little pass I knew just south of the city. I knew about where the <u>Langley</u> was going to be, and I flew underneath the fog, a couple of hundred feet underneath it. I led my section back to land aboard the <u>Langley</u>. We were the only ones who got back; the rest of them all landed at Crissy Field and waited till the next day.

On a previous cruise, the fighter squadrons had TSs, biplanes which had J-5 engines, and the fuselage was sort of halfway between the upper and lower wings. It was not a good fighter. At that time the Army had MB-3s, a Boeing monoplane fighter. It was fast but tricky control-wise. The motor was a 300-horsepower Hisso. It wasn't a popular airplane. I knew several pilots were killed in this plane. It wasn't a good-flying airplane, but it was fast, much faster than the ones the Navy had. So when the TSs flew to Ford Island, the Army pilots just crucified them.* They scared the Navy squadron commander so badly he got right down on the water, and he finally flew into the water. It didn't kill him, but it hurt his pride no end! We all knew about this and were prepared to have revenge.

I had coached my people. I said, "We're going to take those crummy Army pilots to town." Because with the F2B we had enough superiority performance-wise--speed, controllability, and an altitude edge--to outmaneuver their PW-9s. I saw to it that VF-2 pilots had plenty of practice dogfighting. I said, "When you get on a PW-9's tail, you stay on his tail until he lands at Wheeler Field. Don't you let him go." That was exactly what we did. We had 12 planes in the air, and we ran 12 of them right back to Wheeler Field before we let go of them. We had fun. The tables were turned.

That irritated the Army pilots no end. It was only about a week after this, a Saturday morning inspection, when our planes were all lined up out in front of the

---
*Ford Island is in the center of Pearl Harbor, Oahu, Hawaii.

hangar on Ford Island. Here came this PW-9, diving down out of the clouds, and dove right across our line of F2Bs, missing the airplanes by five or ten feet, thumbing his nose as he went by. So I called to Putt and Bill, "Wind up our airplanes." It was a day when there were broken cumulus clouds. Some of them went up to 10,000, 12,000 feet or more, with spaces in between them. I just had a hunch that the pilot who buzzed our line did it as a decoy to get us to take off and chase him. They had other people hiding in the clouds, waiting to jump us from a superior altitude. They'd get the edge on us. We'd get away in time probably, but at least they'd get at us for a while. But they failed.

With Putt and Bill I took off in a hurry. I led them right to the closest cloud handy. I told them to stick close to me, and I used the gyro instruments. All they had to do was keep me in sight and forget we were in the clouds. I spiralled up through the clouds and came out on top, around 14,000-15,000 feet. I started looking for the sneaks, and, sure enough, there were two more. I saw them between clouds, and I knew they were giving us the finger. The first pilot was climbing back up to join the two people who were waiting to pounce on us. We just clobbered them; in a flash we were on their tails, and we ran them back to Wheeler Field. After a couple of futile maneuvers with no luck, they hurried home. When they landed, we were right

Daniel W. Tomlinson #2 - 109

behind them and above them, just thumbing our noses at them and pointing down. We stayed there until they were on the ground.

Then we reformed. I decided on a square loop to a landing. Putt and Bill formed up, and we came across Wheeler Field with beaucoup speed. We pulled up in a loop and flew downwind inverted. When I figured we were in the right position, we came down out of the loop to a formation landing. The show was perfect. We taxied up to the Army line proud as peacocks. And, damn, there was the personal airplane of Commander Jack Towers, who was in command of the Langley. The plane had special insignia on it for the captain's airplane. I could just see him standing there watching us and talking to an Air Corps colonel while we were doing this very non-reg act. That was the first time we had done such tricks where anyone could see us. They could report our show over San Francisco if someone wanted to, but there wasn't any brass right there who could testify. I really was scared. I thought, "Gee, here's my third general court-martial. This is my finish."

We went back to Ford Island. This was in the morning. I knew that every day after lunch Jack Towers would go out and walk back and forth on the quarterdeck for a while. So after lunch I thought, "I'll get this thing over with." I just went out on the quarterdeck and started to wander along. As I came close to Towers, he said, "Tomlinson, I think the Air Corps has been sufficiently impressed."

Q: That's all he said?

Captain Tomlinson: I could have kissed him. That was all that was ever said. But we still had fun with the Air Corps. At a cocktail party some of the Air Corps pilots started yapping about how dangerous it was to fly through the Pali, which was a gap in the mountains. Quite a stream of air goes through it. There is a cliff that drops off about 3,000 feet straight down--vertical. I'd flown through the Pali before; it wasn't <u>that</u> bad. Putt and Bill were standing there, the Air Corps group around, so I said, "Okay, let's see if it is really that bad. At 9:00 o'clock tomorrow morning, we will fly through the Pali in formation, inverted." And we did.

The Army had an ON observation plane at that time, built by Douglas. The pilot's cockpit was just forward of the wing, right in back of the Liberty engine. The ON was circling up above the Pali when we went through inverted.

Q: They must have thought the Navy was producing wild men.

Captain Tomlinson: We had fun and got away with it. After our demonstration, the Navy air was respected. They knew we were not to be fooled with.

Then the thing that finally capped it was in the summer of 1928, when Lindbergh Field was completed in San Diego. They were going to dedicate it.

Q: This is after he got back from Paris.

Captain Tomlinson: Yes. VF-2 came back from Hawaii on the _Lexington_.* In fact, my squadron was the first squadron to land on the _Lexington_. The _Lexington_ joined the fleet in Honolulu. We came back on it. Admiral Reeves again decided to have a grand aircraft parade because a lot of bigwigs were going to be there for this dedication. There was a lot of Navy and Army brass besides civilians. There were elaborate plans for this parade. The first flights to go through were the fighters, two squadrons that made up the fighter wing. Next was to be the observation wing, then the torpedo wing, and the flying boats of the patrol wing.

In the morning there was fog--not a dense fog. We had 1,000 feet of vertical visibility, very little horizontal visibility. Above 1,000 feet, it was approaching dense fog. So we took off as planned.

My section was leading the wing. I said, "We will fly down to the lower bay and keep underneath this fog. I will

---

*The carrier _Lexington_ (CV-2), converted from a battle cruiser, was commissioned 14 December 1927.

Daniel W. Tomlinson #2 - 112

circle at about 500 feet," which I did. All the other planes took off and disappeared. When the time came, according to schedule, I was on time with Fighting Two. I think there was some part of the observation wing. The other fighting squadron never did tell where they went; they never did show up. We went by on schedule.

We'd been told by Gene Wilson, "Put on your show in front of the grandstand."

I said, "This is make or break. Either we go to the air races, or we get general court-martials." In our introductory thing we came in not over five to ten feet apart. I always figured to raise dust with my wheels when I pulled up. Right in front of the grandstand, we did three successive loops and then our inverted stuff. Because of the buildings and obstructions, I didn't fly quite as low as I did at the National Air Races, but I made an inverted pass across at maybe 50 feet or so. The admiral made no comment. Gene Wilson congratulated us, and we were selected to go to the National Air Races to represent the Navy.

Q: That must have been very gratifying after the clandestine beginnings.

Captain Tomlinson: It was. We could have been court-martialed offhand for any number of reasons if the brass

Daniel W. Tomlinson #2 - 113

wished, because nothing of that kind had ever been thought of or done in the Navy.

To cap it off, I trained the entire squadron. To have a little fun, I had 15 planes in V formation. We came in over North Island at about 1,500 feet and looped the whole squadron in formation. People still remember that.

Q: I don't imagine that had ever been done before.

Captain Tomlinson: We had five three-plane sections, the lead section and two on each side. It made a beautiful show.

Q: Was there any kind of official reaction to that?

Captain Tomlinson: There was a lot of talk, but nobody ever said boo officially.

Q: How much time did you have to prepare for the air races?

Captain Tomlinson: I kept them training during the summer of 1928. This was 1928 when the dedication took place.

Q: When did your team become known as the Seahawks?

Daniel W. Tomlinson #2 - 114

Captain Tomlinson: The latter part of the summer of 1928. They had some names people were trying to call us. One day, sitting out in front of the squadron office in the grass, Putt and Bill and I were talking about it. Putt Storrs said, "How about the Three Seahawks?" Then it took. We decided that that was a good name.

Q: Did that have an official connotation to it?

Captain Tomlinson: No, we simply became known as the Three Seahawks, and that was it!

Q: And you were billed as such at the air races?

Captain Tomlinson: Yes. The whole squadron went up, and the squadron put on its show there. It was very interesting. I didn't fool around. I forget just how I worked it, but I had my own airplane over at Earl Daugherty's field. Instead of staying in some hotel like the rest of them did and being subject to a lot of pestering, when the show was over, I just jumped into my Jenny and flew over to Earl Daugherty's field to spend the night. I flew back in time for the squadron flight in the morning. The Three Seahawks flew in the afternoon.

Q: Did you change your routine in any way for the air

races?

Captain Tomlinson: No. I can't remember the exact order in which we did things, but we did this series of loops. I think we used to do four, then a squirrel-cage loop, chasing each other's tails. We did inverted flying, climbing slow rolls, wingovers, flipper turns, and then we did a special simulated dive-bombing attack, a little on the hairy side. We'd climb up and peel off to dive three ways. I can't remember now exactly how it worked out, but I would always come in on the dive over, but away from the stands. Putt and Bill would dive parallel to the stands in opposite directions. We had a target on the runway for bombing attacks. We had a time with it, because it required close timing. I'd come down and go by Bill; Putt then whizzed by. That was a good act, coordinated to a split second. Putt and Bill were dependable. We practiced it, so we never had any what I could dangerous close calls.

Q: It's interesting to note that the Blue Angels are still using that crossover today.

Captain Tomlinson: With the controls and their jet planes, they can do things that we could not. The principle is more or less the same. We did all kinds of vertical turns and such. I can't remember how long it took. The final act was when I would do this inverted flight the length of Mines Field at low altitude.* I never trusted Putt and Bill to fly so low in close formation inverted. At that time, we were at least wearing parachutes, which were of no value at 50 feet. At 50 feet, they'd just be cocked up at angles from me on each side. I'd be upside down. It was fun.

I got to meet a lot of people. One was Jack Maddux, who was president of Maddux Airlines.** He had started Maddux Airlines with Ford tri-motors in 1927. I knew most of the commercial people in the area around Los Angeles as a result of flying the Jenny. I knew all the ones who went to the air meets. I got cups and won cash awards in the various events. The events at the air meets always included a Jenny scramble and a stunting contest. There were balloon-busting contests and dead-stick landings to a mark; it was a lot of fun. They'd release a balloon and time it until you broke the balloon. It's not as easy as you think to dive down and hit that balloon. You'd be amazed how elusive the things can be. They always had a dead-stick landing contest. Somebody always had a fast airplane. There were free-for-all races. Owners would ask me to fly their airplanes for them, especially in the free-for-all. I could beat the others turning at the pylons

---
*Mines Field was the Los Angeles municipal airport.
**John L. Maddux.

marking the course.

Q: That's a terrific way to gain experience, isn't it, seeing everybody else and flying different airplanes?

Captain Tomlinson: You'd talk to everybody about this or that, find a nugget now and then; it all added up.

I flew every plane that was available. I wish I had those log books, particularly the one that has a list of all the planes I flew. There were a couple of them that I flew for five minutes--no more! I took them off and flew around and back to the field. I could have done without that; I was lucky to land in one piece. On one of them the next pilot who flew it--I don't think he was killed, but he washed it out and was bent himself. I tell you, they were curiosities. But I considered it all experience.

Q: One of the recurring themes that Chuck Yeager makes in his speeches these days, in promoting his book, is that the pilot who wins, whether it's a dogfight or a contest, is the one with the most experience.*

Captain Tomlinson: I think that's generally true.

Admiral Moffett was at the national races, and

---
*Chuck Yeager, Yeager: An Autobiography (New York: Bantam Books, 1985).

Daniel W. Tomlinson #2 - 118

afterward he congratulated the squadron and had the three of us at a big formal affair.* He asked what duty I wanted next. I was supposed to have been detached in June of 1928. Admiral Reeves requested that I be held over for the races. I told him I wanted to go to the NAS Anacostia test section. Steve Callaway was the head of the test section and was due to be relieved.** I was senior to Steve.

To this day, I don't know what happened, but when I landed at El Paso, flying back home with the Jenny, I was handed a telegram dispatch. It was to the effect that my orders had been changed, and I was to report to NAS Pensacola to be the chief pilot of training. That didn't interest me; instructing was too routine and monotonous. I knew that I would get into endless arguments with people. Many of my ideas about flying were quite contrary to the accepted Navy standards at that time. Knowing the attitude in the high ranks, people who knew nothing of what I was talking about and trying to do, I wouldn't get anywhere.

So I just went on to western New York. When I got up there, I called the Navy Department and said, "Now, look . . ." My orders were changed back to the test section at Anacostia.

I flew into Buffalo, New York--no problem across the

---
*Rear Admiral William A. Moffett, USN, Chief of the Bureau of Aeronautics from 1921 until his death in 1933.
**Lieutenant Steven W. Callaway, USN.

country. Beyond Buffalo I flew under an overcast, about 300 feet, to Batavia, New York, my old home town, about 30 miles down the New York Central Railroad tracks. I was going to land in LeRoy since Batavia had no landing field at that time; LeRoy was five miles farther east, where there was a landing field. Woodward, a wealthy man, had made this landing field. My father and mother and other people were going to meet me out there. I had the Jenny all loaded up with my personal gear. I was going to spend a week at home. I had 30 days' leave, and then I planned to fly to Anacostia.

I flew over Batavia and on to Woodward Field. I'd never been there before. I took a look at it. It was a peculiar field on a slope, east to west. The wind sock indicated a ground-level wind a little from the west. I was flying right at the base of this overcast. I decided to land downwind and uphill to save taxiing distance--just dive into the wind and do a wingover to a landing uphill. What I didn't take into account was that where I was, at the base of that overcast, the wind was probably going 20-25 miles per hour. But right on the ground the wind sock indicated maybe just five, nothing to worry about. I pulled up and went into the overcast at the top of my wingover. As I dropped down out of the overcast, I could see I was in trouble. The stronger wind in the cloud layer had drifted the plane closer to the rising landing strip than I had expected. I was simply too low to get my right wingtip up. That wingtip guard dragged on the ground, and the plane cartwheeled. That JN really splintered; the ash longeron in front of the cockpit shattered. I went forward, and my face hit the compass on the cowling and knocked out four front teeth.

For several days I stayed in Batavia to get false teeth put in before I reported to Anacostia. I went out to look at the wreckage, and it had been hauled off into a hangar. I salvaged the motor and a few items. The rest of it was hopeless. There was an old cabinetmaker there who did woodwork on the airplanes on the field. He came up and introduced himself to my father. He told my father, "I'd like to point something out to your son."

I said, "Good."

He went over to the old Jenny. It had these old ash longerons about 1 3/4 inches square, which began in back of the pilot's cockpit. They were tapered, glued, and wrapped to the spruce longerons forming the tail structure. Those ash longerons were the main structural members up to the firewall, where the engine mounts were attached. The lower wings attached to the bottom longerons at the front cockpit. Short struts came down from the upper center wing section on each side of the front cockpit and attached to the upper ash longerons. They had shattered. Where there was a bolt hole through these longerons, they looked as though they had been cut through with a knife.

This old cabinetmaker told me, "Live ash does not shatter. Do you realize those longerons were all spruce?" I don't think it had anything to do with the cause of the accident, but I wrote up my accident and sent it to Clarence Young, whom I knew, of the CAA and said that cause of the accident was "cockpit trouble." A year or two later, when I again met Clarence, he said, "Tommy, you submitted the first honest accident report we received."

Sometimes I've wondered, since it ought not to have happened, because I loved that airplane. I flew that JN over 800 hours in all kinds of weather. I had no idea as to the condition of the longerons. I might have flown into some severe turbulence, and it would have come part in the air with fatal results.

Q: It's hard to imagine that being a beneficial result, but it could have been so much worse.

Captain Tomlinson: Yes, that particular accident was pure cockpit trouble but possibly a blessing in disguise.

Q: You mentioned earlier some work on the tailhooks when you were flying on the Langley. Did you have something to do with modifying the hooks on the airplanes?

Captain Tomlinson: No. I said I have this dummy tailhook on my chain which was given to me at a luncheon affair. It didn't have anything to do with that. All I wanted to accomplish on the <u>Langley</u> was to get the pilots to fly onto the deck under control instead of falling in at the instructions of the signal officer. I didn't approve of the standard procedure.

Q: What was your first project at Anacostia?

Captain Tomlinson: The first project that I was assigned to had an observation-type Vought Corsair, which was a beautiful biplane with a Wasp engine. In World War II Vought came out with the F4U, which was called the Corsair, a fighter. But at that time, in 1928, we had this observation plane. It was a lovely airplane to fly; then there was talk of using it for dive-bombing. I relieved Steve Callaway as head of the section, and I decided that any dive-bomber had better be tested at 10-G pullouts at terminal velocity.

Q: Do you remember what terminal velocity was in that airplane?

Captain Tomlinson: I can't remember that detail now. It was whatever registered when you were in a vertical dive at full power and the airspeed had ceased to increase. That was terminal velocity.

Q: The UO-1?

Captain Tomlinson: That was the small one, J-5, purely an observation type, although for a year or so the enlisted (AP) squadron used them as fighters.

Q: The Corsair, then, must have been the O2U or O3U.

Captain Tomlinson: I guess it was. This plane had a Wasp engine. It was a nice airplane to fly, a wonderful cross-country airplane with perfect control at low speed and slow landing speed. In this vertical, terminal-velocity-dive pullout, the structure was subjected to maximum stress. On the pullout, I got elevator flutter. I cut the power off and got the flutter manageable. I had enough elevator control for a safe landing. The left rear stabilizer spar had broken, so the left side of the stabilizer at the flipper hinge point was flopping.

At that time we knew we were about to receive an airplane built by Curtiss, a dive-bomber/observation plane combination which became known as the Helldiver.* I insisted that the factory pilot demonstrate the plane in a

---

*This was the F8C.

terminal-velocity dive with a 10-G pullout.

Q: How did they feel about that?

Captain Tomlinson: There was some huffing and puffing in the bureau, but my recommendation was approved. When that plane was brought down by the Curtiss pilot, he did it. Sure enough, the wings came off. I was standing there with some of these people who had questioned my recommendation, and I said, "Admiral, there's your airplane."

Q: Did the pilot get out?

Captain Tomlinson: Yes, he jumped, and the parachute opened okay. He and the plane ended up somewhere east along the river and didn't do any damage. After that it became standard procedure for company test pilots to demonstrate terminal-velocity pullouts at ten G's.

Q: I remember something about a flying boat that you were testing then.

Captain Tomlinson: Yes, then the PN-11 came along. The boat was built at the Naval Aircraft Factory. It was nice biplane, twin-engine boat, with two Hornets.* I was flying it over the speed course. Navy regulations required them before other performance tests were made, and it had to be in full combat readiness. The plane had machine guns, ammunition, everything in it. I never gave it a thought. You'd level off on a steady flight over the speed course, time the run, check your airspeed, and then you could calibrate your airspeed instrument error on the basis of the actual speed. That's the way you calibrated the instrument for location error as there was a variation due to the position of the pitot tube. You'd fly it at several different speeds, correcting for air density.

This course was up and down the Potomac River. I was flying upriver towards Anacostia. We'd pass the mark at the ends of the course, start or stop our watches, and I'd pull up to reverse course. It wasn't exactly a wingover, but combined with a tight, climbing turn and then back down and level off for another run down the river. Right at the top of this turn, I looked out to the left, and the engine was on fire. I put the plane into a side slip to keep the flame away from the tail surface. I got the plane on the water quickly. The wind was so that I could taxi on the water with full throttle on the right engine toward the

---

*The PN-11 had two 525-horsepower Pratt & Whitney R-1690 engines.

beach. It began to get hot in the left cockpit seat once I got on the water; the fire was roaring. They didn't have flexible gas lines in those days; they just ran the line from the hull to the engine mount. The difference in vibration period between the engine mount and the hull structure caused the line to break, and the exhaust ignited the gasoline.

I headed for the beach, and it was cold. This was in December. I was in the left-hand seat, on the fire side. The crew climbed up the nose in front and took off their winter gear and piled it over between me and the fire. I headed for the beach hell bent. The plane had gas tanks in the hull on each side. I could see that when the motor and wing fell the blades were going to rupture those gas tanks, and hell would break loose. As long as I could keep moving, the fire was back. I just made it to the beach. As we got out, the whole left side collapsed, the tanks went up, and we were all lying on our bellies on the far side of the dike. Then the machine gun ammunition started to go off like firecrackers.

Q: That's enough excitement for one day.

Captain Tomlinson: These were the only two incidents that happened to me at Anacostia. Poor George Cuddihy relieved me. I don't know to this day--nobody's ever explained it--

he was flying a Bristol fighter and something happened. He dived into the ground. George was a top-notch pilot. Whatever caused the crash I do not know.

Q: I never knew that the Navy had any Bristol fighters.

Captain Tomlinson: It was an English Bristol fighter. Maybe they were just evaluating. I don't think the Navy ever bought them. Maybe it was one sent for evaluation.

Q: This was the two-seater fighter from World War I?

Captain Tomlinson: I never saw it. I was told that George went in steep. I could never figure it out, because George was a crackerjack pilot.

Q: What other projects did you do at Anacostia?

Captain Tomlinson: That was all, because I was in contact with Jack Maddux. After the air races, I took two weeks of my 30 days' leave and flew for Jack. He wanted me then to resign from the Navy and take over operations of his airline. It was strictly a barnstorming outfit. There was no organization, no discipline. They picked the best pilots available. They were all fine people, but in those days they never had any plans or any discipline or organization. It horrified me, and I told him so.

Q: Where was Maddux based at that time?

Captain Tomlinson: Rodgers Airport, which was a hell of a field when it rained. The mud was awful. They had no hangar for maintenance; they worked on the airframe in the open and hung canvas over the engines. I wasn't sold on the layout. I told Jack I'd think about it. I went back to Anacostia, and everything was going along well.

Then my good friend Earl Daugherty killed himself. He had a J-5 Laird, which was a beautiful little airplane. I'd gotten Earl a commission as lieutenant (junior grade), Naval Reserve. He and his wife would come down and spend two weeks with me, active duty, with VF-2. He'd fly our fighters, fitted in, liked by all. Everybody appreciated Earl, and he liked all hands. He took his place in squadron flying. He loved to perform acrobatics. He had a particular Jenny, and he'd snap roll that Jenny to the point where he'd stretched the wires so that the turnbuckles wouldn't take them up any tighter. Then he tied knots in the wires. I was horrified. I knew too much about structures and safety factors. I knew what Earl was doing was deadly, and I tried to warn him.

Then he got this Laird, a nice airplane. It had the capability but not the strength. It had performance; it would do these acrobatics that he was doing with our fighters, but it didn't have the strength. One of his favorite tricks was a nice one, something that I used to do with the F2Bs. You'd go across a field doing a precise slow roll. Then when you were on top of the roll, you hauled the elevators full up, kicked the rudder, and did a quick snap roll the opposite direction to that of the slow roll. It was a very pretty but tricky maneuver. He was doing these things with his J-5 Laird. I told him, and other people did, too: "Earl, don't do that. That airplane isn't built for it."

What finally got him was that he liked to practice. He was out practicing to put on a show. He quit and came in, filled the tank full of gas. In time past he had promised a stunt ride to two newspapermen, and they came along and put the arm on him. I guess Earl said, "Oh, hell," and took the airplane out of the hangar after he had put it away full of gas. Now, he put these two men in the front seat, and away he went. He did this trick of a slow roll, then the reverse snap roll. The wings came off. The G's that you put on an airplane, when you do a snap roll with a lot of speed, are way high.

Well, that was the end of Earl. He'd been my mentor--introducing me into commercial aviation, barnstorming, and stunt flying. At a critical period, when the Navy had kicked me out, he'd become a very dear friend, about the closest friend that I had in that period, without any question. He was one of the closest friends I had in my life; we became very close.

The only way I could get out for the funeral was to fly out. Anacostia had several DHs sitting around there that weren't doing anything, and I tried to get permission to get a DH to fly out to Long Beach. Earl had done a lot publicity-wise for the Navy too. There were times when the spotter squadrons had camped on his field to operate off San Pedro with the fleet, and I thought the Navy owed him something. I finally wound up going to old Admiral Hughes, who was Chief of Naval Operations.* When he finally turned me down, I said, "Thank you, Admiral. I will resign from the Navy immediately." And I did. I wired Jack Maddux and accepted his offer to be vice president of operations.

Q: So you had a standing offer?

Captain Tomlinson: I had a standing offer from Jack, and I had decided that if they'd let me fly out for the funeral, I'd probably have stayed in the Navy; I'm not sure. I knew it was a risk; I had a family, two kids. By that time, with the Seahawk background and my barnstorming, I felt

---
*Admiral Charles F. Hughes, USN, served as Chief of Naval Operations from 14 November 1927 to 17 September 1930.

that I was pretty well established in aviation and had a reputation that would stand. When the Navy let me down, I said, "To hell with you." I went with Maddux Air Lines.

Q: How long did it take to make the transition from resigning from the Navy until you started with Maddux?

Captain Tomlinson: Jack said, "Meet me in Detroit in two days." He was taking delivery of their first Wasp Ford. I tendered my resignation and shoved off for Detroit. Jack was there with some of his directors. I got in the Ford, took it out and flew it around the field. Then we took off for the West Coast, heading for St. Louis. We got beyond Indianapolis and ran into a blizzard moving east. I could fly on instruments, but we didn't have any beams at that time. So I was out on my "hands and knees," crawling on ground contact. I knew the route into St. Louis all right, but when I finally got down to about 50 feet over the treetops, I decided, "This is no dice." I saw below me a cut cornfield, a big one, and I just swung around and landed in this miserable cornfield to wait out the storm. There was a town close by.

That night the temperature went to something like ten degrees below zero. Then I started to learn, the next day, how you start three Wasp motors with the temperature ten degrees below. It had warmed up a little bit, now around

Daniel W. Tomlinson #2 - 132

zero. We had to go to all the tinsmiths or hardware stores to obtain pots for heating lead used in plumbing connections. We obtained canvas. It took us until afternoon to get those engines started. Then we got out of there and headed for Los Angeles.

Q: Was that your first experience with a tri-motor aircraft?

Captain Tomlinson: No.

In the two weeks I was with jack, I flew the 4ATs, the J-5s. I flew Jack Maddux down to Guymas, Mexico. He wanted to talk to important people at Hermosillo, Mexico, about an airmail contract. When we got to Hermosillo, I had to chase cattle off the field in order to land. Then they took us to a brewery. They had a fancy room where they entertained VIPs. They had lots of good cold beer. Then, halfway between Hermosillo and Guymas, we were told, "There's an Army post where airplanes land. We'd like you to pick up the general and take him to Guymas."

Jack said, "Do you think you can land there?"

I said, "I'll take a look at it." I could get in all right and could probably get out. The field was L-shaped with a hangar in a corner close to the road and a runway parallel to the road. No problem getting in, but here comes this general--one of those fat Mexican generals. He

Daniel W. Tomlinson #2 - 133

must have weighed 350 pounds. Then he had an aide that he wanted to take along with him. It was now a horse of a different color. I paced the field over. I had just a little breeze coming from the northeast, which would help. This leg was a little bit longer. I couldn't start on it, because I was afraid I wouldn't make it off the edge of that field. So I got back over to the corner of that short leg of the L. I got started on it, and when I had enough speed for aileron control, I turned into the wind with one wheel on the ground and got off. At that it was close.

Q: Had you ever made a takeoff like that before?

Captain Tomlinson: No, and never made another one.

After I joined Maddux at Los Angeles, he was still haggling for a Mexican mail contract. I had only been on the job for about a month in 1929, and he decided to fly to Mexico City. Dwight Morrow was ambassador, and Slim Lindbergh was there courting Anne Morrow.*

I was taken out of my job, where I was trying to get some order and organization, which the airline needed. I flew Jack and a couple of directors to Mexico City, and I took my wife with me. We landed at Guadalajara, and there was some firing going on in the city. It was at the time of the last revolution. Most of the fighting was up around

---
*In 1929 Charles A. Lindbergh married Anne Spencer Morrow.

Daniel W. Tomlinson #2 - 134

Juarez. We didn't worry about it. We didn't have any trouble taking off from Guadalajara, 5,000 feet. It is only about halfway to Mexico City. Then one engine swallowed a valve. The mountains rise to 10,000 feet and over. We made it through the passes into Mexico City on one engine. Morrow and some other bigwigs were out at Cuernavaca, so we spent one night in a hotel in Mexico City. We had a mechanic with us, and he figured he could take the cylinder off and replace it. We carried spare parts for the J-5 engines.

We drove to Cuernavaca, and we were there over the weekend. Sunday Jack was notified officially that the Mexican Government had confiscated the Ford and was flying it over to the military field which was closer in to the city. Jack contacted Slim and Morrow and worked out a deal with the Mexicans.

The final deal was that we had to fly a Mexican general, his aide, a suitcase of gold, and a couple of machine guns to Juarez to pay the troops at the garrison. Again, the general was outsized. And that suitcase of gold weighed plenty at 7,000 feet. The "sewing machine" J-5s were short on power at that altitude, and the commercial field was a little over a mile square. At the far end of it was an irrigation ditch, and on the other side of the ditch was another field. I had to get over the irrigation ditch to the second field to complete my takeoff.

I had been eating hot food. I like that Mexican chow. I had the Mexican "two-step." I finally made a dicker: "I'll take the general and the gold if you've got a plane [and they had one, a Stinson] that will take the aide and the machine guns as far as Tampico. I will land at Tampico, at sea level. I'm pretty sure I can take them all off there, but not here." I knew it was going to be a close one, getting off at Mexico City with the load agreed upon.

I figured I'd just have to "horse" the plane over that ditch on the edge of a stall speed, haul back at the last moment, maybe hit hard on the other side. The Ford just crawled for a half mile before I got the tail lifted off the ground. When we got up to that ditch, I was getting a little on the nervous side. I was looking over, and when I could see the ditch almost under the nose engine, I gave nearly full up elevator, set my belly for the effort, and hauled back on the controls. We staggered over the ditch and headed for Tampico. I laugh now, but there really wasn't anything funny about it.

Everything went okay. The plane staggered off halfway of the second field. We got down into Tampico. We had two-way radio control. I could talk to the field. They said, "You've got to be careful coming in. The rebels are at the west end of the field. Don't stop. We're having little battles all around."

I circled the field. I could see where the gas pump was at the east end. I came in, making a very short landing and turned around in a hurry, away from the west end. You could hear the shooting. I taxied back, and I was thinking, "We must not get caught here." This gas pump didn't stick up very high, so I came in and taxied up with my right wing over and just beyond it. The tank was far out enough to miss the tail surfaces in case we had to leave in a hurry. I cut only the right engine while they were gassing.

I never left the cockpit. I didn't dare go back through the cabin. I figured if the rebels started onto the field, I was at sea level, with two engines running, at the east end of the field. The field was only about a mile and a half long. I could get up enough speed on two engines to turn the right propeller, start the right engine, and get off. I told my passengers, "If anything bad happens, the Mexican putting in the gas better jump off the wing, as when I wind up the two engines, the air blast will blow him off anyway. But we've got to get out of here regardless." But we made it with no serious trouble.

Q: You were with Maddux for about a year before they were merged with TWA?

Captain Tomlinson: TAT--Transcontinental Air Transport. Yes. They started operations on the Fourth of July 1929. By that time, the new Glendale Airport, with paved runways and hangars, had a nice passenger station. TAT had one hangar, Maddux had two hangars, and TAT had the hangar just east of us. The balloon hangar was on the south side of the field.

Everything was amicable to start. Slim Lindbergh came out a couple of times, stayed with Maddux, and I saw him at conferences. He and Anne usually stayed with Jack Maddux.

Q: You mentioned earlier that you had first met him at North Island.

Captain Tomlinson: No, I met him at Claude Ryan's Field the day after he arrived to order his plane and oversee its construction.*

Q: In San Diego.

Captain Tomlinson: In San Diego, yes. When things were slack or the weather was such that the Navy considered too dangerous to fly over North island, nobody ever stopped me.

---

*Ryan built the <u>Spirit of St. Louis</u>, which Lindbergh used for his transatlantic flight in 1927.

I could push my Jenny and fly regardless. I had friends at the commercial fields on Dutch Flats. I always enjoyed going over there and, talking to the pilots, and finding out what they were doing.

Getting back to TAT, they carried mostly deadheads or company personnel. TAT would come in with four or five passengers from New York, and half of them were deadheads. They wanted to get entrance into San Francisco. Maddux had been flying into San Francisco for over a year. Jack Maddux met with C. M. Keys and Dan Sheaffer and Cheever Cowdin. The two airlines merged on October 29.*

I became manager of operations for the western region of TAT-Maddux. That's what was painted on the side of the Fords: TAT-Maddux. This lasted for a year. It was in that fall, late September or early October, that TAT lost its first plane on Mount Taylor. None of the pilots knew how to fly on instruments, much less to fly in thunderstorms. They'd try to dodge around them. You start doing that around 10,000-foot peaks and you can get yourself trapped. The first thing you know, you try to turn back, and it's closed in in back of you. I think something like that happened in this case. He just finally flew into the mountain. It took them several months before they found the damn wreckage.

As a result of that, I inaugurated what became airway

_____
*Daniel M. Sheaffer.

traffic control in the late 1930s. Up until that time, a pilot simply went out to the field to check the weather report and take off. He didn't consult with anyone, no designated meteorological service or anything. I established an airway traffic control service on an informal basis so that one of the older line pilots was ordered to be on duty at the field at the time of takeoff to check with the outgoing pilot. Together they had to agree that the weather was okay. After the takeoff, this duty pilot had to be available and keep in touch with weather conditions until the flight landed, in case there was any question of weather or other problem. He had the authority to tell the pilot to return or to land at a suitable field. We had a duty pilot at Clovis and one at Glendale. My establishment of airway traffic control is covered by Ed Betts in articles he's written, such as "The Making of an Airline."

Then TAT-Maddux merged with Western Air Express, and in October of 1930, that changed everything. Western Air Express had flown out of Alhambra, flew the Fokker F-10s, and they had two of these awful F-32s; they were monstrosities if there ever were any. They operated from the field at Alhambra. Harris Honshue became the first president of Transcontinental and Western Air. TWA came later. The merged operations used the Alhambra field.

Daniel W. Tomlinson #2 - 140

I had been close to Jack Frye from the start of Aero Corporation in the middle Twenties.* In '27 Jack offered me a job with Aero Corporation. I decided it was too chancy. What he had to offer me was too precarious for me with a wife and two kids. Things had to progress. Aero Corporation had the agency for Eagle Rock, Fokker, and a couple of other airplanes. It ran a flight school and did charter flying.

Paul Richter became manager of operations of the western region of Transcontinental and Western Air.** I was out on a limb for a while. I made special flights and acted as a reserve pilot. I checked out in Fokkers, even the F-32, and I made one trip to Oakland in one; that was enough.

Honshue, whether it was health or politics, I don't know, but he sort of faded. Dick Robbins was president of Pennsylvania Central Airlines at that time, based in Pittsburgh.*** In the corporate setup of TWA, Pennsylvania Airlines got 2.5% of the Transcontinental and Western Air stock. General Motors had 47.5%. The other 47.5%, the Curtiss Airplane Company (C. M. Keys) had it; it was not in one block. But when Honshue stepped out, Dick Robbins went in as a compromise president. He was a fine gentleman.

---
*William John Frye.
**Paul E. Richter.
***Richard W. Robbins.

Q: That's R. W.?

Captain Tomlinson: R. W. Robbins, yes. I became very fond of him. He came out on sort of an exploratory trip in the latter part of the summer of 1931. Then I was just flying special flights and as a reserve line pilot. If someone in the movie industry called in the middle of the night and wanted to fly people to Las Vegas or wherever, Tomlinson would fly them. I'd take whatever plane was available, whether it was a Ford or a Fokker. These could be and were dizzy trips, a plane load of drunks.

Q: Who were some of the people you flew?

Captain Tomlinson: I wish I could remember the name of one character. He was a famous cowboy character, and he wanted to go up there to get married. They brought him over and poured him and the bride-to-be aboard the airplane, and I flew them up to Las Vegas. They unloaded and checked into this hotel. I was suddenly called up to be a witness at the marriage. I went up to their room, and here their friends were holding him and his bride up between two beds. They were holding them while the preacher married them. That was a panic. I made several flights like that.

I'd take regular flights out, and then I did a lot of statistical work on the comparative operating efficiency of the Fords and Fokkers--speeds, loads, etc. I had a desk in the operations office.

Dick Robbins came on in the early fall of '31, and he invited me to dinner at his hotel. I talked to him, and he asked me to come back to New York to be his technical assistant and a member of the technical committee for selecting new equipment for the airline, write his speeches, fly, and report on available air transports. In general, I helped him on a wide variety of problems. I was in TWA headquarters until about April of '34.

The first problem in '31 was that we had lost a number of Alpha mail planes. We needed replacements for them and also a satisfactory six-place single-engine airplane that would fly the route from St. Louis to Amarillo, which we were trying to secure. We had inherited the Hornet engines out of these F-32s, the planes having been junked. Each had four Hornets, a tractor and a pusher. If you only lost a nut or anything off the front engine and it hit a propeller blade, it had the velocity of a .30-06 bullet, and it went through the fuselage. We had several narrow escapes, passengers missed by inches.

Incidentally, that F-32 was a miserable thing to land. The longitudinal balance at low speed caused it to be

Daniel W. Tomlinson #2 - 143

dangerously tail-heavy, so it took all your strength to hold the nose down on the approach to a landing.

Q: The trim wouldn't handle it?

Captain Tomlinson: No, the trim wouldn't begin to handle it. It was a serious defect in design.

We had these serviceable engines. Consolidated Aircraft made a bid to build us a parasol high-wing monoplane in the Buffalo factory. I wound up spending six weeks in the early summer of '32 testing these planes. That was also the time when TWA really got into the DC-1 project. Jack wrote his famous letter in '31 setting forth TWA's requirements for a transport to replace the Fords and Fokkers.*

Q: I presume at that time that the only thing comparable would have been the Boeing 247.

Captain Tomlinson: I was sent to fly and report on the 247. Special arrangements were made for me to fly the 247 at Oakland, California. Incidentally, at the 1928 National

---

*Carroll V. Glines and Wendell F. Moseley, Grand Old Lady: Story of the DC-3 (Cleveland: Pennington Press, 1959) provides a history of the airplane that Tomlinson had a role in developing, from the DC-1 onward.

Air Races, Bill and Bertha Boeing had flown to the races in one of their big tri-motor transports. It was one that had a Hornet in the nose and a Wasp on each side.

When I flew the tri-motor, I told Bill Boeing it had two much built-in headwind. It was a big "boxcar" biplane, many struts and wires. I flew the 247; it carried only ten passengers. The plane had a box spar that came across the floor in the rear of the two front seats, and the passengers had to step over it. The spar went right through the cabin--impossible. Cruising speed of the 247 was only about 15 miles per hour better than the Fords. The 247 had no future whatsoever. It was flyable--no question about that--but no future to it.

I flew the Curtiss Condor. I'd flown the old Condor, which was a conversion from a bomber. I don't know how many Curtiss built of these. The Air Corps had some of them as bombers. I think they were forced down TAT's throat, because C. M. Keys was chairman of the board of TAT as well as Curtiss Airplane Company. TAT was flying the condors between Columbus and Winoka.

It was in the summer of '31, after the merger with Western Air, Jack Frye asked me to go back to Columbus, Ohio. He said, "Go back and spend a week flying the Condors to Winoka. Then I want you to come before the board of directors' meeting in New York and give your comments on them." The pilots hated them. The planes were impossible in icing conditions and severe turbulence, and they were obsolete. They landed so slowly that if you had any crosswind, they were very difficult to control. The Condor had a very strange tail rotation; I never knew of such in any other airplanes. For some strange aerodynamic reason, the tail wobbled in flight, sort of a spiral. The center of gravity was about in the center of the cabin. It was steady in flight, when the control surfaces were rotating--a very small radius but enough to be perceptible. Can you conceive to a certain extent the airplane doing this and screwing its way?

Q: A corkscrew motion, yes.

Captain Tomlinson: A corkscrew. What it did to people in the rear seats of that Condor was a fright, always airsick.

Q: I can imagine.

Captain Tomlinson: I told C. M. Keys and the directors what I thought about the airplane in no uncertain terms. Then they called on Slim Lindbergh, and he backed me up 100%. That was the end of the Condors, as far as TAT was concerned. Then later they built the new Condor out of St. Louis with Cyclone engines. That was to be a sleeper plane for American Airlines.

Burdette Wright was president of the Curtiss Airplane Company at that time, and I knew him quite well.* I was sent out to fly the new Condor. Dean Smith had quit American and was the test and sales pilot for Curtiss. I flew with Dean. My report was that the plane was obsolete before it was built. It did fly all right.

Then I flew a Patrician. The Army bought a few of them as bombers; it was a big tri-motor. It had three Hornets in it. It was a monstrosity.

I'm going to digress for a minute. One of the Patricians had been taken out to the West Coast, and St. Claire, a famous Army pilot, was on leave from the Army flying it and demonstrating. Eddie Rickenbacker was there.** Jack Maddux said he wanted me to fly it and see what I thought of it. So I went up with the pilot, who wouldn't let me fly it on the left-hand side. I flew it from the right-hand side.

Coming into Glendale airport, there were some high lines that went across a street below on the approach; they were too high for comfort. Rickenbacker was sitting in the cabin with Maddux and a couple of other VIPs. I flew it and put it through stability and controllability tests. I

---
*Burdette S. Wright.
**Edward V. Rickenbacker was the leading U.S. fighter ace in World War I. He later headed the Indianapolis motor speedway and Eastern Airlines.

turned to the pilot and said, "Take it back." This pilot headed straight for those high-tension wires. I waited as long as I dared, and then I grabbed the control yoke and hauled it back and missed the wires. I was pretty strong in those days. I startled the pilot. He couldn't move. The plane just missed those wires, and I just looked at him.

Q: It makes you wonder.

Captain Tomlinson: I don't know whatever happened to that pilot. I couldn't understand it. He had a good record in the Army Air Corps. I just grabbed the controls and hauled back.

I flew one really weird airplane. Vince Bernelli, the designer and builder, was quite a character and engineer. He was an advocate of the flying wing. Some of the Jewish gentry in New York with money backed him to build this flying wing. He built this monstrosity and had it at Newark Airport in a hangar. As usual, Tomlinson was directed to fly Mr. Bernelli's flying wing. It was the craziest one that I had ever seen. It had two 750 12-cylinder Packard water-cooled engines of the type that the Navy used in the twin-float early torpedo planes; these were built into the entering edge of the thick wing. It had a passenger cabin, in which you couldn't quite stand up, in the center of the wing. You entered the cabin and slipped through a small door. And here was the pilot's cockpit in between these two big engine cells, sticking out ahead of the wing like a couple of horns.

Vince had his pilot there who had flown it a couple of times. I thought, "If this pilot can fly it, I can." I insisted on flying it myself. I checked the plane over very carefully. Several other experimental planes about that time had been lost due to aileron flutter, lack of or improper static balancing. When I looked at the ailerons, there was no static balancing. I pointed this out to Vince. I said, "I don't like it, but I'll fly it around carefully."

It was a foggy day around Newark. I got this plane up in the soup. My description, in my report to Dick Robbins, said, "Flying that monstrosity was like trying to fly an underpowered slab of Navy armor plate. It was horrible." I finally maneuvered it around the field and landed, glad to climb out of it in one piece!

Before we'd taken off, Vince had said, "Tommy, when you come back, you make a dive and a high speed across the field."

I said, "No dice, Vince." I was going to be glad to get that thing back on the ground whole. I think I had it out for about an hour. It took me an hour to find the field again. The two engine nacelles sticking out blanked side vision. Sitting in the crazy cockpit, you could see hardly anything in the thick haze. All you had was some near-vertical visibility straight ahead. It was awful.

The payoff came the next Sunday. Vince wanted to impress some other people. He told his pilot to put on a show, high-speed flying across the field. The pilot did it. Halfway across the field, both ailerons fell off. He crashed in the swamp at the end of the runway. That was the end of Bernelli's flying wing.

Q: So much for that.

Captain Tomlinson: That finished Vince and the flying wing for a while.

Q: Apparently, most of the people in the industry at that time believed that a tri-motor was the answer to air transport.

Captain Tomlinson: At least the pilots did. But I was absolutely against that nose engine, because it introduced vibration directly into your main structure, your passenger cabin, plus noise, odors, fire hazards. And from the pilot's standpoint, you've got that propeller whirling around right in front of you. With the inevitable leakage of oil, it gets on your windshield. Also the nose installation is relatively inefficient--much less efficient than your wing engines, decently streamlined. The nose engine was way up off the ground, difficult to reach for maintenance. I was adamant against it.

Finally, I won my point. A contract was worked out with Douglas with the requirement for taking off from Winslow and cutting one engine after rolling 1,000 feet, then flying across the Continental Divide to Albuquerque. At that time, putting together the TWA specifications for the contract was all done in my office at New York headquarters. I didn't like the Winslow requirement the way it was written, but I'd had such a time winning the point on bi-motor that I decided I'd better go easy on the Winslow point. I considered it extreme and unnecessary to cut the switch, because as it was set up it was too marginal. We made it. The propeller tips missed the ground about six inches, according to witnesses. TWA had one every 100 feet down the runway to the 1,000-foot point.

Q: Was Douglas the only manufacturer who was willing to design a twin-engine transport?

Captain Tomlinson: Yes. We had two conferences with Martin, but they were half-hearted, and we dropped it.

Daniel W. Tomlinson #2 - 151

They weren't enthused, and we weren't either. Dutch Kindelberger, Art Raymond, and of course Don Douglas himself were in on it.* They were satisfied that the combination of retractable landing gear, improved NACA cowling, new wing design, and new two-position propellers would turn the trick.

Q: Constant speed.

Captain Tomlinson: No, constant speed didn't come for a couple of years. Two position only.

Q: Just two-position?

Captain Tomlinson: Two-position: one takeoff and landing or emergency and another for cruising. Fowler flaps for short takeoff and slow landing speeds. Douglas did a lot of wind tunnel work on the project. Bailey Oswald, aerodynamicist special, deserves credit. I was convinced Douglas could meet their predicted performances. They came in with their data. Finally, Art came back again and talked it over. Then Doug and Dutch came back, and they brought more figures and data. I went over it, and I gambled. As I say, I had my fingers crossed on the severity of this Winslow test, but they said they could do

---
*J. H. Kindelberger, Arthur E. Raymond, Donald W. Douglas.

it, and they did. I would not do it again for love nor money; it was unnecessarily dangerous. But the airplane did it. They made their guarantees and even exceeded them. The DC-1 and the DC-2 at critical power for cruise altitude of 14,000 feet at full throttle would cruise better than 210 miles per hour.

Q: I didn't realize that.

Captain Tomlinson: Landing speed about 65, full flap.

Q: You had mentioned earlier that Lindbergh was noncommittal about the selection of the DC-1.

Captain Tomlinson: He was noncommittal with respect to the tri-motor and bi-motor. As I say, quite a lot of discussion went on.

After World War II, I attended a TWA reunion. Ernie Breech was there.* While the DC-1 and the General Aviation tri-motor were building, I regularly visited Jay Schoonmaker to check on the tri-motor progress. He was president of General Aviation at Baltimore. Herb Thaden was his chief engineer. He was a good man, but he had never done anything really outstanding in aviation. He had

---
*Ernest R. Breech, chairman of the Ford Motor Company before going to TWA as chairman.

built one all-metal single-engine airplane in Pittsburgh, but this project was just over his head. I told him at the start that it was a waste of money, but nobody would listen to me. General Motors put half a million down that rathole. Also Ernie told me that it was at Lindbergh's behest that General Motors insisted TWA contract with General Aviation to build the tri-motor as competition with the Douglas DC-1.

Q: And those were 500,000 real dollars in those days.

Captain Tomlinson: Yes, they were.

Q: Did you spend much time out at the Douglas plant while the DC-1 was being built?

Captain Tomlinson: I went there every six weeks, no less.

Q: Do you recall how long the construction period lasted?

Captain Tomlinson: We signed the contract sometime in the fall of '32. I went out to Santa Monica to be TWA's representative and test pilot, rented a house in Santa Monica, and spent the summer of '33 out there. The DC-1 flew 1 July '33.

Q: So obviously you knew the design crew and the management pretty well.

Captain Tomlinson: I lived with it. At the same time, we had contracted with Northrop Aviation to build six Gammas before the cancellation of the mail contract. We were going to initiate transcontinental mail service, overnight across the continent. These Gammas were to cruise at 235 miles an hour, and we figured we could do it practically overnight. The mail cancellation came, and we changed the contract with Northrop, cut it down to three. I ran the tests on those, all the factory tests.

Also Northrop built, at the same time, an airplane which he called the Delta. There was only one built. It had the Gamma wing, but it was a high wing. It was all metal. It was a good, comfortable, six-passenger plane, and it had a Cyclone engine in it. The pilot sat up in front of the cabin, a cramped cockpit right in back of that Cyclone engine. I disliked the cockpit.

Q: You did quite a bit of high-altitude work in the Gamma, didn't you?

Captain Tomlinson: Yes. That came after the high-altitude

work with the DC-1. We put the DC-1 through extensive service testing. For one month it was flown every night one way or the other between Kansas City and Glendale as a mail plane. Paul Richter and I alternated. He'd make a round trip, and I'd make one during the winter of '33-'34. We had trouble with the heating system. We nearly froze to death a couple of times, flying in blizzards over the mountains, temperature way below zero, and that heating system would go out. It was bad. But the problem was finally worked out.

We also had trouble with the landing gear collapsing. Douglas insisted that the hydraulic pressure alone in the landing gear extension device was adequate to ensure that after it went over dead center, the landing gear could not retract. The first time it collapsed was over Mines Field. There was reasonable assumption that that was the result of negligence on the part of the copilot, who was this Bailey Oswald, sitting in the copilot's seat.

We had several near-collapses landing at Clover Field. We'd land and while taxiing one could see the landing gear "knuckle joint" had moved out of dead center toward the "up-gear" position. It didn't happen every time, but you'd land and particularly from the left-hand pilot's seat you'd see that landing gear knuckle joint jumping in and out of dead center.

Q: Flexing back and forth.

Captain Tomlinson: Yes. We'd very tenderly taxi up to the ramp in back of the factory. The crew would come out with jacks and jack the plane up. I was adamant that we had to have a positive mechanical latch to secure the gear in landing position. Douglas got his back up. I don't know why. He just absolutely refused to make this change. When I was checking out TWA pilots at Glendale, the gear collapsed. George Rice was flying, Eddie Belande the copilot. I was standing in back of George, checking him. He started to taxi off the runway, and the gear folded up. TWA accepted the DC-1 with deep reservations on this point.

The crowning event was when Paul Wicker and I took it to Wichita to take the city fathers up for a ride. It was a beautiful sod field. Paul was pilot; I was copilot. I pumped the gear down; the gear was actuated by a hand pump. You had to hand pump the gear either up or down, and it was not easy. When within 50 yards of the passenger station, all the bigwigs were waiting, and the airplane just gently knelt down on the grass. It was an easy step down for the mayor. This embarrassment finally got the mechanical latch installed. Douglas wouldn't give us any explanation of the sources of the problem.

A friend of mine, Johnny Guy, a very capable mechanic, was our inspector at Douglas and later at Boeing and then at Lockheed. I had talked it over with Johnny, and what we decided was that when you would take off at ground level, the system was then full of hydraulic fluid, sealed. After a climb to altitude, where you would have a substantially lower temperature, this would cause a contraction in the volume of the hydraulic fluid so that at some point in the sealed system, a little vacuum was created. If that little pocket of vacuum happened to be in the landing gear extension piston, you were in trouble.

Q: Insufficient pressure there.

Captain Tomlinson: Yes, insufficient pressure in a way. If it were filled full of incompressible hydraulic fluid, okay, but heated hydraulic fluid had contracted, causing a vacuum and no longer completely filled the system.

Q: The altitude and the weather flying that you did in the DC-1 and DC-2 must have been pioneering at that time.

Captain Tomlinson: It was. After completion of these service tests, I flew the DC-1 back to Kansas City. Then I flew it east on several trips and demonstrated it to VIPs.

Then I went back to the New York office. So far as I was concerned, the DC-1 disappeared out of my life, because at that time we knew what was going to happen to the management of the airlines in order to recover the airmail contracts; top management was in a turmoil. I didn't know what was going to happen to my position. By that time it was into the summer of 1934. So I talked it over with Jack Frye and Dick Robbins. I was number 13 on the pilots' seniority list, so I decided that until the dust settled, I would exercise my pilot's seniority and fly as a line captain. I loved to fly. In fact, I'd rather fly than sit in a swivel chair at a desk.

At that time, due to the fact that we hadn't received all our DC-2s and reduction with the airmail cancellation, pilot jobs were pretty scarce. I thought, "I'll just ride as a copilot until things clear up." So I spent the summer of '34 flying copilot between Kansas City and New York. I served lunches; I did everything. It was fun, as far as I was concerned. I knew something was going to work out.

Then fall came along. There was a pilot position open for the night mail, and I grabbed it. So in October of '34, I started flying the regular single-engine night mail "graveyard" run every other night between Newark and Columbus. That was absolutely fascinating, because the night mail was never canceled. If you canceled, you were out! You could delay a little while. You could take off and maybe come back or parachute out, if you had to, but you never canceled.

I learned a lot about weather while pushing through that miserable stuff: fog, ice, hail, turbulence, temperatures 30 to 40 below, in an open-cockpit airplane, the Alpha. At times with the DC-2s, they'd cancel all flights. I'd go through. Sure, it might kick you around a bit, but I'd laugh at the meteorologists when I came in. It was no real problem.

Q: I suppose that as a result of that experience, you probably knew more about actual conditions than the meteorologists, didn't you?

Captain Tomlinson: Yes, in certain practical aspects.

Q: Their knowledge, I suppose, would have been more theoretical than practical.

Captain Tomlinson: That's right. Very definitely. They were all my friends, and I loved them. I said, "You're just conscientious liars. You're doing the best you can." I appreciated their limitations.

I really had only one bad night. I took off from

Newark, flying a Consolidated Fleetster; it had a hatch cover over the cockpit. It was a nice airplane to fly. When I got to Harrisburg, I had probably 1,000 feet in heavy rain, but I knew I was going to have icing conditions at Pittsburgh, because they'd been reporting light freezing rain, ceilings of 400 to 500 feet, and half a mile visibility. I used to say if I had only 50 feet ceiling to a quarter mile visibility, I'd make a stab at it. That was enough to land a small, maneuverable mail plane. But the ice concerned me. I was heading for Pittsburgh. I passed the south leg of Belfonte and was heading for Crescent on top of the Allegheny Mountains. I started to pick up ice, flying at 9,000-10,000 feet.

Two years before, Andy Andrews, heading east in an Alpha on the night mail run, encountered ice approaching Allegheny Ridge, on which TWA's radio station was located at Crescent. Dean Buford in another Alpha was headed west. They both encountered severe icing and bailed out. At the time I wondered why they had not either turned back or headed south.

Pittsburgh reported, "We're down to 100 feet, almost zero visibility, and freezing rain." I knew what that meant. I was picking up heavy rime ice at 9,000 feet; it was a frequent winter condition. Above 1,000 feet, you'd have a layer where the temperature would be up to 40 degrees or a little over. But it was the cold air under 1,000 feet, and the rain was coming out of clouds up around 7,000 to 8,000. Falling first through the warm layer, then into this lower cold layer, becoming super cooled, causing icing mixed with sleet from about 1,000 feet to the ground. We'd make our approach, staying up in that warm air to get the airplane structure warmed up. So you'd come down into this layer of cold air. You had enough time to make your offset turn, come back over the cone of silence on final approach, and land before the airplane would pick up enough ice to be dangerous. Sometimes this trick was a matter of do or die, because if the plane did pick up too much ice, there was no go-around.

Q: Were these techniques distributed to other pilots on the line, or was it sort of learned by yourself?

Captain Tomlinson: Word of mouth. Not all of them would do it. I did it--not too many times. It was close.

I decided to turn around. I decided, "It's no go. That's too close. I'll go back to Harrisburg." Well, by then Harrisburg weather was down to 200 feet and a half-mile visibility and light freezing rain. The old Harrisburg field was a sod field on the west side of the Susquehanna River. At the west end of the field was a graveyard, then quite a hill just beyond. I got on the radio; its south beam lay directly across the TWA route. I got on Belfonte and found that Baltimore had broken clouds. I always figured with this icing business, "Go south, young man, go south."

By that time, I started to lose altitude, from 9,000 feet. I staggered along with the throttle wide open. The plane continued to lose altitude as I headed south. I wasn't coming down too fast and had good control. In about half an hour, the first thing I knew, ice was starting to come off the wing. I was flying a high-wing Fleetster. I had opened the cockpit hatch so I could bail out if necessary. Finally, one big chunk of ice came off, and it bounced off my head. Soon the ice was gone, and I went to Baltimore with no trouble.

This was at the same time that a tri-motor Stinson with passengers was trying to crawl underneath, through the icing, flying from Washington to Pittsburgh. I could hear him on the radio. He was having trouble; finally he made a forced landing someplace and crashed the airplane, but no one was killed. I went into Baltimore and held the mail, sat there for two or three hours until the front had passed Pittsburgh. Then I flew to Pittsburgh with the mail. That was my only bad-weather flight.

An interesting thing happened with the Alpha. I went

into the Harrisburg grass field. The area had had a lot of rain. It was just before Christmas. I had a full load of mail. I made my usual landing, always landing short as a matter of habit. I was on the ground, put on the brakes, and I could literally feel it seem to speed up. "What's going on?" I never had anything like that happen before. That grass was slippery, and the Alpha was hydro-planing. I could see the graveyard coming up, and I cut the switch. The Alpha finally stopped. I was nosed into the graveyard between a couple of tombstones. The station crew came out with a truck and hitched on the tail and pulled me out to the station. They serviced the plane, and I took off.

Now, to get back to the DC-1. In April 1935 Jack Frye had taken over as president of the company. He contacted me and said, "I want you to come back to Kansas City as my assistant to carry on in the test, research, engineering end." I moved my family to Kansas City. I had the office next to Jack. It had two doors: one to the hall, one into Jack's office.

The DC-1 disappeared for a while. I never knew whether Howard Hughes or the CAA had it, but they took the seats out and put in extra tanks for some long-range flights that somebody planned but never executed.*

---

*Howard R. Hughes (1905-1976) was an American industrialist who gained fame in the 1930s as an aviator and motion picture producer. He later gained a controlling interest for a time in Trans World Airlines.

Again, the ownership at that time has never been clear to me, but it suddenly came back to TWA. Jack said, "What are you going to do with it?" In a conference he said, "We don't know much about thunderstorms, Tommy. Why don't you take it and fly it through thunderstorms?"

That suited me perfectly. So for most of the summer of 1935, whenever there were strong thunderstorms moving between Kansas City and Chicago, or St. Louis, or east of us, I'd take the DC-1 out and fly through them. Before we did that, we obtained from the Wright Engine Company two special engines with two-speed blowers. We put on special propellers to give us better performance at high altitude. I could get the DC-1 up to 27,000 feet. Sometimes I could get some pilot to go. They were a little bit leery of that, but I corralled a few of them as copilots. I finally collared a couple of meteorologists and said, "Now, you better go out with me and see what these things look like from the inside."

Before that, I had flown in thunderstorms between Amarillo and Kansas City in the Fords and Fokkers. I had developed the practice of ignoring the readings of the air-speed meter, altimeter, and rate of climb. These would fluctuate over a wide range. If you should try to correct according to their readings, you simply made matters worse. I simply set the artificial horizon, flew at constant altitude (angle of attack), and reduced speed somewhat. I cut the speed down in the Fords and Fokkers 10-15 miles an hour and 30 miles an hour in the DC-1. I would just sit there and hang on and fly the plane, using only the artificial horizon and the gyro-compass. Generally, I'd go through the storms at 10,000-15,000 feet. Sure, you get kicked around. You generally came out the back side of the storm, close to the altitude at which you went into it.

Then I started going up higher. I flew through the anvil heads. I'd get up 25,000-27,000 feet and fly into one of the anvil heads and out the other side--no problem. But at the base of the anvil heads, in most of these thunderstorms that I encountered, was the damndest collection of black and purple in the clouds, evidencing severe turbulence. You could see that those clouds were just boiling green, blue, black. I never stuck my nose in there. I gave that area of the storms a wide berth!

I don't know of any systematic, determined research in thunderstorms prior to that time.

Q: I have not heard of it.

Captain Tomlinson: A couple of times I tried flying between thunderstorms. I used to fly the Boeing 307

Stratoliners about 21,000-22,000 feet.* At that altitude, you had around 12,000 feet pressure altitude in the cabin. In my better days, I could fly an airplane without oxygen up to around 25,000 feet before starting to feel it. As a result of this flying, we knew that we had to get up into the stratosphere eventually, fly on top for real passenger comfort.

I made one flight with the DC-3 with our TWA chief pilot. He rode as my copilot. We knew that there was a hurricane coming into New York, so we took off to fly at 25,000 feet to Newark. It was quite interesting. We flew between several different layers approaching this hurricane center. Finally we reached the Pittsburgh area, and I could see the dome-shaped top of the storm center to the southeast. We had heavy rain over Newark. There were four or five inches of water on the field; we had no trouble with that. It was an interesting flight to see all these different layers of clouds. We experienced moderate turbulence. The center didn't go right over Newark but was a little south. We stayed at Newark a few days.

To demonstrate the accuracy of instrument flying, I made a fully hooded takeoff at Newark and flew under the hood to Kansas City, making an instrument approach. When I

---

*The Stratoliner was a four-engine passenger plane with a length of 74 feet and wing span of 107 feet. Its loaded weight was approximately 45,000 pounds. It had a top speed of 241 miles per hour and maximum range of 1,750 miles.

figured I was 100 feet off the ground and lined up with the runway, I took off the hood. We were in perfect position to land. We had two newspaper reporters with us. As we progressed along the route, I predicted my ETA over the usual radio reporting points, and I never missed it by more than 30-45 seconds on the way back.*

Q: Were scientists or meteorologists interested in making some of these flights, or did they have to be thrown aboard?

Captain Tomlinson: Parkinson--he's still alive and Mentzer, I took them. I took several of the pilots. I took Joe Bell, another meteorologist. I had a very competent male secretary who made a number of flights. He would go along to record the data.

These tests ended in September, and then came new types of rubber boots for de-icing. Goodyear wanted us to test them. They had also come out with a propeller de-icing arrangement. Strips of rubber about six inches wide were cemented on the entering edge of the propeller; these had grooves that led from the hub up to the tip. Then there was a slinger ring on the hub of the propeller, into which a mixture of alcohol and glycerin was fed. I

---

*ETA--estimated time of arrival.

tested this, and it worked quite well. I made many flights in November and December, whenever severe icing was reported. I'd take the DC-1 to the area where the icing was reported and fly through at varying altitudes.

One of the most interesting observations that I made was that no way could meteorologists give you any accurate advice as to where and how much icing would be encountered. I'd be flying on our route; on United, 50-75 miles north, some pilot would be crying his eyes out about ice, and I wouldn't have any, and vice versa. Icing was extremely elusive. I never worried about getting out of it. You did need de-icers for a while. In ice a pilot should try other altitudes. Never remain at one altitude; either go up or down, depending on then-existing conditions.

One interesting flight in the DC-1, I went east and hadn't found the predicted icing. I stayed overnight in Columbus. The weather bureau reported, "There's going to be icing over western New York and around Albany." So I took off the next morning and flew to Albany. Also, the weather was bad at Newark, and we could see it to the east. When I got up 20,000 feet, I was around Syracuse and ran into a very peculiar condition. It wasn't ice; it was very fine ice crystals. It was so fine that through the slightest air leak the crystals would come in. It would form like puffballs where it came into the cockpit. It was the most unusual weather phenomenon I ever saw.

It happened on one other flight that I made going east from Chicago in a DC-1 passenger flight. On this flight, when I was south of Syracuse, as I was angling towards Albany, I was on the instruments. Suddenly one engine quit completely, and the other one slowed down. I knew that my carburetor air intakes behind the ring cowls on the DC-1 did not have the alternate air intakes in back of the cylinder baffles, something that was standard in the DC-2. This fluff had filled up the air intakes to the carburetor. There wasn't a thing I could do. It wasn't ice in the carburetor, just in the air intake. I tried to get the engine to backfire to blow out the intakes. Then I checked my map. I could see that at 20,000 feet I was within gliding distance of the airport in Syracuse. I began to align myself for a do-or-die approach to Syracuse. When I got down around 10,000-12,000 feet, one engine came back and finally the other, so I went on to Albany.

We stayed overnight at Albany, because it was really bad, zero-zero, at Newark. We took off the next morning to go to Chicago. Weather was reporting ice along that route. When we reached the south shore of Lake Erie, I was down between 3,000 and 4,000 feet. A peculiar ice formation started to build up. The de-icing boots were working and taking care of it. But wherever there was an unprotected surface, the rime ice grew out against the air pressure like a mushroom. The stem of the ice mushroom grew out of any bare spot on the wing or elsewhere, and a head grew on the stem.

Q: I've never heard of that.

Captain Tomlinson: I was starting to get a bad buffet on my rudder. On the DC-1 a relatively large diameter directional radio loop antenna was right on top of the fuselage, back of the navigation hatch. Ryan was my assistant engineer and copilot. I said, "Open that hatch and see what is affecting my directional control." There was the loop, 18 inches in diameter, and the center of it was solid ice. There was no de-icer on this loop, and the turbulence from it was buffeting the rudder. I was about halfway between Detroit and Chicago, and the ice was fantastic. I informed our people in Chicago and said, "I've got the oddest load of ice I've ever seen on an airplane. When I come in, have the tower give me a clear landing so I can grease the plane on without jarring the ice loose. Have photographers on hand." I landed real smoothly but fast. Some of the ice fell off, but there was enough left for pictures of it. Everybody just shook their heads. I flew in ice after that but never experienced anything like it again.

That's one of the things about flying in weather. Many pilots don't realize there are hellishly odd things that can occur in these storm areas which are unpredictable as to when, where, and how much.

I saw one of the most remarkable sights one morning when I was flying to Chicago. In back of where a couple of big thunderstorms had passed, extending for 30-40 miles on the ground, was this strip of hail that I would estimate to be over five or ten miles wide. It appeared like some monster with a big pitcher had gone along and poured the hail on the ground. I'd been caught in hail before in DC-2s and DC-3s, and my recommendation was that if you hit hail, be careful about turning back. You may double your exposure. Just decide the way the storm is moving, if you can. Cross its pass at 90 degrees, and if you hit hail, just grit your teeth and hold your course, because if you make a turn, you can double the exposure to the hail. It's not going to cover any great width. It is like a wall coming down that you have to go through.

Q: Did NACA or any government agencies express any interest in this type of information?

Captain Tomlinson: No. I sent copies of that report to the Army Air Corps, the Smithsonian, the Navy, and other people who we thought would be interested. My office copy's in existence; the Naval Aviation Museum at Pensacola has it.

We had to get into the stratosphere. The DC-1 made 27,000 feet, not high enough. So we decided on the Gamma. Through my friends, I had close contact with the Air Corps at Wright Field.* I could go over there and fly any airplane they had. I knew that they were working on the exhaust turbo supercharger project. We had tried out the two-speed blower; it was too limited.

Wiley Post and his stratosphere flying was a joke. We knew that he was using a Wasp engine with a two-speed blower. I went out to talk to Wiley and find out if he had any data that would be helpful. I found Wiley sitting alongside the Winnie Mae, parked along the edge of the Lockheed landing strip. He was all dressed up in his stratosphere suit. I asked what he was using to pressure it, but I couldn't get any answer or other useful information. He was a fine subject for publicity. Wiley made several high-altitude flights. He said he went over 30,000 feet. We decided that the Vega with this Wasp engine and two-speed blower might make 30,000. He had no data on his engine temperatures, pressures, or anything else pertinent. Wiley said it was all secret. Phooey!

Q: Sounds like more of a promotional gimmick than anything else.

---

*The Army Air Corps's research and development center was at Wright Field, Dayton, Ohio.

Captain Tomlinson: That's what it was--publicity for Wiley. Too bad. He had so much publicity that Will Rogers believed in him.*

We knew TWA had to get the exhaust turbo supercharger. I think Ellsworth Lincoln flew a Gamma over the North Pole. Jack washed one out. He ran into carburetor ice and crashed in New Mexico near Gallup. He washed out the airplane; then TWA had just one. We figured from that data that Wright Field gave us that we could get well up into the stratosphere; we weren't sure how far. With a special Cyclone engine with pressurized carburetor and the exhaust turbo properly installed in the Gamma, we'd be able to explore the stratosphere. I went over and arranged with my friends at Wright Field to borrow an exhaust turbo supercharger.

In the winter of 1935-36, by hit and miss, cut and try, TWA installed the special Cyclone engine, turbo supercharger, and inter cooler. It was a complex job. We had a very competent metalsmith by the name of Jim Easton, an extremely able man. He did the job. He finally had the Gamma ready in the spring of '36. The first few flights, I'd get up to 20,000 feet and lose fuel pressure. We finally installed electrically driven drowned pumps plus

---
*Humorist/entertainer/columnist Will Rogers died with Wiley Post in a plane crash during a flight to Alaska in 1935.

several other changes so there would be dependable and adequate fuel pressure above 20,000 feet.

Then we ran into problems with the engine surging. The power wouldn't be steady; it would be up and down. The turbo speed was not constant. We had an automatic device that was intended to control it but did not work. We took that out. We installed a positive hand control from the exhaust bypass valve to the turbo, so that when I reached critical engine altitude and needed turbo boost, my engine throttle was then wide open. I'd start feeding in the turbo boost, using that control. Gradually and carefully, I could control it on up to service ceiling, about 35,000 feet.

I did most of the flying around Kansas City between 30,000 and 35,000 feet. That's where and when I discovered the jet stream. I'd fly a triangular course from Kansas City to St. Louis, to Kirksville, and return to Kansas City. I could keep on the beam so I knew what my drift angle was. I knew my airspeed; I could thus calculate the wind strength and direction exactly. On landing I would report 100-125-mile-an-hour winds. Meteorologists knew nothing about winds above 20,000 feet. Actually, that was about their limit; 20,000 feet was the extent of wind knowledge at that time.

Q: Was the jet stream even acknowledged at all?

Captain Tomlinson: Not at that time. Nobody knew it was the "jet stream" until after the war. Then there were enough jets flying at different places that meteorologists could put wind current data together, and it was realized that the jet stream circled the earth. All I could say was that I was flying in these unknown high winds. It was kind of upsetting when you're not used to winds of that strength.

One night was particularly bad. I was going over to Wright Field and got a pretty good fix at altitude. I went by Marshall, Missouri, and there was a beam station there and a cone of silence. I was picking up unusual speed, about 75 or 80 miles of wind. I reached St. Louis much too soon, and I ran my next estimate to Terre Haute. I hit Terre Haute four or five minutes early. I calculated the wind was close to 200 miles an hour. I was going over the country hell bent. I was flying at 32,000 feet.

I used that calculated speed for my next checkpoint. I didn't go over the cone at Indianapolis, but I checked when passing the south leg, which gave me a good check. I hit it just about on the button. That was the biggest wind that I encountered, ground speed near 475 miles per hour. I had a 1,000-1,500-foot ceiling over Wright Field, and I let down there and landed.

The final flight with the Gamma was the crowning trip. I was at Wright Field in January of 1937, working for North American. That's a separate story. I thought I had finished with the Gamma; I'd put about 30 hours in the stratosphere in it. The Gamma was stored in the hangar at Kansas City; no one was using it. No one else had ever flown it with the turbo installation.

There was to be an aircraft exhibition at New York. Jack Frye called me on the telephone at Wright Field. He said, "Tommy, if you're not too busy over there, would you come back to TWA for a few days? I'd like you to fly the Gamma through the stratosphere for publicity back to Newark. Then we're going to put it in the aircraft show in New York."

I said, "Sure, Jack. I'd gladly come back."

The show was to open on Monday. I took TWA from Dayton to Kansas City on Friday, planning to make the flight on Saturday. Something had gone haywire with the oxygen system. I can't tell you today what it was, but they said, "Tommy, you can't go. We've got to get this oxygen system in perfect order."

Sunday morning, okay, they had it repaired. But Kansas City's weather was zero-zero in a blizzard. All United and TWA operations were canceled east of Chicago and Kansas City. I checked with the meteorologist and asked,

Daniel W. Tomlinson #2 - 177

"What is the weather at Newark?"

"Newark will probably hold up to 1,000-1,500-foot ceiling until the afternoon."

I said, "Okay, I'll go." Taking off in that blizzard was no problem for me. I could creep out to the end of the runway and line up and make an instrument takeoff. There were six fuel tanks in the Gamma.

The Gamma, unhappily, did not have one of the anti-static radio directional loops. They put them on all the DC-2s, but they didn't have one to spare to put on the Gamma. I had no trouble after I reached the top of the storm. I rode the Kansas City beam east, got a good check at the Marshall beam. I was at 32,000; that was as high as I could get fully loaded, and I was on top. Everything was fine, no static. But in the clouds were ice crystals, and the static cut out all the beams and the two-way telephone.

The cloud level was rising. With the full tanks, about 35,000 feet was as high as the Gamma would go at that point. I was in the clouds. I had enough reception to make a good check over the north leg of the St. Louis beam. After I crossed that, I lost all radio communication. What was I going to do? I thought, "Well, this storm ought to have breaks in it someplace. I can surely fly by DR to Newark."* I flew the DR course toward Pittsburgh. After

---
*DR--dead reckoning, a system of determining position by projecting forward from one's last known position.

about an hour, during which there was no radio reception, I decided to try a lower altitude, hoping I could get between layers. At that time, I was staggering at 35,000 feet. I dropped down to about 10,000 feet, absolutely solid cloud, and I still couldn't hear any radio. Back up again, back up to 35,000. Finally, about the time I estimated I was somewhere near Pittsburgh, I began to get a little two-way reception. I heard Pittsburgh report there were high, broken clouds over Albany, New York.

By this time, I was getting a little bit squeamish, sitting up there in ice-crystal clouds. So I changed course 45 degrees to the north, which I figured would take me to the Albany area. I flew about 15-20 minutes and suddenly got breaks in the clouds. By that time, I was at 37,000 feet. The outside temperature was 70 degrees below and about a half inch of frost all over the inside of the Gamma; the plane had no insulation. I had a flexible hot-air tube that I could direct on my feet or move around as required. I was breathing pure oxygen by that time. You had to breathe pure oxygen above 32,000. I was heated up to about 60 degrees. I thought I was going along fine. I looked up and estimated the top of the storm was about 41,000.

In these breaks, Elmira radio came in. I knew the ranges. Elmira had one pointed up toward Albany, another one toward Newark, one toward Pittsburgh, and the other one toward Buffalo. So based on what the Kansas City meteorologist told me, I hoped Newark was still open. I'd get on that southeast leg of Elmira, follow it, and pick up the west leg of Newark. What I didn't realize was that by that time I was getting a little soft in the bonnet. I changed course 90 degrees to bring me to the west leg of Newark--somewhere. As I slowly descended, radio beam reception became spasmodic.

Finally, I came out the east edge of the storm. The front of the storm lay northeast and southwest. By that time, I had descended to a little over 20,000 feet. I looked back at one of the strangest sights I've ever seen. It was just like an absolute wall of clouds, as though cut by a knife. It went from 41,000 down to the top of the next layer, which was about 14,000 feet, as far as I could see. When I came out of the storm, radio reception was perfect. I looked at my map, and I saw the south leg of the Albany beam. I crossed that with the southwest leg of the Boston beam, and I had a pretty good fix. I estimated I was about 60 miles at sea off the Delaware Capes, and I had 45 minutes of gas left.

Well, Bermuda was a little far out. I decided the only chance I had was to head north. I had no idea what the winds were. I'd been encountering high winds. How strong or in what direction, I had no way of knowing. Heading north between layers, with the top of the lower layer about 2,000 feet, I had perfect radio reception. I hoped to cross the east leg of Newark, then from my time to cross the beam, I could get a fair estimate of how far I was east of Newark. I sat there. I was on my last tank, and I estimated by the gauge I had about 10-15 minutes of fuel left. Newark was coming in strong.

It seemed ages that I'd been flying north. I had no idea what the wind was. I crossed the leg and timed it. I estimated I was over Brooklyn, so I flew west on the beam, letting down. The engine was still running okay. After I dropped out the bottom of the upper layer, rain was falling, and I was in a warm layer. My radio reception was okay. I was on the beam, heading for Newark. Then I contacted Newark for the weather. They had a quarter of a mile of visibility and 100-foot ceiling, freezing rain, which was a horse of a very different color from what I had expected. I expected I'd have probably a 500- or 1,000-foot ceiling, maybe a mile of visibility. And here I was, about to be out of gas at any moment.

I was flying just at the top of the lower layer, then about 4,000 feet, which was all right. I was watching that gas gauge. I hit the cone of silence and figured I'd have to make an offset and come back for my final approach over Elizabeth, New Jersey, and shoot for the field. When I went over that cone, the gas gauge was showing empty. Well, I was still at 4,000 feet. So I decided not to attempt to land at Newark. Jim Easton, my mechanic-observer, was riding with me; we both had parachutes. If the engine quit, we would have to bail out. Both our cockpits were well back, planned that way in case of a crash landing. I told Jim, "I'm taking the west leg of Newark, and I know there's open country out there." From my night mail flights into Newark, I was familiar with it. I wrote a note to Jim and said, "I'm going to ride this down at low speed, and we'll make a crash landing. Buckle yourself in."

I had the fuel mixture control full lean. This big three-bladed prop was turning over about 1,100 RPMs, the engine was still hitting on all barrels, and that gas gauge needle was hard against empty. With those gauges, you might run for five minutes, three minutes; you never knew. I dropped half flaps and stabilized the airspeed at about 65. That was just above the stall. I was settling at a couple of hundred feet a minute, easing down. I had my hatch cover open so I could feel my windshield to check for ice forming. That was the old trick; you'd feel the windshield and detect the first formation of ice. I started to pick up ice at about 600 feet--not too bad, but it was coming. I could not see the ground. Five hundred, 400, 300, 200. Then suddenly I saw a polo field right underneath. The engine was still ticking weakly. I decided to do a quick offset turn to reverse course. I rolled her and then came back in a flipper turn. I thought if I could get my wheels on that polo field, we wouldn't crack up too bad.

Right in the middle of the turn, poof! The engine stopped; there was nothing to do but level the plane. The old adage I always believed in: take what's ahead and make the best of it. Changing one's mind-plan under such a condition is often fatal.

Q: You bet.

Captain Tomlinson: I had about a quarter mile of visibility. There were high-tension wires to clear. I just missed them. Ahead there lay the hill, sloping to the right, sagebrush, a row of trees at the bottom of the slope. I landed on the side of that hill, slow and easy. The plane started to turn toward the trees. I kicked the left rudder hard to turn uphill. When the plane responded, the wheels dug into muddy ground. It sounded awful with the flaps down hitting the sagebrush. The Gamma nosed up gently and bent one blade of the prop. I had my trailing edge antenna out and called Newark. The station received me, and he asked, "Where are you?"

I said, "Wait a minute. There's a farmer coming."

Q: That's how you could tell.

Captain Tomlinson: I didn't know where the hell I was. I was about two miles east of Princeton, near a polo field. Many radio stations had been trying to reach me, and they had gone crazy, with what directional radio apparatus was available, trying for hours to locate me. With no radio reception, the efforts were wasted. Most of the way across they knew that I was lost, and the conditions in which I was flying. They could hear me, but I couldn't hear them. The airline was in a panic. Across the years I have met people who listened to my attempts to communicate throughout the flight.

An hour after I landed, two trucks came with mechanics. They took the wings off, tail surfaces off, the prop, and then towed the plane to New York. The Gamma was in the show, fully assembled for inspection, the next morning at 9:00 o'clock. Paul Richter had been at Newark; he came to Princeton. He was in the first truck. They were plain going crazy; they didn't know where I was. We got pretty tight that night at Princeton.

Q: And not without reason.

Captain Tomlinson: That was the last time I flew the Gamma. I told Paul, "Look, somebody else can do it from here on out. I've had it!"

In 1934 my good friend Dutch Kindelberger, chief engineer for Douglas during the DC-1 and DC-2 project, left Douglas to become president of North American Aviation. It actually was the former General Aviation Company (owned by General Motors), which had withered after the tri-motor flop. In the summer of 1934, at odd times when my TWA duties permitted, I went to the North American factory at Baltimore to test-fly for Dutch two small experimental biplanes. These were fighter types, built in hopes of obtaining Navy contracts. These planes had an early small two-row Wright engine. They flew okay but were not up to Navy expectations. At this time Lee Atwood had left Douglas to be chief engineer for North American. I knew Lee well from the DC-1 days.

I went to Washington sometime in 1935. While I was there, I picked up a newspaper. There was an account in it of a couple of naval aviators being tangled up in weather, getting lost, and cracking up. I knew that there were a few people--Frankie Akers, whom I knew, and a few others--who had taught themselves to fly instruments.* But there was no instrument course at Pensacola or provisions for properly training naval aviators to fly instruments. So I decided to see what I could do about it. I've always believed in going to the top dog.

---
*Lieutenant Frank Akers, USN.

Daniel W. Tomlinson #2 - 185

Ernie King was Chief of the Bureau of Aeronautics.*
I called on King. I'd never met him. I had heard he was
an SOB. Anyway, I went to his office and introduced myself
and said, "I'd like to talk to Admiral King about an
aeronautical matter which I think is important." I was
ushered into Ernie King's office. He was quite pleasant.
I gave him a dissertation on why naval aviators should all
be trained as instrument pilots. It was inevitable that
they would get caught in bad weather, and in wartime there
were bound to be times when it would be necessary to take
off in bad weather to get to an enemy, or when out on a
mission the weather might close in between them and their
base. I talked for at least a half an hour on this matter.
King listened very attentively, and when I got through, he
looked at me and said, "Tomlinson, if you can't see, you
can't shoot." I got up and walked out of his office.

That SOB later--too late, in fact--had a change of
heart. He flipped the other way and did get instrument
training started, but it was too late. The Navy lost too
many pilots in the early years of the war due to lack of
instrument flight training and lack of experience in
weather flying.

Q: I guess even the YEZB homers weren't widely understood,

---

*Rear Admiral Ernest J. King, USN, served as Chief of the
Bureau of Aeronautics from 3 May 1933 to 12 June 1936.

Daniel W. Tomlinson #2 - 186

even when they did enter the fleet.*

Was that the only time you met King?

Captain Tomlinson: I met him after I was ComNATS Pacific.** He came to Honolulu. It was my duty to meet him on his arrival. I had no other contact with him.

Q: Did he remember your first meeting?

Captain Tomlinson: His only comment was, "Nice to see you, Tomlinson. Nice to see you." That was the end of that.

About early December 1936, after the Gamma stratosphere tests were concluded, Dutch, after clearing the matter with Jack Frye, asked me to take leave from TWA to work for North American, which had no regular test pilot at that time. North American had two Army Air Corps projects under way. The first was a twin-engine bomber. It had two Pratt & Whitney experimental two-row engines, each equipped with an exhaust turbo supercharger. At that time I was the only commercial pilot with exhaust turbo supercharger experience. The second project was the BC-1, a two-place, single-engine monoplane with retractable gear,

---
*These devices transmitted Morse code signals in pie-shaped sectors so pilots would know where their aircraft were in relation to the carrier.
**ComNATS--Commander Naval Air Transport Service. Tomlinson served in this billet while on active duty in World War II.

Daniel W. Tomlinson #2 - 187

flaps, and controllable-pitch prop. The Air Corps called it the basic combat trainer.

When I arrived at the North American factory, at Inglewood, California, on the west side of Mines Field, the BC-1 was ready for test. The bomber construction was behind schedule. I test-flew the BC-1 and put it through a strenuous program of flight tests to ensure that it did not have the least tendency to flat spin. The BC-1 had excellent flight characteristics and met the Air Corps specifications. It did have a slight tendency to "wing-tip" stall at maximum safe angle of attack when landing. We knew how to correct this in production airplanes: simply alter the wing jigs so the wing tips would have a bit less angle of attack.

Early in January '37, I flew the BC-1 to Wright Field, told them about the wing-tip stall. Colonel Echols, head of Wright Field engineering, understood.* I proceeded to put the BC-1 through the Wright Field required documentation tests. The final one proved critical. It was the acrobatic demonstration at low level. The board of Air Corps officers charged with inspection and approval of the BC-1, a general and several colonels, lined up on the warm-up line to watch me. I decided to do all the normal required acrobatics, then as a grand finale do a loop, my wheels raising dust directly in front of the board, with a

---

*Lieutenant Colonel Oliver P. Echols, USA.

snap roll on top of the loop. This called for plenty of excess speed. I had it. When I yanked the stick back and kicked full left rudder for the snap roll, I knew I'd hit high G's. Next morning the major, head of the structures branch, sent for me. He had the VG recorder record. It showed 14 G's. All wing inspection plates on the BC-1 were removed. A slight "set" in the left rear spar, just outboard of that spar's attachment to the center section, was evident. The board accepted the BC-1. In production it became the Air Corps AT-6 and the Navy SNJ.*
Thousands were built. It was a fine airplane; some are still flying.

I returned to Inglewood to flight-test the bomber. First off I demanded suitable steel deflection plates be installed on the exhaust turbo mounts so that if turbo blades flew off--it happened with the Gamma--the pilot and copilot would not lose their heads. The bomber's flight characteristics were good in all respects. The experimental P&W engines were subject to mechanical failures, and the experimental Curtiss Electric controllable-pitch propellers were undependable.

---

*This was one of the Navy's primary training planes in World War II. The initial version had a wing span of 42 feet, length of 27 feet, gross weight of 4,440 pounds, and a top speed of 167 miles per hour at sea level. All told, North American produced more than 16,000 of this plane in its various versions. More were produced in other countries.

The Air Corps contract for the NA-21 bomber required it to be delivered to Wright Field on X date; I can't remember what it was. That day came. Dutch wanted me to fly it back to Wright Field at 20,000 feet to impress the Army. The plane had been rushed to completion. With one of the project engineers and an experimental mechanic as crew, I took off from Burbank in January '37 about 0730. All okay till near Tucumcari; then the left prop went into low (takeoff) pitch. I had to drop to 15,000 near Wichita. The right prop went toward feather position but not quite. Stabilized at 3,000, making about 125 miles per hour. If I landed, the flight was ended. No hope of repairing the propellers in time to make the deadline at Wright Field. We wobbled east. The props held the pitch where it was.

We landed at Wright Field after dark. When I tried to use the engines to taxi, they both quit cold. A truck towed us to the line. Dutch had been there all day waiting for us, tearing his hair. The bomber passed the routine flight tests but experienced another engine failure while on the large bomb-drop approach to the target, which I made okay and impressed the colonel who was my copilot. Then, after all this, it was discovered that the bomber had been built for a safety factor of 4.5. The Army specs called for 5. Lee Atwood of the engineering department was responsible. Lee threatened to jump out his window at the Dayton Biltmore. My wife-to-be and I spent the night calming down. Lee is still alive.

Burdette Wright, Curtiss Airplane Company, was assembling a plane. It came from Buffalo by truck, a monoplane fighter, P-36, to compete with Seversky's P-35. Seversky for several days had been jazzing his P-35 over Wright Field. Burdette was in a sweat to get his plane in the air. It had not been flown. The P-36 had a 12-cylinder Allison engine. Below it was an exhaust turbo supercharger, "tucked in," streamlined into the bottom cowling. Burdette asked me to test-fly it. I did, around the field, up to about 10,000 feet, with the usual stability and controllability tests. I did turn on the turbo. The tests were excellent. Then Burdette asked me to take the plane up to 20,000 and get a high-speed check, using the turbo. I can't remember the exact airspeed, but it was well above that of the P-35.

Burdette also asked that when I came in to give them the old dive and zoom. At the top of the pullup, I realized there was a fire underneath the engine. I decided to try to slideslip, maybe blow the fire out; a fire extinguisher had done no good. Suddenly, when I was too low to jump, flames were coming into the fuselage ahead of the cockpit. A freshly plowed field was handy. I put the plane on the ground almost sideways to wipe off the gear. It did and stopped close to a farmhouse. A farmer rushed out, and together, using our hands, we extinguished the remaining flames underneath the engine section. The aluminum cowling around the turbo overheated and had caught fire. I had two broken ribs.

That plane was rebuilt as the P-40, with the turbo, and the pilot's cockpit was moved one bay forward. This closed a fascinating and rewarding session at Wright Field. I returned to TWA, having made a number of Air Corps friends.

In July 1937 Burdette asked me to come to Buffalo, where the Curtiss Airplane Company factory was then located, to run the terminal-velocity dive tests with 10-G pullouts on the SBC, a biplane dive-bomber for the Navy.* He also wanted me to do the demonstration terminal-velocity and 10-G pullouts at Dahlgren, which was where the Navy made ordnance tests then.** These tests covered the bomb-load configuration. The final tests were with a 1,000-pound bomb. For all the tests the plane was loaded to its normal operating gross weight. The plane was a two-cockpit job with an observer-gunner in the rear seat. For test purposes there were 200 pounds of lead shot secured in the seat.

On this last test after I made 10 G's by the accelerometer, I tried to level off. I discovered the

---

*The SBC Helldiver had a wing span of 34 feet, length of 28 feet, gross weight of 7,632 pounds, and a top speed of 237 miles per hour. It began entering Navy squadrons in 1937.
**Naval Proving Ground, Dahlgren, Virginia.

control stick was partially jammed. The rear seat had collapsed, limiting up elevator movement of the stick. With power off, the plane wanted to go into a dive. The slowest speed at which I could stabilize, using partial power, was about 120 miles per hour. This meant that to land I would have to "fly on," have my wheels on the runway before cutting the engine. It was either that or bail out. As on a couple of previous tests, I chose to land the plane and hope for the best.

I alerted the control tower as to my predicament and requested the meat wagon and fire department at the end of the runway. It was a dicey landing. The plane stopped abreast of the fire wagons at the end of the runway. John Ballentine, a Naval Academy classmate, was CO.* He was by the crash wagons to greet me with, "Why are you, 40 years old, doing this kind of flying?"

I told him, "I enjoy it, and who else do you know who can consistently hit 10 G's, plus or minus .01G? And the pay is good, 1,000 smackers a dive."

This was my last terminal-velocity, 10-G pullout. In August I married Margaret Castelline, whom I had met in the Kitty Hawk Room of the Dayton Biltmore. I had done so when Dutch Kindelberger and I were having a late dinner following the delivery flight of the NA-21 from L.A. to

---
*Lieutenant Commander John J. Ballentine, USN, was probably there at the time as a representative of the Bureau of Aeronautics.

Wright Field. It marked the beginning of 33 wonderful years.

Now to my next job with TWA. We knew that we had to develop a new transport with four engines--the best as far as engine dependability is concerned. It would have the capability to fly substantially higher than the DC-3s and have a pressurized fuselage--cabin and pilots' cockpit. I knew from what I'd done with the DC-1 and the Gamma that we weren't going to get up to the stratosphere yet, but another step up was possible.

That was about the time that the first Boeing B-17 bomber was to be delivered to Wright Field. I discussed it with Jack, and I said, "It may have possibilities. I'll go over to Wright Field and fly it." A colonel whose name I do not recall and the Boeing pilot tried to take the B-17 off with the controls locked, with the result that they were killed and all on board. So it was a week or so before the next B-17 was delivered. An Army Air Corps officer rode as my copilot. They gave me a cockpit check. I took the B-17 out and flew it around for about an hour, making careful stability and controllability tests.

There was one new development it had that we were particularly interested in. Boeing had developed a new idea for keeping the control forces within reason. They put on small flettner tabs on the ailerons, rudder, and elevators, so that when you first moved your controls, the flettners moved first. It was a differential device; as the controls moved, the more these flettners moved to reduce the force required to move the main surfaces. It worked all right. The airplane was all I hoped it would be.

I went back to Kansas City and told Jack Frye, "Let's get Boeing engineers here and see if they can't put a pressurized cabin on the B-17 wing." It wasn't ten days before there was a Boeing delegation at Kansas City. One fellow by the name of Collins was from the sales office, with several aeronautical engineers. I can't recall their names, but Collins was the head of the delegation; he represented the sales and administrative. He's still alive in Seattle. Jack, several others, and I made our suggestions. The Boeing group were very interested.

Collins said, "We'll go back and study this. It was a couple of weeks after that when another group came, including Collins. They had the answers we wanted. They said, "We can use the B-17 wing jigs and center section and those for the landing gear and the engine cells. We'll have to design and build new tail surfaces to give you adequate control and stability for the increased size of the fuselage. We can pressurize it so that you can fly at 16,000 feet with 8,000-foot pressure altitude in the

Daniel W. Tomlinson #2 - 195

cabin." This would be a real forward step, because flying out west in the summertime, and over the country generally, if you can fly to 16,000 or a little over, you're on top of the worst convectional turbulence and enjoy a smooth ride. Out west, any time under 16,000 feet, the turbulence just kicks hell out of a plane--especially on clear, hot days, flying across the desert or over the Grand Canyon. The majority of the passengers become airsick. That sounded good.

Unfortunately, at that time a fellow by the name of Hertz, a taxi man, had control of TWA and was chairman of the board.*

Q: I had no idea there was any connection.

Captain Tomlinson: Yes, he was chairman of the board of TWA at that time. Jack Frye got the contract through the board of directors for the Boeing 307. American agreed to take three or four, and we wanted seven. There were 13 to be built. Boeing got started in 1935, and I was pretty busy, '37 to '38, going up to Boeing. Construction was getting under way in good shape in '36. Hertz had no aeronautical vision. The company was in trouble financially. We weren't making money with the DC-3s,

---

*John D. Hertz was founder of the Yellow Cab Company.

skimping by with the mail revenue, plus what we could take in by passenger fares. Because of Hertz's control, TWA was forced to cancel the order when the 307s were about a third completed. The program was in turmoil.

I had always disliked the fact that in the DC-2s and DC-3s the landing gear was stiff-legged. You had to be pretty careful about landing those planes; they had a tendency to bounce. When you're coming in at night with snow and rain and it's miserable; to try and make a smooth landing is almost impossible. I knew what had been done after leaving the Navy, where the manufacturers had softened up the action of the hydraulic landing gear strut. The Navy had finally come to what I had wanted them to do on the <u>Langley</u>--fly onto the deck, don't come staggering in and fall onto it. Come in under control and land with a landing gear which would take that without bouncing.

So I wrote in the specifications for the 307 that "the action of the landing gear and the shock absorbers must be such that the airplane can be landed without shock or bounce at a rate of descent of 500 feet per minute." I figured 500 feet was ample leeway; actually a 200- or 300-foot rate of descent was all you needed. I did it. When the 307 came into service, you'd fly onto the ground, ease the yoke forward, no bounce. That revolutionized air transport landings.

Daniel W. Tomlinson #2 - 197

Q: How long did the Stratoliners stay in service?

Captain Tomlinson: They were the only four-engine airplanes in existence at the beginning of World War II which were capable of intercontinental operation. True, they could only carry a dozen passengers. They had to hike the gross load materially. Roosevelt made one trip over to Africa in one of them. It was a shame that there weren't 100 or so of those planes built. They were beautiful airplanes. They flew for years after the war. The last I heard, there were several flying in Southeast Asia. Pilots loved to fly them.

Q: I would imagine some of the engineering in that airplane must have shown up later in the B-29.

Captain Tomlinson: Quite possibly. I never got to fly one of those planes. I saw them when they came out to the Pacific.

Q: Among the Northrop designs, you flew the Alpha and the Gamma?

Captain Tomlinson: Yes, and the Delta.

Q: How do you compare those three? Were they similar?

Captain Tomlinson: The Gamma was an excellent flying airplane, and so was the Alpha. The Alpha had a peculiar characteristic. Just two or three miles of airspeed before the stall, you suddenly got a slight tail buffet, which was a good warning. The Gamma had nothing of that kind. It was stable, easily controlled. The control forces were just right.

The Delta was a good flying airplane; it was a high wing. My only adverse comment about that was that the pilots' cockpit, right in back of the firewall, was a hellhole.

Q: Yes, I can imagine.

I suppose TWA's next airplane would have been the Constellation, wouldn't it?

Captain Tomlinson: The next one, after we got the 307, was a Douglas. The other airlines were interested. Douglas started building what was supposed to be the DC-4. We got into that in about late '38 after the contract with Boeing was canceled. I was tired of flying a swivel chair. I had remarried, had a fine wife, and I asked Jack Frye, "Things are quiet here. How about my going back flying the line and having some time off?" I worked every day in the office, and if they had test or special flights they'd call me. I said, "I'm going to take a regular run and enjoy life."

I flew the line until the spring of '39. Then I was hooked for the Douglas prototype DC-4 development. Pan American, Eastern, American, and United were involved. We had many conferences regarding it. When the plane was ready for test, there had been too many chief engineers with their fingers in the pie. For instance, one thing was the electrical system, a 400-volt experiment with a separate gasoline engine-powered generator in one of the engine nacelles. There were a lot of other questionable items. It was a hodgepodge.

I flew it. I thought I was going to be at Los Angeles all summer and rented an apartment. Bennie Howard was the Douglas test pilot at that time. I flew it with Bennie. The plane had a two-wheel landing gear. They were big wheels and tires. We landed at Burbank. As we slowed down and Bennie was starting to taxi, one of these tires blew out. I don't know how much pressure it had in it, but it blew a hole about four feet deep in the runway.

After I'd made a couple of flights with Bennie, I telephoned Frye and said, "This plane is no good." All the airlines turned it down.

That's when Doug got mad and said, "You can all go home. I'll build an airplane." And he did. That was the successful DC-4. There were substantial changes. The first monstrosity was sold to Japan, and some Jap cracked it up. It was a flyable airplane, and aerodynamically it was all right, but it had too many half-baked innovations in it. It did have the first nose wheel landing gear, a key change in passenger transports, and this was one of TWA's proposals. I had flown at Wright Field a DC-5 in which the Army Air Corps had installed a tricycle nose gear. I recommended we use it.

Q: The DC-4 became the C-54 in military circles.

Captain Tomlinson: The C-54, R5D for the Navy.*

Q: Right.

Captain Tomlinson: Then the next thing, of course, was the Constellation.

Going back to '35, when we were working on the contract and specifications for the 307, Jack said Howard Hughes was going to come in to go over some of the data with him. At the time, I was TWA chief engineer, test and research pilot. I had never met Hughes. I knew who he was. This odd-looking character came through the door of

---

*The four-engine R5D Skymaster carried a crew of four and up to 30 passengers. It had a wing span of 117 feet, length of 93 feet, gross weight of 65,000 pounds, and maximum speed of 281 miles per hour.

my office. He had flown from L.A. in a JRB, a stagger-wing Beech. He looked like an apparition, a tramp: long hair, half inch of whiskers, dirty clothes, and he smelled bad. My eyes bugged out. I said, "Sit down." There was a chair opposite my desk. I had no choice other than spend a couple of hours discussing our plans for the 307, the performance specs in particular. Hughes gave me no trouble re the specs. I was surprised at his detailed knowledge of the matters we discussed. He was well-informed and asked sensible questions. I went over the performance requirements and what we were asking. Finally, he was satisfied, got up, and left.

I went right over to Jack Frye's door and rapped. Jack hollered, "Come in."

I walked over to him. Jack was sitting there with a lot of papers on his desk. I said, "Jack, that man is crazy. Do I have to put up with him?"

He looked up and me and said, "Tommy, he owns the airline." What Jack had done to circumvent Hertz was to send Hughes the list of stockholders. Hughes had bought control of the airline to throw Hertz out. That was what enabled TWA to reinstate the contract with Boeing and have the 307s built.

Q: For the Stratoliner?

Daniel W. Tomlinson #2 - 202

Captain Tomlinson: Yes, the Stratoliner. I've always laughed about Hughes. I said, "I tagged that man in '35 as being crazy." And I think subsequent events proved that I was correct.

Q: That's just about right.

Were any other airlines interested in the Constellation?

Captain Tomlinson: Let me tell you--the first conference involved Jack Frye, Walt Hamilton, Howard Hughes, Bob Gross, Lockheed's chief engineer Hibbard, and me. They had the brochure prepared to present us. It was based on four small two-row Wright engines. Apparently Pan Am had approached them earlier independently, and they had prepared this brochure. I took one look at it and remembered my experience with Navy aircraft procurement, when invariably the airplanes would end up overweight and underpowered. What Lockheed claimed for this plane with these four small engines would be impossible. It would be overweight and underpowered.

Before this conference, I'd been in touch with an ex-Navy friend of mine, George Chapline, who was vice president of sales for Wright Aeronautical. I knew George well. In fact, he was one of the officers who was at

Pensacola with me, along with Tommy and Ziggy Sprague.* Chapline kept me posted on new engine developments. I knew about the 3350, which was then on the stands and had practically completed the tests for use in the B-29s at 3,000 horsepower. I said, "Whoa! Now, see what you can do around four of the 3350s." I told Jack, "I will write the performance specifications on this airplane, based on only 50% of the power. If they meet that, the parameters of performance will follow through."

The first stumbling block was Howard Hughes, who was afraid to gamble on an engine that had never been flown. We finally talked him into going along with this. Several weeks passed, and when we went back they had the first proposals using the 3350s. I had prepared the TWA specifications: the cruising speed, takeoff, range, payload, etc. We finally got Howard to approve it. This was the basis on which the Constellation design rested.

There's an interesting story. During the final workout of the contract, Howard Hughes developed this secrecy complex, and his idea was that only the minimum people necessary were to know anything about the construction of the Constellation until it flew. He didn't want any of the other airlines to know about it. To finalize the contract he rented a villa with many rooms at

---

*George F. Chapline was a Navy lieutenant in 1920. He resigned his regular commission in 1929 and later came back on active duty as a reserve officer in World War II.

the Beverly Hills Hilton. Then we were literally locked up there. Jack Frye, president of TWA, was exempt, but Paul Richter, Walt Hamilton, Jack Franklin, and I, with opposites from Lockheed, had to be locked up there.

The fun of this thing was when somebody said, "Who's going to be the secretary to handle this top-secret project?" Hughes made no suggestion, and Jack didn't have anybody to offer. Happily, my wife had been a court reporter, and she was a crackerjack. Fortunately, we'd been married long enough at that time so Jack and the people in TWA knew that she was a gal who could keep her mouth shut.

I said, "How about Margie?"

Jack turned to Hughes and said, "I'll buy that." So she was locked up with us and took all the dictation and typed the original contract for the first Constellation. I said, "At least I got to sleep with the secretary."

This secrecy thing, due to Hughes's obsession, was a panic and a pain. However, no one in the industry knew about it until around '41. A very high-level board was sent out from Washington, directed by Roosevelt, with orders that they had to be shown everything that was being considered, built, or at what stage of development in all aircraft factories.

Interview Number 3 with Captain Daniel W. Tomlinson IV,
U.S. Naval Reserve (Retired)

Place: Captain Tomlinson's home in Silverton, Oregon

Date: Wednesday, 11 September 1985

Interviewer: Barrett Tillman

Q: I'd like to skip back a little bit to your trip to Europe in 1938.

Captain Tomlinson: Yes.

Q: How did that come about?

Captain Tomlinson: That came about because I'd spent more time in the stratosphere than any other pilot in the world. I prepared a paper on what I'd learned by the stratosphere flights, and it was read at this high-level meeting at the Lilienthal Gesellschacht meeting, which is the German counterpart of our Institute of Aeronautical Sciences. I was suddenly told that I'd been selected, along with Igor Sikorsky and another engineer who operated a test basin where flying boat hulls were tested to determine their efficiency.* He was an expert on designs for pontoons

---

*Igor Sikorsky, an immigrant from Russia, was an aircraft manufacturer and one of this country's pioneers in the development of helicopters.

and flying boat hulls. We were there as the guests of the German Government. It just happened that Slim Lindbergh and Anne were there. I knew Paul Pihl, and his wife, who was the sister of Wendell Willkie.* Paul was the naval air attaché at the embassy in Berlin. We had a marvelous time in Berlin.

Slim and I went through several of the military factories, and he was invited to fly the military planes. I was invited to fly the Ju-99, which was a large four-engine transport which the Germans were flying between Berlin and Vienna. It carried 60-70 passengers, with four big BMW fuel-injection engines. They were using it on this one service experimentally. It was a huge thing.

I looked it over carefully. Looking at the elevators, I noticed that they had a spring-loaded flettner on them to lighten the control forces. I could see it had springs under tension. I did not like the spring device. That did not look good; it could flutter. I decided to find out about it, because I was curious. Slim was going, and we were both given a chance to sit on the left-hand side and fly the plane. Slim flew first. He had precedence over everybody except God in those days. He just flew the plane maybe ten minutes, level easy turns. Then he said, "Tom, you get in there and fly it."

I did. I was thinking about these questionable

---
*Lieutenant Commander Paul E. Pihl, USN. Willkie ran for President in 1940, when he was defeated by Franklin D. Roosevelt.

flettners, and I thought maybe the device would become critical at high angles of elevator control when landing. I thought, "How am I going to approximate that without getting the passengers alarmed?" So I just started working into flipper turns so I could get higher elevator control angle and anxious to see if any reverse control force appeared. I finally had the plane close to a 45-degree bank, a steady turn, and all of sudden those elevators went into flutter. They were serving tea in the passenger cabin. Anne Lindbergh and my wife were back there with dignitaries from Lufthansa.* It really messed things up. They were tossed around.

The German pilot must have known what was coming. I thought he was getting a little antsy when I was into the maneuver, so he got to the throttles before I did. He pulled the power off, and the flutter stopped. Slim Lindbergh was standing in back of me; his feet were off the floor due to the flutter, pitching of the plane. It was a hell of a big monoplane. They knew about that condition, and yet they were flying regular service with passengers. The pilots were probably extra careful how they used those elevators when landing.

Q: Maybe it was a prestige type of project which they figured was worth the risk.

---
*Lufthansa is a German airline.

Captain Tomlinson: Yes, it was undoubtedly that.

Q: Did you get a chance to talk to any notable German aviators?

Captain Tomlinson: Yes, Milch and Udet.* I talked to Udet at a few parties. Of course, we went through the Messerschmitt factories that were turning out fighters, 20 a day. All were not even test flown but put in storage, fuselages complete, wings and tail surfaces disassembled. Slim told his Air Corps friends, and I told my Navy friends, "The U.S. has never built airplanes on a production-line basis like the Germans are doing." I'll never forget Paul Pihl's parting shot, "Tommy, for heaven's sake, tell those stupids back home what is going on."

Q: Was anybody interested?

Captain Tomlinson: No.

Q: They didn't want to hear that.

Captain Tomlinson: No. I made a special visit to the Navy

---

*Erhard Milch was essentially the operating head of the German Air Ministry in the 1930s. Ernst Udet had flown for the German air force in World War I. He was later head of procurement for the Luftwaffe.

Daniel W. Tomlinson #3 - 209

Department to tell them. All I got was, "Is that so? Well, isn't that interesting?" That was all.

Q: Were you in Britain or France on that trip?

Captain Tomlinson: I flew from Berlin to Paris for a couple of days. Then from Paris I went to Amsterdam and met the managing director of KLM.* I went through their maintenance and overhaul shops and saw what they had at Schipol airport. I went to England for a couple of days; I had lunch with Gray, the famous editor.

Q: C. G. Gray.

Captain Tomlinson: C.G. Gray, yes. He was an interesting person. I liked him. He took my wife and me to Windsor Castle to lunch. He was really a live wire. He took what I told him re the Germans seriously.

Q: To get back on schedule, then in June of '41 you requested return to active duty status.

Captain Tomlinson: I went back to Washington in April, but I had in mind June 1 as a propitious time to report.

Q: So you were convinced at this time that war was coming?

*KLM is a Dutch airline.

Captain Tomlinson: Definitely. In '39-'40'-'41 I was often required by TWA to make many talks at functions--lunches, dinners, etc. I always managed to tell them, "Don't fool yourselves. Hitler means business.* War is inevitable, and the U.S. had better be ready. Our concerned people in Washington, D.C., are either too stupid or have their heads in the sand, ostrich-fashion."

Just to go back a little bit, I returned to Kansas City in '35. When I was in New York, I had command of the reserve squadron at Floyd Bennett Field. I liked to keep up my Navy contacts. I could always use a Naval Reserve airplane and fly most anywhere. It was a privilege. So I conceived the idea--I had good friends in the bureau at that time--I said, "I'm going to be in Kansas City with TWA. There's a lot of Naval Reserve pilots flying for TWA. If there's a Naval Reserve base established there, I will see to it that a group of experienced pilots join it." In no time, Frank Weld, who was exec of the reserve base at St. Louis, was transferred to Kansas City to establish a reserve squadron at Fairfax Airport in '35.** As soon as it was set up, we organized the reserve squadron. I lined up old friends of mine, TWA pilots or copilots, top-notch men.

---
*Adolf Hitler was Chancellor of Germany from 1933 until his death in 1945.
**Lieutenant Frank E. Weld, USNR.

Q: What type of aircraft did you have?

Captain Tomlinson: When we started out, we had the old Curtiss Helldivers, Wasp-powered. Then we got a single-engine, two-place Grumman fighter with retractable landing gear.

Q: SF-1?

Captain Tomlinson: Something of that sort. We probably got those in about '36, '37. We never received any better planes than those. They were a bit clumsy and awkward-looking, but they flew; they were all right. We could really fly with them--formation, simulated dive-bombing, gunnery runs, etc. For three consecutive years before the war--'36, '37, and '38--the squadron I commanded won the Noel Davis Trophy for proficiency.

Q: That's for all the reserve squadrons in the country.

Captain Tomlinson: Yes. The pilots were really interested, much like when I was training the Seahawks. If one was out of line, he heard about it. I cursed on occasion in those days. The pilots took pride in their reserve flying. We put on demonstrations that were first class. The Navy annually sent an inspection team around

Daniel W. Tomlinson #3 - 212

the country to all reserve bases. Individual pilots had to take a written exam. Also the squadron performed prescribed air maneuvers. The trophy was awarded for the best performance; we did it three years in succession. We all enjoyed it. The organized reserve drill pay was an item. I got extra command pay. It was worthwhile and a change from airline operations.

We had two weeks' active duty each summer, and I'd arrange for the pilots to have two weeks off with base pay, and we'd just have a circus. We'd have parties in the wardroom in the administrative building. We finally took over the old Curtiss flying school building at Kansas City, Kansas, Municipal Airport. That was a nice setup--hangar and nice offices.

Q: After we got into the war, did your base become a training facility right away?

Captain Tomlinson: It was a training facility before. They trained cadets and soloed them, then sent them on to Pensacola or Corpus Christi for basic training.

Q: So it was an elimination base then, primarily?

Captain Tomlinson: Yes. I wore two hats when I went back on active duty. I was in command of the Naval Reserve Aviation Base at Fairfax and in command of the Naval

Reserve Aviation Base under construction at Olathe, Kansas. I'd go back and forth between the two places. NAS Olathe was a well-built station. I got the contract, got the approval and the contract approved before the war. The principal buildings at Olathe were made of brick; they were all first class. All the other NRABs that were built after the war began were wartime construction, primitive, second-grade material and construction.

Q: Quonset huts and that sort of thing?

Captain Tomlinson: A few were used as the wartime bases were built.

When I took over the command, prior to the war, the reserve base operations were more or less on the country-club style, easygoing. I took command and decided, "To hell with this." We were at war. I reorganized the operations on an efficient basis. One of my beliefs for a long time had been that more primary training should be given at night so there wouldn't be any mystery about it. Right from the start, they'd learn the principles. So I changed the schedules. We began flying at 8:00 o'clock to 12:00. We knocked off until 1400, then we flew until 1800 and secured to dinner. Then we flew from 2000 to midnight. This schedule practically doubled the output of students.

Another thing I did--instead of having plane crews for each airplane, we had a small line crew that serviced all the operating planes. Then in the hangar I established an overhaul production line. I put the maintenance crew on three shifts around the clock. That made a big difference in availability of aircraft.

Q: Sure thing.

Captain Tomlinson: The men knew they had a certain watch for a set time. Watches were changed at least every two weeks so that they weren't all on the late shift. The output doubled.

Q: What did you have--N2Ss and N3Ns?

Captain Tomlinson: One or two N3Ns and a JRB.* The N3Ns were made by Consolidated; they called them the "Yellow Perils." We also received Stearmans, a good plane.

I got the base going, and then Raddy Radford, an old friend, was ordered back to Washington to be director of training.** The Kansas City NRAB was turning out twice as many students as any other base, so Raddy called me to Washington and wanted to know what was going on. I told

---
*The N3N was a trainer manufactured by the Naval Aircraft Factory. It had a wing span of 34 feet, length of 26 feet, gross weight of 2,792 pounds, and top speed of 126 miles per hour. The Beech JRB, designated SNB as a trainer, had a wing span of of 48 feet, length of 34 feet, gross weight of 7,850 pounds, and top speed of 225 miles per hour.
**Commander Arthur W. Radford, USN, became director of training in the Bureau of Aeronautics in December 1941 and was promoted to captain in January 1942.

him what I'd done. He said, "I want you to set up a conference in Kansas City, where all the base commanders and a few other key people may convene. You're to describe your new base organization and operating schedules, and it's going to be made standard."

That's what we did. We set up the conference. Raddy and several other key people came back to Kansas City. I had the program carefully organized with pamphlets, charts, etc. My base reorganization and operational training schedules were approved. I took off after the conference to visit each NRAB to be sure each CO understood. I took Lieutenant John Harlin with me.* There were 13 naval reserve air bases and four preflight schools. The cadets went to these colleges for a month or so for indoctrination and elementary military training.

The new changes nearly doubled the output of cadets into basic training at Pensacola and Corpus Christi. Then the war started. We were ready for it. We could not increase our output without more personnel, more facilities, and more planes. Then we began to get the Stearman, a fine plane. Needed personnel came in. The show was on the road!

I had a comfortable home on the north side of Kansas City, Missouri. From it I could drive to the TWA headquarters at the Municipal Field, Kansas City, Missouri

---

*Lieutenant John E. Harlin, USNR.

Daniel W. Tomlinson #3 - 216

or go across the bridge over the river to reach the base at Fairfax, Kansas, easily. I had one traffic light to go through either way. I knew I was going to be in command of the new NRAB at Olathe the first of October. I got a note from Admiral Towers, just a personal note.* At that time I had just taken command of the NRAB at Fairfax, and we were under the director of training in Washington. The Navy was going to set up the Naval Air Primary Training Command with headquarters at Fairfax. He wanted me to go as chief of staff of the NAPTC. In anticipation of this, I had rented a house in Olathe, figuring that I'd rent my house in north Kansas City and move, but he sprung this on me. I said, "Admiral, I'm all set up to live in Olathe. May I use Beechcraft or other suitable type plane to fly back and forth?"

He said, "Use anything you want."

Q: This was Admiral Buckmaster?

Captain Tomlinson: No, this was Rear Admiral Jack Towers. After Buckmaster lost the Yorktown at Midway, they ordered him to be in command of the NAPTC.** He was a nice old gentleman. We'd inspect the NRABs, and he'd tell me to handle the inspection and hold a conference with the base

---
*Rear Admiral John H. Towers, USN, served as Chief of the Bureau of Aeronautics from 1 June 1939 to 6 October 1942.
**Captain Elliott Buckmaster, USN, commanding officer of the aircraft carrier Yorktown (CV-5) when she was sunk in the Battle of Midway in June 1942.

heads of departments. He'd sit off on a chair to one side and listen to what was going on. We got along fine. We lighted a fire under the NRABs. Delivery of the Stearman trainers made a marked improvement. There were 75,000 people in the command.

Q: We're talking about 1942 now, right?

Captain Tomlinson: Nineteen forty-two, yes.

Q: By this time, I would imagine, the training syllabus had evolved to the point where the washout rate was pretty low once the student got past E-base.*

Captain Tomlinson: Oh, yes. The washout rate, after we sent these cadets down to Pensacola, wasn't bad. We washed them out at the NRABs. I was always in favor of being pretty tough, get rid of them before they crashed really expensive equipment.

I inaugurated one test that there was some holler raised about. I said, "The graduation test that they're going to have before they go to Pensacola will separate the men from the boys. They're going to have to make a night cross-country flight alone. I threw the BBT flood lights

---

*E-base--elimination base, which performed a screening function before students went to Pensacola for flight training itself.

out for night landings. I made it standard to use smoke pots, outlining a rectangle on the runway 600 feet long and 100-150 feet wide. We turned out all the other lights on the field. I took one of my TWA reserve officers with me. On each one of the NRABs I'd take the CO by the ear and say, "Come. You're going to learn this right from me, and I'll demonstrate."

Well, I convinced them that you could come in, line those lights up, using the angles, and know exactly where you were and how high. Don't even look at the ground; just look at the angles those lights make, level off, and the ground will be there. I finally got that started. The thing that caused me to start this procedure was a report from the Pacific forward area, where many of the night fighters had returned to the field, which had only BBT floodlights, and the CO was afraid to turn them on in the combat area. The pilots jumped out. They wouldn't even attempt to land without their BBT floodlights to illuminate the whole field. They just got in over the field and jumped out. I got ahold of Raddy and said, "This crap's got to stop." And I had his okay.

This goes back to my time with the night mail. When you're sitting up there all alone at night, you find out whether you can take it or not. I got some static; this final graduation flight was the one that counted at Olathe. The cadets flew Stearmans with running lights and radio and went to St. Louis. They'd turn at St. Louis and fly to

Daniel W. Tomlinson #3 - 219

Omaha, Omaha back to Kansas City, all by their baby selves. If they made it, they went on to basic. So far as I know, we didn't lose any of them. But my argument was that that separated the men from the boys, and it was a damn sight cheaper, if you lost one, to lose a Stearman than the expensive combat airplane later on.

Q: Sure thing, yes.

Captain Tomlinson: That was carried on through the program, at least as long as I was chief of staff of the NAPTC.

Q: Do you remember the ratio of night flying to day flying hours?

Captain Tomlinson: No, I can't remember exactly. They had roughly ten hours' instruction before they soloed. At least two hours of that was at night.

Q: Did your position change through 1943?

Captain Tomlinson: No. I was chief of staff from the spring of 1942; in June I was promoted to captain. In the fall of 1942 I knew something was going to happen. I'd been there at the NRAB at Kansas City, Kansas, since 1 June 1941.

Out of a clear sky, I received orders to report to the Navy Department for indoctrination. My first orders read to relieve Captain Don Smith as Commander Air Transport Squadrons Pacific.* I went to Washington, where the department outlined the tremendous expansion that was going to come, and acquainted me with the NATS organization. I actually got down on my knees and begged the director of personnel in naval aviation to let me command a carrier. My rank was right, and I had flown off three carriers. I certainly was entitled to at least a baby carrier.

He said, "Tommy, your experience is in transport aviation. We haven't got anybody else."

So I proceeded to Honolulu and relieved Captain Smith. He was trying to run this show across the whole Pacific as a wing commander. Under Navy regulations, the respective squadron commanders were responsible for the flying, operation, and maintenance of their airplanes. It was completely inapplicable to the organization and efficient management of an integrated airline--utterly impossible.

Q: Did you ever learn how this existing setup had been established?

Captain Tomlinson: Simple. Don Smith was following Navy regulations. The Navy had never before been faced with a project of this special magnitude and scope. As soon as I
_____
*Captain Donald F. Smith, USN.

relieved Smith, the first thing I did was sit down and rough draft an organization of how the squadrons were going to operate, what the duties of each squadron commander would be, and the same for my staff. Just like a ship's organization, when anyone is reporting aboard, you can hand him a pamphlet and chart of the organization. He knows exactly who is who, who he reports to, and what his responsibilities are. That took me about ten days to promulgate. I called the squadron commanders in and we had conferences. I had all my staff people together. I explained the new organization in detail. Each had an organization chart, and I had a booklet printed that clearly set forth the duties of everybody.

I told Admiral Towers what I was doing. I said, "I'd like to have an appointment with Admiral Nimitz, because little of it is according to regulations."* He arranged it and introduced me to Admiral Nimitz, a wonderful gentleman.

I said, "Admiral, I've been sent out here to run an airline for you, and I've found that none of the setup is applicable to the efficient conduct of a large, widespread airline operation. So I have set up my own organization, based on my 12 years with TWA. Here's the chart and booklet of duties and responsibilities. I have already put it in operation."

---
*Admiral Chester W. Nimitz, USN, was Commander in Chief Pacific Fleet.

I'll never forget. Admiral Nimitz looked at me and said, "Tomlinson, it better work."

I said, "Thank you, Admiral," and excused myself. No more was ever said.

It was vital that the control of all operations be vested in my staff operations officer. He had two assistants. One was flight dispatch, responsible for coordinating and dispatching all aircraft; the other was the flight control officer. The dispatcher was responsible for knowing the locations of all the airplanes, the availabilities of the crews, and the readiness of the aircraft. He had to see that they were at the loading area on time, with crew on board and ready to take off. When the pilot was released for takeoff, he came under flight control until he landed; then dispatch again took over. We were in an office in the tower, a part of the passenger station at John Rodgers Airport, which was my headquarters. A passenger station was on the ground floor, with offices on the second floor.

The NATSPac operations officer was Lieutenant Charles Dolson.* When I tagged him, he was chief pilot for Delta Airlines and had wide experience with airline operation; he had two assistants, both experienced TWA pilots. Dolson directed dispatch and flight control, which were on the third floor, in the control tower. He was a junior reserve

---

*Lieutenant Charles H. Dolson, USNR.

pilot in VB-2B at the time of the national air races in 1928. I knew him as a very junior pilot; he was a sharp one, and I liked him. I had inquired about his work with Delta, and I knew that he was tops. In his offices were charts, devices, and information such that ComNATSPac could quickly learn the status, location, and capability of all aircraft and flight personnel.

Q: How many aircraft did that involve when you took command?

Captain Tomlinson: Not many. In the big boat squadron at Alameda, VR-2, they had 20 or more four-engine Coronados, PB2Ys.* These flew through the South Pacific to Brisbane. We had received four or five R5Ds. VR-10 was operating between 20 and 30 Martin PBMs, twin-engine boats, in the South Pacific.**

Q: The Mariners.

Captain Tomlinson: Mariners, yes; that's what they called them. Part of those were temporarily based in Espiritu Santo, ferrying people from Guadalcanal to Noumea, to New

---

*The Consolidated PB2Y flying boat had a wing span of 115 feet, length of 79 feet, gross weight of 68,000 pounds, and a top speed of 213 miles per hour.
**The Martin PBM flying boat had a wing span of 118 feet, length of 80 feet, gross weight of 58,000 pounds, and a top speed of 198 miles per hour.

Zealand, and sometimes to Sydney. The individual squadron commanders were responsible for their operations. Don Smith didn't have the organization or the facilities to keep in touch with them. I obtained a crackerjack communications officer, and we soon had an elaborate and efficient communications system of our own throughout the Pacific. You cannot operate an airline without dependable communications. We got everything NATS needed. I never took "No" for an answer.

With this operations organization, when Admiral Nimitz's staff would call and want to know if we could supply X airplanes at a certain time and place, we had the information right now. We could tell him exactly what we had, because Dolson, with his dispatch and flight control, knew where the airplanes were. We knew where the crews were, whether they were in Brisbane or at intermediate islands. We knew how much flight time was available in the airplanes, maintenance-wise. It was all right there in NATSPac headquarters.

Part of this change was the squadron commander's duty. VR-2 was responsible for the training, discipline, and readiness of flight crews, other squadron personnel, maintenance, and overhaul of the PB2Ys at Alameda only. In VR-11, which flew the R5Ds, the squadron commander had nothing to do with maintenance; he was simply the land plane chief pilot, responsible for training, discipline, and readiness of flight crews. At the end of the war he had 3,000 pilots. VR-10 at Honolulu was the system maintenance department, the main overhaul base. It supplied trained mechanics at forward area stations and at Guam a special unit of about 1,000 men and six nose docks for R5Ds.

Q: In one squadron?

Captain Tomlinson: In one squadron.

Q: My God.

Captain Tomlinson: One squadron.

Q: He was running an airline himself.

Captain Tomlinson: VR-11 had a check pilot for every ten pilots, all former airline pilots. Before they were allowed to fly the Pacific, the R5D pilots had special training and were called to Crow's Landing in California, a special school. I had two outstanding former TWA pilots there in charge. I told them, "You will apply to the pilots you check out the same criterion that we had with TWA: When you check a man out, would you be content, if you had brought your family down to board a flight and saw this pilot in the cockpit as the captain, and the weather was a little marginal, would you put them aboard the airplane with him? If you wouldn't do that, he is out so far as NATSPac is concerned."

The Navy Department then sent these dropouts somewhere else. The check pilots were plenty tough. I never got any flareback, and we weeded out quite few. After completing at Crow's Landing, they had to put in 100 hours flying cargo across the Pacific before they could fly regular passenger schedules. We lost one cargo R5D at Guam. The pilot encountered exceptionally bad weather at night. It was perfectly understandable.

Q: I've been on Guam at night when it's raining, and, boy, you can't see a thing.

Captain Tomlinson: It could be miserable. That was the only one we lost.

Q: Just a little side trip. How did the need for airline pilots in the military affect TWA's operations during the war.

Captain Tomlinson: Right after I took command of NRAB, Kansas City, Kansas, I received another note from Admiral Towers. He said, "I want you to come back to Washington to head a board to contact the airlines and set up an orderly procedure whereby, in the event of war, we can call back needed pilots." Artie Doyle was one of the members.* I was the senior one. I went back and talked with Artie and the other member; there were three of us.

I asked the admiral if I could have an airplane to fly to New York and Chicago, because in New York I could contact Eastern, Pan American, and American headquarters. Then I'd fly to Chicago that night to talk to United in the morning.

I talked to them, and we evolved this procedure. There were three categories into which the ex-Navy pilots were placed. The immediately available pilots were those who had been with the airlines only six months. In the second category were pilots who had been with the airlines a year or more. In the third category were pilots who were necessary, qualified, well-experienced captains, who had regular runs. They would be exempt except in the case of the gravest emergency. The airlines all agreed that was a fair agreement.

Q: Do you recall what the ratio would have been on TWA pilots who had been naval aviators?

Captain Tomlinson: No, I don't.

Q: Would it have been very high?

---
*Commander Austin K. Doyle, USN, Bureau of Aeronautics.

Daniel W. Tomlinson #3 - 228

Captain Tomlinson: I can't even attempt to tell you at this late date.

Q: I've heard from other sources that apparently there were quite a large number of TWA pilots.

Captain Tomlinson: Yes. I convinced quite a number of pilots to volunteer for duty with me. These would not have had to go. Doc Mesker was one; he was one of the old pilots.* Wendell Peterson and Johnny Harlin were two others.** They volunteered at my request to take special important assignments, and there were others.

Q: Did your staff personnel change much during the war?

Captain Tomlinson: No. No need to change.

One vital matter happened right after I took command. I had been out there a week or so when I received a dispatch from the Chief of Naval Operations, with a copy to Admiral Nimitz. The Navy had contracted with Consolidated Aircraft for 150 of what the Navy called the RY, which was a commercial version of the B-24 bomber.*** The Air Forces

---
*Lieutenant Douglas L. Mesker, USNR.
**Lieutenant Wendell F. Peterson, USNR. Lieutenant John E. Harlin, USNR.
***This four-engine plane was designated PB4Y in the Navy's bombing version. It had a wing span of 110 feet, length of 67 feet, gross weight of 60,000 pounds, and top speed of 279 miles per hour.

called it the C-87. I knew from letters and conversations with people who had flown them that they were lousy airplanes to fly. They had some very bad features. When I received this dispatch, one of the RYs was already in the air, flying from Oakland, and another was scheduled to leave in a couple of days. I was horrified that I was going to have to operate such unsuitable aircraft.

I contacted the prospective squadron commander who would have these planes. He was one of my key TWA pilots, Wendell Peterson. I said, "When this airplane comes in, if it's okay for flight, I want it loaded to full gross weight, and I'm going to fly it. You will ride as my copilot."

I'd never been in one of the planes before. A quick cockpit check was all I needed. I took the RY, flew it about an hour and a half, and put it through all kinds of stall conditions, flaps up, gear up, gear down, simulated landings. I made several actual landings and thoroughly checked stability and controllability under a wide range of flight conditions. I found it to be unstable under several conditions. Coming in to land, the RY could drop a wing very easily. It had twin rudders. If you lost an outboard engine on takeoff, there was no way that you could maintain straight flight with the small rudders. I'd been warned about that. I made notes on all the tests. I still cannot understand how and why the RY was accepted by the Navy Test

Section at Patuxent.

I went back up to my office, and I wrote an official letter to the Chief of Naval Operations, copy to Admiral Nimitz. I won't attempt to tell you all that was in this list of defects. I listed these very carefully. Aside from the undesirable flight features of the airplane, I pointed out that the cubic capacity of the fuselage was totally inadequate for either passengers or cargo in the Pacific operation. I said, "If this command be required to operate these airplanes, the undersigned will not accept responsibility for the loss of equipment or life which will inevitably result. D. W. Tomlinson." I doubt if anybody in the Navy ever wrote a letter like that to the Chief of Naval Operations. They could either cancel the order or fire me. I had a job waiting for me at TWA with better pay anytime.

Ten days later I got a memorandum from the director of the Naval Air Transport Service in Washington: "Dear Tommy, Contract for the RYs has been canceled." It wasn't until three or four years ago, at one of the Golden Eagles reunions, that I got the rest of the story. I cornered Don Smith, former director of NATS, and I said, "Don, just what happened in the Navy Department when that letter of mine about the RYs hit the fan? Who handled it?"

Daniel W. Tomlinson #3 - 231

"Duke Ramsey."*

Duke was another one of my friends. I said, "What did Duke do?"

Don said, "Duke immediately convened a special test board at Patuxent. We went there, and they flew an RY, checked out the points covered in your letter, and agreed."

What burned me up was that I never did know who approved the RYs in the first place.

Q: That's what I was going to ask. Where did this come from to begin with?

Captain Tomlinson: I never knew. No way to find that out. Here they made this contract, and two of these things were coming out.

Q: What was Ramsey's position at that time?

Captain Tomlinson: He was Chief of BuAer. Ernie King never got my letter; at least I doubt it. I don't know whether Ernie King would have stood still for that last paragraph. But Duke Ramsey knew me; he was a good friend. He knew that I wasn't kidding.

___
*Rear Admiral Dewitt C. Ramsey, USN, served as Chief of the Bureau of Aeronautics from 7 August 1943 to 1 June 1945.

Q: Did your headquarters remain in Hawaii through the war, or did you move up to Guam?

Captain Tomlinson: They were always in Hawaii. For the first few months, until late 1943, they were on Ford Island, because John Rodgers Airport was not completed. When it was completed, they were two nice quarters built there. One was for me and the other for Dave Ingalls, CO of John Rodgers NAS, who wanted the job that I had but didn't get it.* I still do not know the politics involved. I was tipped off when I was back in Washington for my indoctrination. It didn't make any difference to me. I had my chief staff officer, administrative assistant, and operations officer quartered with me. I had a fine Filipino steward and two messboys for the rest of the war. We had an ideal setup.

One time while I was there, Slim Lindbergh came over to have dinner with me. We had a long chat. Before he left, he told me what he was going to do in the forward area. I said, "You are a damn lucky character. I never envied you flying to Paris, but I envy you getting a chance to fly out there and really see some action." He went out on combat missions and had fun. He shot down one Jap by himself.

---
*Captain David S. Ingalls, USNR. In World War I Ingalls became the Navy's first fighter ace. From 1929 to 1932 he was Assistant Secretary of the Navy for Aeronautics.

Q: Yes, flying P-38s.*

Captain Tomlinson: They were flying those P-38s, and the kid pilots didn't know how to fly them, cruising economically, fuel-wise. If you want to secure max efficiency, use full throttle, keep RPM and proper cruise setting and open the mixture control until the engine loses a few RPM, and watch cylinder head temperatures. Then you get max economy. It makes a tremendous amount of difference in the fuel used.

Q: A couple of good friends of mine flew P-38s out there and were in the fighter group Lindbergh was with, the 475th group. I think they said their group commander was 27 years old, and he was over the hill, because most of the pilots were 22 to 24.

Captain Tomlinson: How old was Slim at that time?

Q: Lindbergh at that time, I think, was 40 or 42, and they said he was really ancient.**

---

*The Lockheed P-38 Lightning was one of the Army Air Forces's top-notch fighter planes of World War II. It had a top speed of 420 miles per hour and was armed with four .50-caliber machine guns plus a 20-mm. or 37-mm. cannon.
**Charles Lindbergh was born in 1902.

Captain Tomlinson: I always admired Slim. He was a good pilot and had lots of guts. He annoyed me on the DC-1 problem, when he wouldn't take sides. He was a diplomat, more so than I was. I never fooled around; things had to be cold turkey!

Q: In March 1945 was there a consolidation of all the NATS units? I'm a little uncertain as to how your status changed during that time.

Captain Tomlinson: My status was always ComNATS Pacific. Raddy Radford wanted me to come back to relieve Don Smith as overall commander of NATS in December 1944. There was a star in it. My wife learned I had turned this assignment down and was disappointed. I said, "Look, I've got 30 years' service. I receive the same pay I would as a commodore or junior rear admiral, and I'd have to buy a lot of gold lace and a fancy cap. To hell with it." I got everything I wanted out there as a captain with four stripes. I had what was needed to get things done. My reputation in aviation was more valuable than rank. A lot of those who had high rank gave me such a pain, I wasn't particularly desirous of being in that group. As a result of the Navy kicking me out of naval aviation, I had been forced to go it alone, depend on myself.

Q: Didn't much want to join them?

Captain Tomlinson: Never interested me. I didn't give a damn.

Q: Were you able to fly fairly often in that capacity?

Captain Tomlinson: I always flew on my inspection flights when I went to the Pacific forward areas. I always flew the plane myself. I'd put the captain over in the copilot's seat. It was one of my basic principles: "Do as I do." I had to set the example, and I did. If there ever was an instrument approach to be made, I always made it. I always made the takeoffs and landings. There were enough of these pilots who rode with me so that the word got around that I would not expect any pilot to do anything I would not do myself.

Besides the required inspection trips, I made trips in between. When we went into Tarawa, Kwajalein, Saipan, Guam, Okinawa, the Philippines, or wherever we went in the Pacific, I checked every one of the places myself, night takeoffs and landings, the facilities, the NATS detachment. Two months after I took command, MacArthur was screaming his head off because VR-2 was flying à la Pan American, and the Pan American pilots wouldn't fly at night.* Also, no way they would fly through the stationary front between Palmyra and Canton. Pan American operations were part of NATSPac, not their San Francisco base.

I sat down with my chief staff officer and the operations officer. When the complaints from MacArthur were received, I prepared a complete new schedule between Pearl-Honolulu and Brisbane. Pan American, so far as schedules of operations in the Pacific, was operating under my command. I had nothing to do with the hiring or firing of its personnel or its operations at the Treasure Island base; that was under their local manager. But when their planes operated in the Pacific, they flew when and where I ordered. That was in their contract with the Navy.

On my first trip to the south Pacific, I had a PBM Mariner with a special crew, flew it myself. Before I did, I made a couple of night landings with it at Pearl Harbor. I flew to Palmyra at night, where there was a lighted buoy area for landing. It was okay. I laid over one day and waited till the next night. Then I took off and flew through this stationary weather front from Canton. That front didn't amount to anything. It was nothing like flying through cold fronts in the States with 20-30-degree

---
*General Douglas MacArthur, USA, Commander Southwest Pacific.

Daniel W. Tomlinson #3 - 237

temperature drops.

I laid over at Canton, where Pan Am had a posh hotel for passengers. Then I flew at night to Funafuti, next to Espiritu Santo at night, laid over there, checked all the buoy lighted landing areas. I went to Brisbane, landed in the river, and called on MacArthur. I told him, "I have already sent a dispatch placing into effect a new schedule. The planes will now fly straight through. There will be no more overnight layovers." Pan American screamed to high heaven, but they complied. Pan Am sent high executives out to Admiral Nimitz, complaining about this crazy man Tomlinson questioning the wisdom of their super pilots. They advertised that their pilots were all supermen. That was a big deal in those days--the Pan Am super pilots. That was a joke so far as I was concerned. I always laughed and said, "I do not believe in Super Pilots."

A couple of Pan Am pilots came up to me and said, "You're going to have trouble. We don't have to comply with that."

I said, "You don't have to. You can quit any time you want. I've got Navy pilots that are only being paid a third of your salary, and they're flying it and enjoying it."

Finally, a Pan American plane crashed at Funafuti. We had an RY not operating on regular flight. I immediately flew it to Funafuti. It had the range to reach it nonstop. I took an experienced TWA pilot with me. This is my opinion of what happened. There were adequate lights there, but on this particular night there was a tug which was anchored to the right of the lighted runway, about two-thirds of the way down the runway. There was a light on the tug jackstaff. I made a takeoff to see it, and it was a little confusing, as it was in between another light farther down, a marker at the end of the lighted takeoff area that a pilot should watch on takeoff. This Pan Am pilot apparently took off and mistook the tug light for the end runway marker. He began his right turn too soon, and his low right wing hit the jackstaff and flipped the plane into the water. This cut about 15 feet off his right wing.

Pan American really screamed. This night flying and that this pilot's right flap had failed. With Pan Am it had to be a mechanical failure. Pilot error was impossible in Pan Am. By the time I got there, they had recovered the cleanly clipped cut end of the right wing. A Navy court of inquiry was convened, as an admiral and his staff, plus all the plans for the next move north of Guadalcanal were lost.

The angle of the cut, where the wing tip was sheared, clearly indicated that in the turn the Pan Am plane was "skidding." Had the flap failed, as Pan Am agreed, the plane would have been slipping, and the angle different. I disapproved Pan Am's accident report, "clearing the pilot of any error." That caused another uproar. Pan Am VPs again pestered Nimitz, bless him. He'd tell them to see Tomlinson, and that burned them up.

Later, at Auckland, I developed solid evidence that Pan Am pilots were deliberately canceling flights to have another night with a girl. When I had a real dossier on them, I terminated Pan Am's operation at Honolulu. They had to pull all their people out of the South Pacific. This really galled them, but their screams were to no avail. Once again, Admiral Nimitz backed me up.

Q: Did you see Admiral Nimitz very often?

Captain Tomlinson: My only other contacts with him were when I attended his briefing conference every morning.

Q: One of the items Paul Stillwell particularly wanted you to discuss was how the Martin Mars was "accidentally" killed in a discussion with Artemus Gates.*

Captain Tomlinson: Right from the start, after I became ComNATSPac, people would kid me, "You're going to get 25 of these Mars." On top of that, they'd say, "You're going to operate Howard Hughes's Spruce Goose." I was not worried about the "Goose," but the Mars were a real possibility.

---

*Artemus L. Gates was Assistant Secretary of the Navy for Air from 5 September 1941 to 1 July 1945.

Daniel W. Tomlinson #3 - 240

The extended operation of even the PB2Ys (Coronados) through the Pacific, first to the South Pacific, then through the Central Pacific to Manila, was a major headache and inefficient. Handling the big boats on a dolly, ramps, in and out of the water at forward area stations took a lot of men and equipment, and it was always tricky. Water conditions for landing and takeoff were frequently marginal. Landing or taking off a big boat under rough sea conditions is a very tricky task. A few pilots will have the ability and extra "feel" to do it. In VR-2 I think there were at least 300 qualified captains; among them there were bound to be some lacking in the special skill and experience to cope with these situations.

Examples. When NAS began PB2Y operation from Ebye Island at Kwajalein I made my usual survey and told Admiral Towers, then Deputy CinCPac, that when the northeast trades blew in Kwaj Atoll the sea conditions were bad, and we were apt to lose a plane.* I said that NATS should operate from Majuro, which was safe. Soon thereafter we lost a PB2Y, and the NATS move to Majuro was approved.

Then came Tanapag Harbor at Saipan. I made my survey and told Towers that under one wind condition takeoffs were going to be very critical. Just as I feared, NATS lost another PB2Y, but there was no alternate in the Marianas.

---

*As a vice admiral Towers served as Deputy Commander in Chief Pacific Fleet from February 1944 to July 1945.

I could imagine the time when a Mars would be lost under these unavoidable hazardous conditions.

So every time I could collar Artemus Gates, I begged him to cut the order for the Mars; at best they would be inefficient white elephants. In my opinion then, even earlier, in the Thirties, the day of the big boats was over. I would not allow the first Mars to fly beyond the protected sea runways at Honolulu.

Well, the very first time that Artemus Gates showed up out there, I met him at a cocktail party. I got his back up against the wall one time, and I told him the problems of operating these big flying boats, particularly out into the Pacific forward areas, and all the other problems we had with them. I begged him, saying, "If you can't cancel the order, cut it down. The thing is a monstrosity and uneconomical. The manpower required to handle them on the ground and in and out of the water to maintain them is way out of proportion to their usefulness. They're a menace."

He finally cut the order to five. One Mars finally did appear. We had to set up a special squadron and facilities to handle that monstrosity, which was a sacred cow. Lieutenant Coney was the pilot, and he thought he was God. He came in to report to me. I said, "Coney, I want you to ready the Mars. I will fly it, and you will ride as my copilot. I will decide whether it is safe to be flown in this service."

Coney said, "You can't do that."

"The hell I can't." I flew it, I stalled it. I put it through all kinds of slow-speed stalls to make sure it was okay. I let it fall off on a wing each way, to be sure there was no problem there. Stability was okay, controllability okay, but heavy on the controls.

When with TWA, I checked out the chief pilots on new equipment. I'd let them stall and make a quarter turn of a spin. No sense in letting a large airplane wind up in a full spin. The danger with a large plane in a fast spin in the inertia. Once you get the inertia built up, it will make one to two turns before it can be stopped.

Q: It's that much harder to correct.

Captain Tomlinson: Yes, to get the spin stopped, I wanted to make sure that any transport plane that we were going to fly would fall off properly and recover properly and promptly.

Q: What sort of cargo would that normally carry?

Captain Tomlinson: I can't remember. We carried about 125 people on one trip to Alameda when I made the takeoff and landing. It didn't compare with the monstrosity of the DOX, which I briefly flew at the behest of GM. You talk

Daniel W. Tomlinson #3 - 243

about decibels. The noise in the DOX cabin was absolutely deafening. It was impossible.

Q: Did you have a preference concerning flying boats versus land-based transports, or did it matter?

Captain Tomlinson: Definitely. The boats were a problem. Landing on water at night, you had to keep the lighted buoys functioning. You had to have ramps and dollies. You had to have men in waders in position to get the planes on to the dollies. The manpower required to handle them was wasteful. They served a military purpose, but so far as scheduled air transport was concerned, I thought they were anathema.

Q: What would have been the ratio in NATS between land-based planes and flying boats?

Captain Tomlinson: In the Pacific we had 55 Coronado boats. The best utilization we could obtain with them was about 5.5 hours a day per boat. The R5Ds averaged 7.5 hours a day. I was told the best Army ATC C-54 utilization was about 3.5 hours. The four-engine Coronados weren't bad-flying airplanes; they were appreciably faster than the Boeing 314. I rode one of the 314s to Treasure Island--21 hours from Honolulu to get to Oakland.

Q: A PBY will do it that fast.*

Captain Tomlinson: A PBY took about 15 hours. With R5Ds we were making it in 10 to 12 hours. Dutch Schildhauer was on the Washington, D.C., staff of NATS.** He had trouble selling me boats. I took him on one trip to the South Pacific; I invited him and Paul Richter to accompany me. I said, "I want you to see what the conditions are: landing at night, landing on the buoy-lighted landing and takeoff areas, hauling boats in and launching them on makeshift ramps. I didn't know what Schildhauer's flight status was, but I said, "Dutch, you brag about these boats. Get in this seat and fly. See for yourself."

Do you think he'd fly it? Do you think he put his hands on the controls? Hell, no! He wouldn't touch them.

Q: But he was trying to sell them.

Captain Tomlinson: He was trying to sell me on the Mars. We went to Brisbane and Sydney.

Q: How do you remember life in Honolulu during the war?

---

*The PBY was a two-engine flying boat with a maximum cruising speed of 110-115 miles per hour.
**Commander Clarence R. Schildhauer, USNR.

Daniel W. Tomlinson #3 - 245

Captain Tomlinson: I didn't see much of Honolulu.

Q: What about in Hawaii generally, after the early period where the invasion scare had died down?

Captain Tomlinson: I was out there two years. I went into Honolulu about six times.

Q: Obviously, you had your hands full.

Captain Tomlinson: I had plenty. I had an admiral's steward. I don't know how I happened to get him. He was tops. The meals he served couldn't be equalled at the best restaurant in Honolulu. We had two mess boys who really took care of us in grand manner.

One of the events of that period was that Rear Admiral Baldy Pownall, ComAirPac, asked me to come to his office on Ford Island.* He said, "CNO directs me to establish an evacuation squadron at Guam to fly wounded out of Okinawa to hospitals in Guam, Pearl, or Stateside. This command is not prepared to handle it. We do not have personnel, planes, maintenance facilities, or knowhow. What would you suggest?"

---

*Rear Admiral Charles A. Pownall, USN, was Commander Air Force Pacific Fleet from 28 February 1944 to 17 August 1944.

I replied, "NATSPac can handle it easily."

Pownall then added, "CNO planned it as a group: 50 airplanes, three squadrons, and Captain Skee Erdmann has orders to Guam to be the wing commander."*

I said that would not be my way. For NATSPac it would be a sideshow, one squadron with an experienced, capable former airline pilot as CO. I named Lieutenant Commander Jack Thornburg, who was then with VR-1 at Patuxent.** That closed the discussion for that day.

A few days later Pownall called to advise, "CNO concurs. You have it. Get busy. This also involves a complement of about 50 nurses. Assignment of these will be handled by the medical department. You'll handle their quarters and duty details, et al."

Being sure that NATSPac would get this job, I had already arranged to obtain Thornburg. I got fast action from Washington. What did plague me was Skee Erdmann. I'd had trouble with him when he was on Admiral Halsey's staff at Noumea. He came into Espiritu Santo on a scheduled PBM flight. While the PBM was fueling at the dock, he stood there smoking a cigarette. He was in a no-smoking area, well marked. The NATSPac officer in charge of the unit asked him to stop smoking. Hell broke loose. Erdmann threw a tantrum, cursing the officer in charge for his

---
*Captain William L. Erdmann, USN.
**Lieutenant Commander Jack W. Thornburg, USNR.

"impudence," disrespect of a senior officer, ad infinitum. The officer in charge was an excellent, competent reserve lieutenant, and this outburst scared him. He secured statements from witnesses and reported the incident to me. After discussing the matter with Rear Admiral Radford, who was then chief of staff for ComAirPac, I forwarded the file to Bull Halsey for his information. I learned later that Halsey took him apart.

To my surprise, Erdmann appeared on the scene to be the wing commander. The wing commander with 50 airplanes. This was asinine. All I needed was one good squadron commander. It was stupid, but he had his orders, and he considered himself over Thornburg. Jack had gone to Guam on my orders and got this operation going. Erdmann tried to order Jack what to do. He'd go to the airplanes and try to instruct the pilots. Erdmann was drunk much of the time. To make matters worse, he had secured an old crony of his to be chief staff officer, because he really had visions of grandeur. This crony was his drinking pal. Together they made scenes in the passenger terminal when intoxicated, excoriating NATS in general and me in particular. Erdmann was really making a mess out of things; it was an intolerable situation.

I wrote to Jack: "Get a dossier on this man." Several weeks went by, and I got the file on Erdmann. It contained reports of many nasty episodes with statements of witnesses--enough to justify a general court-martial.

Admiral Jakie Reeves was made ComNATS, which eliminated the Director NATS in Washington.* Jack Whitney, who had the director job, received a star as commodore.** He became chief of staff. I had no trouble with Jakie. I sent this file to him with a letter which read, "I'm sending this to you, because I feel that for me to go out to Guam and conduct an investigation would look bad for a Naval Reserve captain, to be proffering charges against a regular Navy captain. Number-wise, Erdmann was junior to me. I said, "Unless I hear further from you, I will proceed to Guam on a scheduled flight and will investigate this matter. If I find the contents of this file correct and adequate, I have no choice but to recommend a general court-martial on the charge of conduct unbecoming an officer and a gentleman."

I received a dispatch from Jakie: "I will join you."

On the way to Guam, I said, "Look Jakie, you run this investigation. I'm going swimming. I see no need for me to be a part of it. You're ComNATS, and I pass the buck to you." So I went swimming.

When I came back, Jakie said, "We are having dinner with Admiral Nimitz tonight." Nimitz had moved his

---

*Rear Admiral John W. Reeves, Jr., USN, served as Commander Naval Air Transport Service from March 1945 to March 1948.
**Commodore John P. Whitney, USN.

headquarters to Guam by then. So we went up and had a pleasant dinner with the admiral. After dinner, the admiral invited Jakie and me out on to the lanai. Reeves briefed Admiral Nimitz on Erdmann's position and reprehensible conduct. Admiral Nimitz took time to think it over, then said, "Captain Erdmann will be reassigned somewhere else tomorrow morning."

I was more than shocked, because this was high-level buck passing. Since the incident in the South Pacific, I had learned through several sources that Erdmann was a first-class stinker and alcoholic, hated by those who had to serve under him.

My job, as ComNATSPac, was to file a fitness report on Erdmann. Later, when I was again in Guam, Forrest Sherman sent for me. He had been a classmate of mine at the Naval Academy, and he was now a deputy to CinCPac.* He had Erdmann's fitness report on his desk, the one I had submitted. I had described Erdmann, using polite language, in no uncertain terms, with the closing opinion that he was a disgrace to the naval service. Sherman said, "Tommy, this report damns Erdmann. Can't you soften it somewhat?" With that, I blew my stack and told Fuzz (his nickname) what I thought of the Navy's practice of passing the buck.

---

*Rear Admiral Forrest P. Sherman, USN, deputy chief of staff (plans) to Nimitz. Sherman was later Chief of Naval Operations, 1949-1951. He and Tomlinson were Naval Academy classmates.

By then word had come back to me from Okinawa, where Erdmann had been reassigned as a group commander, that his command was on the verge of mutiny. The way Erdmann abused and mistreated his subordinates was unbelievable.

I had a grudge against Navy buck passing. While CO of the NRAB at Kansas City, I had reported to BuAer that one aviator was a menace--alcoholic, emotionally unstable--and I had grounded him. BuAer reassigned him to an Aleutian command in flight status. A few months later, after a night of drinking, he flew an R4D into a mountain, killing all aboard. On my next trip to BuAer, I saw Rear Admiral Honus Wagner, whom I knew well. He was deputy chief of BuAer. I let him have it, and all Wagner said was, "I'm sorry, Tommy, but we need aviators."

When Erdmann retired after the war as a rear admiral, he came back from the Pacific on a carrier and brought a large quantity of booze that he had bought in Guam. He was royally hated by all who had served under him. Somebody tipped off the proper authorities in San Francisco, and they apprehended Erdmann. I was disgusted. I was sick, because about a week before this happened, Fuzz Sherman dropped dead in Naples. I would surely have made a trip to Washington, just to walk into Sherman's office and give him a piece of my mind--to no purpose, other than to clear my mind.*

Q: What would be Sherman's reason for protecting him?

Captain Tomlinson: I don't know. I don't know how this character could have had anything on Fuzz, who was a shrewd character and brilliant. He was the one, for instance, who persuaded key people against the plan to take Formosa but to take Okinawa instead.

This business with Erdmann took place in 1945. By mid-summer of that year, the war was winding down. Halsey was rampaging up and down the coast of Japan with impunity, hardly a rifle shot distance from the beach.** In my opinion, invasion of Japan would not be necessary. It might take a bit longer, but the home islands of Japan would become a jungle like bypassed Rabaul. I began making plans for return to the "Flying T" farm in Arkansas.

Then ComNATS, Rear Admiral Jakie Reeves, dropped a hot one in my lap. He had decided the meals, adequate and edible in wartime, which NATS Pacific was serving were not sufficiently elegant or tasty. He proposed to convert the R5D galleys to serve warmed-up frozen meals. The packaged meals would be processed somewhere on the East Coast and

---
*Sherman died in 1951; Erdmann did not retire until 1960.
**Admiral William F. Halsey, Jr., USN, Commander Third Fleet.

shipped to wherever required. Then they would be stored in "reefers," large frozen food containers installed almost everywhere in the Pacific. I opposed this with a passion. Number one--throughout the Pacific these reefers had a habit of failing, which would be discovered in a day or two and the reefer restarted. Too often some of the contents had passed the point of no return. I knew about the scattered cases of ptomaine. Number two--the R5Ds were urgently needed in scheduled service and would be out of service a day or two to effect the major galley alterations. Number three--the cost of the change (I do not now recall the exact amount) was way out of proportion relative to betterment of NATS service. Number four--I could see that one day a planeload, crew and passengers, would be taken violently ill in flight.

My screams were wasted. The project went forward. About a year later, when I was back on my farm in Arkansas, a friend who had chosen to remain on active duty wrote me from the Pacific: "Tommy, It happened just as you said it would. We just had a planeload violently ill from ptomaine, the pilot barely able to land. The frozen meals program is finished, and we are back to simple box lunches."

Q: Did you ever have a chance to discuss the Battle off

Samar with Tommy or Clifton Sprague?

Captain Tomlinson: No, I never saw them after that. Tommy Sprague, who was in command of a carrier in '43, came into Pearl several times.* I would have lunch with him on board his ship, and he came over to have dinner with me a couple of times. But Ziggy and I never met again after we left Pensacola in '21.

Q: It's kind of unusual, considering how small naval aviation was in those days.

Captain Tomlinson: Many naval aviators served on the East Coast. My 12 years with TWA broke many contacts.

Q: Did you run across any of your other Annapolis classmates during the war?

Captain Tomlinson: No.

Q: At the end of the war, how many squadrons did NATS have in the Pacific?

---

*Captain Thomas L. Sprague, USN, was the first commanding officer when the USS Intrepid (CV-11) went into commission in August 1943.

Captain Tomlinson: VR-4 was the secondary maintenance squadron at Oakland; VR-2 the big-boat squadron at Alameda. In Seattle I had VR-5, which served Alaska. In Honolulu I had VR-10, the maintenance squadron. There were two big nose hangars in Guam, 1,000 personnel as a detachment of VR-10. A very capable commander was CO of VR-10. There were about five planes, R5Ds, in the VIP squadron. At Noumea, Isle New Island, there was another detachment of VR-10, with about 20 PBMs. It maintained them and operated scheduled service between Espiritu Santo, Noumea, and Auckland. In late 1944, when the delivery of new R5Ds had ended, NATSPac had received 150. The scheduled use of the R5Ds in regular service was such that maintenance-wise, with 10,000 hours of flight allowed between major overhauls, and expecting the invasion of Japan in 1946, NATSPac Alaska needed a major overhaul base with facilities and space to complete two R5D overhauls daily.

It was proving impossible to get this across to BuAer. No one seemed able to appreciate the rate at which R5Ds were being used. In this regard I gave Tillman a comprehensive record of NATSPac operations, prepared in early August 1945 by an expert analyst. I discussed this at length with Admiral Towers. One day he called me to have lunch at his quarters with him and Rear Admiral Duke Ramsey. That was my golden opportunity. I convinced Duke that the figures I had were not lying. He agreed a major overhaul base had to be prepared as quickly as possible. They had been using my nominee for such work, Walt Hamilton, TWA's superintendent of maintenance.* In three years he had been promoted from lieutenant to captain. I asked that he be assigned to my staff to get the urgent task completed. He was.

With the full backing of BuAer and Ramsey, the job was completed--too late. Just before the war ended, the south dirigible hangar at Moffett NAS had been turned into a major overhaul R5D base. Two railroad tracks ran through the hangar. Two R5Ds entered at one end. Landing gears came off as the fuselages were secured to a carrier on the tracks. Then the carriers began moving through successive work areas. Engines went to lean-to shop south; instruments, electrical, plumbing, to shops in the center of the hangar; wings, tail surfaces to lean-to shops on the north side.

Q: Was it in August or September of '45 that you left the Navy again?

Captain Tomlinson: I forget the exact date of my detachment, probably early September.

Q: Did you maintain a reserve status at that time?

―――――――――
*Captain Walter A. Hamilton, USNR.

Daniel W. Tomlinson #3 - 256

Captain Tomlinson: Upon release from active duty I was ordered to a hospital in Oklahoma for examination and survey. Then to home to await orders, then to a survey board in Washington, D.C. Finally released to inactive duty in the Naval Reserve with my rank of captain about June 1946.

Q: How did you come across a retirement location?

Captain Tomlinson: It was a compromise. When I flew over the Willamette Valley in 1923, I looked down and thought that this area was perfect, beautiful country. There were big, luxuriant fields on both sides of the valley. It was perfect hunting and fishing, an ideal place to retire. I wanted to have a home for Margie and me when the war was over. It was beautiful country with many springs and streams. But in 1939, when I knew war was inevitable and my office and work were at TWA headquarters in Kansas City, Missouri, the Willamette Valley in Oregon was too far away for us to find what we wanted, buy it, and start developing it. So we found this real pretty spot in the northwest corner of Arkansas. It was close enough to Kansas City that we could get down there on weekends.

After the war we rented our house in Kansas City and moved to near Cave Springs, Arkansas. The farm, as we

Daniel W. Tomlinson #3 - 257

called it, was 120 acres; it was a pleasant, quiet life, nothing to worry about, taking it easy. I was then simply worn out, constantly flying since 1920: the Navy, barnstorming, stunt flying, back in naval aviation, the three Seahawks, test at Anacostia, Maddux Airlines, TWA, airline pilot, night mail pilot, test, research, and vice president of engineering. There was the development of the DC-1, the Boeing 307, and finally the Constellation. As the only one in TWA who had said "No" in no uncertain terms to Howard Hughes on a number of critical points, I was sure he'd get me, Paul Richter, and Jack Frye. Paul and I beat him to it. He fired Frye PDQ.

Unbeknownst to be, in 1946 Congress changed the retirement laws affecting naval reserves in my category. On my release from active duty, I had 17 1/2 years of active duty, but due to my organized reserve status before the war, I had 30 years' longevity. At the time of my release I would have had to stay on active duty five years to qualify for a 75% pay retirement. Under the new law only two and a half years; I could take it after a year's rest.

Also ATC and NATS had been combined to form MATS, involving a big personnel shakeup. I had friends in the Navy Department who wired they had a spot for me as deputy commander, Continental Division of the Military Air Transport Service, to be based at Kelly Air Force Base, Texas.

So I wired back, "Rig the deck. I'm coming aboard." I reported just in time to be caught in the Berlin Airlift.* Major General Tunner tapped me to be his deputy.** I'd be flying and having fun for two and a half years before retirement. As it turned out, the Berlin Airlift was something else, more problems.

I flew to Wiesbaden with Tunner and most of his staff. The Air Corps, at least the ATC during the war had no concept of the vital work performed by the departments of flight dispatch and flight control in NATSPac, which I had established to effect orderly, efficient control and use of large numbers of airplanes operating on fixed schedules. Tunner planned to have two wings at Rhine-Main, five squadrons in each. A group commander, two wing commanders, their staffs, ten squadron COs, and no idea how to handle the problem.

I told Tunner that at Rhine-Main at Frankfurt a central office with adequate communications should be established to function as follows. Flight dispatch with a

---
*On 1 April 1948 the Soviet Union began a land blockade of the Allied sectors of Berlin, preventing overland transport from West Germany. U.S. and British airplanes then began and airlift that flew food and coal into the city until the blockade was lifted on 30 September 1949.
**Major General William H. Tunner, USAF.

liaison office at Rhine-Main in close contact with the squadron commander, who would keep dispatch informed of the planes and crews available. Dispatch working closely with flight control told Rhine-Main the interval at which to release planes, which was contingent on how the planes were progressing through the corridor to Berlin and landing at Tempelhof. Flight control kept in touch by radio with each plane as it flew the corridor. It was essential to maintain an orderly flow and a safe interval between the planes flying on instruments. This worked.

Early in the airlift operation, the first month I was in Wiesbaden, the pilots flying into Tempelhof complained to General Tunner that when flying the corridor IFR, frequent relatively mild thunderstorms, which I had flown through, were encountered.* And while in them bright flashes of light were seen to strike the wing tips and were burning holes in trailing edges of ailerons. The pilots claimed fighters were flying on top and dropping phosphorus bombs on them. Tunner reported exactly that to Air Force headquarters in Washington. Finally one evening he called me into his room to inform me of this top secret matter. Also present was Major Jim Hearn, the senior squadron commander at Rhine-Main, who was there to support the charges of his pilots.** To me and any experienced

---
*IFR--instrument flight rules.
**Major James A. Hearn, USAF.

airline pilot, this was old hat, no more than St. Elmo's fire, maybe a mild lightning strike now and then. I told Hearn to check carefully the holes burned in the trailing edges and he'd find evidence that the holes were burned from inside out, static discharge, and to install flexible wire bleeds at the edges where the holes were found. That ended that.

In November '48 I spent about ten days in bed at the Army hospital in Wiesbaden with a miserable back condition. In my 1921 crash and collision my lumbar vertebrae had been injured. It did not show up until I was in my 50s as arthritis. I then felt I had done about all I could for the airlift, which was accomplishing its mission by brute force. The waste of manpower due to the group-wing-squadron organization was appalling. It was an Air Force regulation. I tried to explain to Tunner how in NATSPac I had modified similar Navy regulations organization to function as an airline. He was horrified that I would consider departing from sacred regulations. He said it would ruin morale not to have each airplane serviced and maintained by its own crew.

I asked to be relieved of TDY, as the Air Force defined my position with the airlift, and restored to my planned duty as Deputy Commander, Control Division, MATS under Major General Bob Nowland at Kelly Air Force Base.*

---
*TDY--temporary duty. Major General Bob E. Nowland, USAF.

My request was approved. Before joining the airlift I had taken time to move my wife and son to San Antonio and into nice comfortable quarters at Kelly Field.

The airlift was flying pilots 150 or more hours a month. It was strenuous duty. Tunner had requested Major General Kuter, Commander MATS, that a special school be established to insure availability of replacement pilots, all with IFR ratings and experience in all-weather flying-- a large order for the Air Force.* By the time I was pleasantly settled at Kelly, this school had been established at Great Falls Air Force Base, Montana, and operating for about a month. The outfit was way short of expectations with respect to numbers and flight capability, weather-wise.

Nowland sent me to Great Falls to survey the situation and report back as Kuter was screaming. I found what I expected, the standard Air Force organization and the horribly inefficient practice of each airplane being serviced and maintained by its own crew, which wouldn't touch another airplane--no way. I called Nowland and told him the situation, and if he'd inform the CO at Great Falls that I had full authority to reorganize the school as I saw fit, I felt that in less than a month the situation could be turned around.

---
*Major General Laurence S. Kuter, USAF.

Bang! I wiped out the wing commander and the three squadron COs and most of the supernumerary cohorts. Instead of a lieutenant colonel for school superintendent, I put in three majors for general administrative, ground school, and flight training. Adequate hangar space was available to establish production line maintenance on a three-shift basis. Another major was in charge of maintenance, a captain as liaison between maintenance and flight training to schedule R5Ds between the line and shop. For a few days I had quite an uproar on my hands, but the plan got going, and by the end of a week, men and officers began to understand the advantages of the new organization.

Formerly training flights had been canceled if there was any evidence of snow or rime ice on the planes. I demonstrated several blind takeoffs under a hood in conditions previously considered unsafe. I demonstrated, as I had at Rhine-Main, slow flight, stalls, incipient spins, landing to a mark with the wheels on the ground, airspeed not over 95 miles per hour and within 100 feet of the mark. The pilots began to take pride in their plane handling.

In a month school output was on schedule. Kuter was pleased. With my work completed re the school at Great Falls Air Force Base, I returned to the headquarters of Continental Division of MATS for two years of pleasant duty, enjoying life with my family and many fine Air Force officers and wives who became life-long friends. Of them only one is now alive, Colonel Jim Hearn. When I retired, the Air Force awarded me another Legion of Merit, which I knew was Kuter's work.

In July I prepared for final retirement. Plus other considerations affecting my decision not to return to TWA was that my father at age 75 had suffered a stroke and had fallen down a flight of stairs. He recovered partially, but he was never to be himself again. He had spent his life making first the Baker Gun and Forging Company a profitable endeavor, secondly the Batavia Metal Products Company his final life's work. He had never really taken time to enjoy life. His last nine years were spent housebound. Such was not for me. I would fully retire while in good health to enjoy my family and friends, travel, meet people, have fun, while at the same time performing the healthy outdoor life of an active farmer, but without the financial worries and rigid farm routine.

After receiving my retirement orders at BuPers in Washington, my wife and I headed north to drive around the Gaspe Peninsula in Canada.* On a pleasant beach on the south shore of the St. Lawrence River we saw a house trailer parked. We paused to talk with the engaging couple who were on their first trailer trip. We compared what they had convenience-wise with what we were experiencing in
_____
*BuPers--Bureau of Naval Personnel.

motels, also the cost of travel. Promptly on our return to Arkansas, we started looking for a suitable second-hand travel trailer to try it out. In the spring of 1952 we had a 21-foot aluminum travel trailer.

In June of 1952 with our son, then eight years old, we took off with the trailer, using a 1947 Chrysler straight 8 New Yorker as a tug. The planned itinerary included the Black Hills, Yellowstone, Seattle, the Olympic Peninsula, and down the West Coast to San Diego, the Grand Canyon, Pueblo, Sky City of Acoma, Carlsbad Caverns, and home. It was a wonderful, rewarding trip. We were confirmed travel trailerites, covering 8,500 miles. It was a great experience for our son; today at age 42 he happily recalls incidents of that trip.

We used the trailer to winter in Florida, wandered a couple of months during the autumn. In 1954 we replaced the 21-foot Curtis with a 26-foot Airstream and continued our rambling. We became unhappy with Florida weather and crowded conditions. In the winter of '57 we headed west to try the desert and wound up near Indio. The Palm Springs trailer parks were for adults only, and our son felt humiliated. As the school term came along in the fall of '58, our son entered the Missouri Military Academy at Mexico, Missouri. Later we took off to winter at Blue Skies Trailer Park, Cathedral City, California. There we met three congenial couples ready to try old Mexico. In the early winter of '59 four trailers rendezvoused in Tucson and headed south on a look-see tour. We paused at Guymas and Maztalan--too cold and windy. We tried San Blas, but there were too many museums. On through the mountains to Guadalajara, a beautiful city with good trailer parks. There we split; one couple went to Audiencia Bay at Manzanillo, two headed home. Margie and I went to Mexico City, San Luis Potosi, Monterey, and home. On this trip we carried a 12-foot boat on top of the car and a 15-horsepower outboard.

From the couple who went to Manzanillo we received glowing reports of Audiencia Bay, an ideal beach to swim and launch boats, warm water, perfect weather, and the hospitality of local Mexicans. So after Christmas of '59 we headed for Manzanillo via Laredo, Monterey, Saltello, San Luis Potosi, and Guadalajara. A hurricane in October '59 had raised merry hell with Manzanillo. The roads and bridges washed out in the three mountain ranges between it and Guadalajara. It was very tricky in places, but we made it. Winds up to 150 miles per hour had stripped trees of all foliage along the coast. At the Audiencia Bay trailer park there was no fresh water or electricity for over a month. Bottled water came from Colina. Twelve couples, all trailerites, made it--determined, kindred souls.

Weather was perfect; swimming delightful; great fishing, including dorado, sailfish, marlin, and mackerel; rum plentiful and inexpensive. The trailer park cost a dollar a day. Supplies, except for good beef, marvelous vegetables and fruit, plenty of tasty pork, the dorado and mackerel excellent eating. Margie really took to the fishing, a proud gal when she hooked her first sailfish; it took her over an hour to get it alongside the boat. It was no easy task for a neophyte to gaff and have that nine-plus-foot sailfish over a 12-foot boat. (I have pictures to prove it.)

We were hooked on Audiencia Bay; from then on it became a winter hideout. We took the winter of '65 and flew to Frankfurt, Germany, where we took delivery of a VW "square back," headed for Aliconte, Spain, and rented an apartment on the beach, one of life's mistakes. We all but froze to death; Rome had 14 inches of snow. Don't let anyone fool you. The sunny coast of Spain from October to May is like a morgue--ten-story hotels with no heat, no elevators, closed up tight. In the spring of '66 we did Rome, Germany, Austria, Denmark, back to Hamburg and home on a freighter and the car.

Winter at Audiencia became routine. We made many wonderful friends; four couples still survive, and we keep in close touch. Tragedy struck in May '70. Margie was found to have brain cancer. Fitzsimmons Army Hospital in Denver operated and tried cobalt treatment, to no avail. She died in September. I went to Audiencia to be among dear companions. I returned in the late fall of '71 with a new wife, the widow of an old trailerite friend. We returned again to Audiencia in the fall of '72. The marriage was not working out. We moved our home base to Oak Harbor, Washington. After Margie died, I deeded my retirement home in Arkansas to my son Larry, then an established architect. In October 1973 I was granted a divorce, no alimony.

I decided to search for the lovely girl whom I had met in Port Townsend, Washington, when attached to the USS Oklahoma in 1922. I had taken her for her first airplane ride in May 1923, then kissed her good-bye to marry a lieutenant in the Army. Though she disappeared from my life, so far as anyone ever knew; deep down in my heart there was the tie to Francel Hill.

So, 50 years after that farewell kiss, I was wandering around Port Townsend, trying to find someone who had any memory of the Hill family. It was disheartening. Could find no one who had lived in Port Townsend over 25-30 years. Finally, in a florist's shop, a woman told me a Miss Sally Hill lived a few blocks away. Luck was with me. She was Francel's sister. I introduced myself, as I had not met Sally, who had taught school in San Francisco. I could see she was studying me. She said, "I know who you are. You are the Navy man my mother hoped Francel would marry. Francel just left here a half hour ago to return to her home in Seattle. Her name now is Walter, a widow for 20 years, and she has three marvelous sons." Sally and I had a happy talk. She gave me Francel's address and telephone number.

I called her that evening. She was naturally startled. I told her I had accommodations at the Sand Point Naval Air Station. I told her I would like to take her to dinner the next evening. We met as planned. All was well, and we married in October. Happily together at long last, she returned with me to Audiencia in November. At that time I had a comfortable 32-foot travel trailer. All my family and friends were delighted with Francel. She had a nice home in Magnolia, a choice suburb of Seattle. We had seven wonderful happy years together. Then in May 1979 she died of cancer of the liver. I was heartbroken.

For two years I was a virtual hermit, living in a mobile home on the ranch of a granddaughter deep in the Trinity Mountains near Hyampan, California. Winter I spent in a housekeeping room at an excellent motel in Yuma, Arizona. Age was creeping up. I was lonely and needed companionship. When one is 84, finding a wife is a tricky and risky matter. Again Lady Luck was with me. Purely by accident at an old Audiencia friend's New Year's dinner in 1981 I was introduced to two widows sitting side by side on a divan. One I observed carefully the rest of the evening, then offered her a ride home. She was living in the 32-foot park-type trailer she and her deceased husband had bought in the Capri trailer park. Her husband had died in October 1980. I trod carefully but persistently. It developed that Peg Feller and I had several close mutual friends. I did some inquiring, and they were enthusiastic about our meeting. I was wary as the marriage before I found Francel had foundered on the rocks of extreme and unreasonable jealousy. Peg and I were having happy times partying with our friends. February 19, accompanied by the couple in whose home we had met, we headed for Las Vegas for a simple, quiet, legal marriage and a fun evening on the town.

Peg had taught school in the Salem area and had a comfortable home in Salem. Her youngest son is a prominent dentist in Silverton, 15 miles to the northeast. Besides his practice, as an avocation he does 4-H training for his two sons and a daughter. He has a 20-acre sheep project on the edge of Silverton.

Neither Peg nor I was happy with the Trinity Mountain hideout. Peg sold her house in Salem. Her son Wayne offered us an arrangement whereby we might use one and a half acres of his sheep place to set a double-wide mobile home with a two-car garage in the rear. Ample ground for an attractive yard, two garden spots, a small orchard, a row of raspberry bushes, and flower beds. Peg, a farm-raised girl, has a green thumb and loves the outside. So here I am, settled in the finest of the Willamette Valley agriculture area, walking distance of Silverton, a town of 5,000, and most of the staples we need. Salem is only 30 minutes' travel. The Portland area is one hour away.

It took me 63 years to achieve my dream of retirement in the garden valley of the West. The dream of an ex-naval aviator winging his way to a career of adventure has been fascinating, productive, and rewarding, and finally blessed by a loving wife, companion, and caretaker. Finis.

Daniel W. Tomlinson #4 - 271

Interview Number 4 with Captain Daniel W. Tomlinson IV,
U.S. Naval Reserve (Retired)

Place: U.S. Naval Institute, Annapolis, Maryland

Date: Friday, 18 September 1987

Interviewer: Paul Stillwell

Q: Captain, it's a real pleasure to meet you, after having read about you and seen the transcript of your previous interviews. Barrett Tillman concentrated on your flying, of course, and didn't go into too much on your Naval Academy days, so I'd appreciate it if you could provide some recollections of what it was like to be a midshipman here at the academy.

Captain Tomlinson: Being a midshipman at the Naval Academy was an escape from problems in high school. I was often in a bit of trouble, nothing serious, but the board of education thought that I'd be better off somewhere else. So my family obtained an appointment for me to the Naval Academy. To pick up a little extra change in preparation, I developed a business of climbing flagpoles in my home town to replace worn and broken halyards. That didn't last long after my father found out about it.

Before entering the Naval Academy my ambition was to

become an aviator. I had watched Cal Rodgers making the first transcontinental flight when he flew around the south outskirts of Batavia, New York, in a Curtiss biplane. During plebe summer at the Naval Academy in 1914, the only entrance to Bancroft Hall the plebes were allowed to use was the main entrance. The ones at the ends of the original wings were always kept locked. I had a room on the terrace level east wing. It was the one closest to the door leading to the gymnasium and the Santee Basin. We used to have to go there to take boats to the rifle range.

To cut down the foot travel, I studied the construction of Bancroft Hall and decided that the crevices between the stone blocks, the way the building is built, I could slip along with my feet in the one level with the bottom of the window sill. There was a similar device for handholds up above. I could just slither back and forth to my room from the terrace and save a lot of walking, which I had done a number of times, no problem. But one morning we went to the rifle range after it had been raining all night. When we came back, I walked across the corner of old Farragut Field and got the soles of my shoes wet. When I got about halfway across this ledge to my room, one foot slipped, and I wound up in the moat, with my left leg broken in three places. As a result, I spent most of plebe summer in the naval hospital and came out with a leg three-quarters of an inch shorter than the other one. That was a bad start. So I gave up all pretenses of being a human fly. I decided that was strictly for the flies.

I made midshipman cruise in 1915 in the USS Ohio to San Francisco. There I watched Atwood fly and perform acrobatics. I was determined to be an aviator. Before we left the harbor in Annapolis aboard the Ohio, I jumped off the superstructure and got an infection in my left ear. I came down with pneumonia while in San Francisco. I'd been in the black gang, passing coal out of a bunker from Guantanamo to San Francisco, breathing mostly coal dust. I was transferred to Mare Island Hospital and came very close to dying. My father received a telegram advising that, "Your son is not expected to live." I lived, however.

Youngster year, when I got back, I knew for sure aviation was my destiny. I saw an ad somewhere for a slightly damaged Bleriot monoplane which could be bought for about $250.00. Sinclair Gannon, a lieutenant commander then, was assistant to the commandant. So I girded my loins and decided to ask him if I bought that airplane whether I could put it together and fly it off of Farragut Field. I stood in front of his desk, finned out. He looked at me and said, "Mister, are you crazy? Get out of here!" So I got. That ended that.

Then I started building model airplanes. I built my first, assembled it. It came in parts, and I assembled it and flew it off the floor of Dahlgren Hall. It had rubber bands for power. It would take off, make about a 270-degree turn to a crash landing. That was really the beginning of my aviation career. I knew the principles of flight and action of controls.

My hearing went bad when I came up for the next annual exam; I didn't make the second-class cruise. I was on sick leave for treatment during the summer. I just skimped by the hearing test when I came back in September for second-class year.

Another thing of interest. About the time I was thinking of this Bleriot monoplane business, in 1915, Glenn Curtiss had set up a school in Buffalo, New York, to train pilots to go to England as instructors. Without consulting my family, I put in an application for this training and was accepted. I wrote my father and told him I wanted to resign. He refused to give his permission. I felt obligated to complete my studies at the Naval Academy. From that point on, my Naval Academy career was uneventful. I never studied too much. I was thinking of airplanes, but I managed to graduate 40th in the class.

Q: You must have done some studying, because that's a notable achievement.

Captain Tomlinson: Actually, if my class had taken the regular fourth year, first-class year, I would have had a star my last year. I barely made it in English and Spanish in the first plebe exams. I got a 2.5 in each, and that scared me half to death. Then I started studying but not too much. I graduated September 1, 1917, after a three-year course and was assigned to the USS Dubuque, as I covered in my first interview.

The real panic in that ship was that we had a half-breed Hawaiian skipper who, I think, had been retired early and was recalled to duty because of the war. He was a veritable sundowner, just a miserable cuss. He would be up on the bridge, and we'd start to lose the convoy. The only means of communication in those days with the engine room was by voice tube; you hollered back and forth. A classmate of mine, Guy Townsend, was the engineer officer. The skipper would get Guy on the engine room end of the voice tube, and what he would start telling Guy damn near melted the tube. Guy would pat his firemen on the back, shoveling coal into the Scotch boilers, and all of a sudden the twin stacks would torch. Towering flames would come out of cigarette-type tall twin stacks, probably 50 to 100 feet in the air. When that happened, the skipper blew his own stack. It was terrific; it was a farce.

There was no hope of our ever seeing Europe because at that time any ship to go across had to carry enough coal for the round trip. I was thoroughly disgusted. I wasn't particularly interested in the surface Navy anyway--never

Daniel W. Tomlinson #4 - 276

had been. I still wanted to go into aviation, so I had to use a devious trick to get away. This SOB, the CO, used to come up on the bridge a few minutes before 8:00 o'clock every morning and get the 8:00 o'clock report. There were two ladders on each side of the center office that came up to this bridge. He would always come up on the lee side. And the weather used to be miserable. I sure as hell wasn't an admiral. I was the most seasick character you ever saw in the USS Dubuque.

You probably heard this story, but it was actual in my case. I had a bunk with a porthole close to my head, and a lot of times I had my head urping out the porthole. When we were getting up close to Halifax one time, I decided, "This is absurd. I've got to get off this bucket." So about 15 or 20 minutes before this character was due to appear, I sent the quartermaster down for a big plate of scrambled eggs, which I just literally rammed down, and then I stood by. This thing was pitching around, and I was all in position. When I saw this guy coming up, I just let him have it, see. So I got my orders off the ship all right.

When we got in to New York, I had orders to report to the commanding officer of the naval training station at Hampton Roads, Virginia, in June of 1918. When I reported for duty, there was a fine old gentleman, Captain Crose, who had been recalled from retirement to command the training station. I'll never forget, I was all finned out in front of his desk. I was then a senior lieutenant, which I made before I was 21. He looked me over and said, "Mr. Tomlinson, do you know anything about airplanes?"

I said, "Yes, sir, I've made a study of airplanes. I've built flying models; I know all about their components and operation."

Captain Crose said, "I've got just the job for you." I wound up as officer in charge of the aviation mechanics school for quartermasters, which was then being set up. At that time, men were enlisted into aviation as quartermasters. Right across from the administration building, on the other side of the big parade ground, which was also used as the land-plane field in those days, was Naval Air Station Hampton Roads, commanded by Lieutenant Commander Pat Bellinger.*

I established contact there and found that they were in need of people to go out on antisubmarine patrols as copilots. They had pilots, but they just had hardly anyone to ride as copilot. I volunteered, and that was where I learned the basics of flying, because the pilots wanted a copilot who could fly. The patrols were three to five hours, and the pilots wanted relief at the controls. They found out that I had no trouble flying the airplane. It

---

*Lieutenant Commander Patrick N. L. Bellinger, USN, later a vice admiral in World War II.

came naturally. "Well," the pilot thought, "suppose something happens to me. Maybe it would be better if this guy could land the plane." So they gave me both landings and takeoffs.

Q: What was your experience with Lieutenant Halsey when you were a plebe at the Naval Academy?

Captain Tomlinson: It was typical. He was a marvelous battalion officer--tough but absolutely square. Everyone loved Bull Halsey. At breakfast formation one morning, I had just jumped into my blue uniform. I can't remember just why or how; I never did it before and sure as hell didn't do it afterwards. I didn't even have socks, shirt, or collar on, much less underclothes. Well, I was standing there in breakfast formation. Bull Halsey came down, looking with a gimlet eye. He looked at me and he said, "Mister, unbutton your uniform." Gee, there he was, looking at my belly button. I drew 25 demerits for that. But the payoff came a long time later. When I was calling on him when I was ComNATS Pacific/Alaska, I stayed at his quarters. I was there several times. I had to inspect the several Pacific areas every quarter. I ate in his mess and reminded him of the time that he caught me in a bad situation. He laughed and damn near fell off his chair.

Daniel W. Tomlinson #4 - 279

Q: You'd been wearing just a blue uniform?

Captain Tomlinson: Yes. Buttoned up here.

Q: Had the high collar on it.

Captain Tomlinson: High collar, yes. That's all I had on, plus shoes.

Q: I'd be interested in more about your cruise in the Ohio. Where all did that go?

Captain Tomlinson: Well, it was the Ohio, the Missouri, and the Wisconsin. There were three. We went first to Guantanamo and then through the Panama Canal.

Q: The canal was quite new then.

Captain Tomlinson: Ah! That's where, if you'll excuse me, the stuff hit the fan. Because I think it was Admiral Fullam who was in command of the old Missouri. He had it all set up to be in command of the first battleship to go through the canal. By some misunderstanding of the canal personnel, the Ohio slid into the Pacific ahead of the Missouri, and there was hell to pay.

I had been assigned to the black gang. Being plebe

cruise, we drew the worst details. We weren't even on the floor plates of the boiler rooms. We were back in the bunkers, getting the coal out onto the boiler room floor plates for the fireroom to stoke the boilers. When we arrived in San Francisco, we had about ten days there to see the Panama Pacific Exposition. I watched Atwood, who was flying, doing all kinds of acrobatics, and I was all steamed up to become an aviator.

Then I came down with pneumonia and nearly died.

Q: Did you get any liberty there?

Captain Tomlinson: Yes, I had several days' leave to visit an aunt in Sacramento.

Q: What were living conditions like on board the Ohio?

Captain Tomlinson: I think it was the last cruise that midshipmen slept in hammocks like the enlisted personnel. If you weren't out when reveille sounded, a good tough boatswain's mate with a 2-by-4 fixed as a sort of club came through the sleeping compartments. You got it on your rear end in the hammock, and you came out in a hurry. It was a tough cruise.

Q: Did you get involved in coaling ship?

Captain Tomlinson: Yes. We used to coal ship on the USS Dubuque, an all-hands affair that was a miserable job. We would hardly get the ship clean before the coal barges were again alongside.

Q: And you probably didn't have showers to clean up afterward.

Captain Tomlinson: A bucket of salt water!

Talk about coaling ship, I remember the Texas. When I was kicked out of aviation and assigned to duty on the USS Oklahoma, I was horror-struck when the exec told me that I was the senior watch officer. I had only stood OOD duty on the USS Dubuque, a spitkit. I was scared stiff. I think I had one day to talk about the duty and talk to people familiar with the ship. We were going to get under way at midnight the next day and proceed to San Francisco. So I thought, "It is going to be a black night. I'll put myself on the bridge as OOD. Maybe the skipper will be asleep." So I had to get the old Oklahoma under way. The hell of it was we had to follow the Texas, which was the flagship and a coal-burner.

My experience with a stadimeter was rudimentary. I was supposed to keep the "Okie" in position 500 yards astern of the Texas, which could no way keep a constant speed. I think the distance variation allowable was 50 yards. I almost lost my mind issuing orders to the engine room. Take off five RPMs, increase seven RPMs. It seemed that the "Okie" was either about to ram the Texas or lose the flagship. I was used to maintaining position in an airplane formation with a throttle, and trying to take two or three turns off or add two or three turns to these old reciprocating engines was a nightmare. I thought that midwatch would never end. Likely the captain was a sound sleeper and stayed in his bunk.

Q: I presume you became a competent watch officer after that.

Captain Tomlinson: Let's say I survived.

Q: Did they have you strictly in deck duty, as opposed to any aviation?

Captain Tomlinson: I had the port 5-inch battery. It was a division. I always got off the ship on Friday afternoon. We were anchored off Long Beach. I returned Monday morning in time for quarters after barnstorming and carrying wing-walkers, plane-changers, all that kind of exhibition flying over Earl Daugherty's field. This was to draw a curious crowd, the source of our passengers at $5.00 a ride.

Q: The duties on board ship must have seemed tame by comparison.

Captain Tomlinson: Very frankly, I never cared for sea duty. Aviation was my line of work, and I wanted to stick with it. I didn't give a damn about anything else. I had certain things that I wanted to accomplish, and along the way I got them done.

Q: Captain, today's interview has been a really enjoyable experience for me and a useful addition to the ones you did earlier with Barrett Tillman. Thank you very much for this.

Captain Tomlinson: Okay, now let's go over and have lunch at the O-club. It's on me.

Index

to

The Reminiscences of

Captain Daniel W. Tomlinson IV
United States Naval Reserve (Retired)

AT-6
 Army Air Corps trainer developed from the BC-1 by North American Aviation in the mid-1930s, 186-188

Accidents
 Tomlinson landed a Navy Jenny on a street in Coronado, California, in the early 1920s after the engine failed, 35-36; while flying a VE-7 out of North Island in the early 1920s, Tomlinson had a mid-air collision that resulted in the death of the pilot of the other aircraft, 37-40; a Marine Corps flight team experienced a crash during the National Air Races at Spokane, Washington, in 1927, 100-101; Tomlinson cracked up his Jenny when flying into Batavia, New York, in 1928, 118-121; a Navy PN-11 patrol plane caught fire during testing at Anacostia in the late 1920s, 124-126; Earl Daugherty died in the crash of a J-5 Laird in 1929, 128-130; a B-17 crashed during tests at Wright Field in the 1930s, killing all on board, 193; Pan American plane crashed at Funafuti in World War II, 237-239

Air Force, U.S.
 Role in the Berlin Airlift in 1948-49, 258-261; instrument training in the late 1940s for Military Air Transport Service pilots, 261-262

Alpha
 Northrop-built commercial aircraft flown by Transcontinental and Western Air in the 1930s, 142, 159, 162-163; flying characteristics, 198

Anacostia (D.C.) Naval Air Station
 Site of Navy aircraft testing in the late 1920s, 122-127

Antisubmarine Warfare
 The Norfolk Naval Air Station sent flying boats out on patrols over the Atlantic in 1918, looking for German U-boats, 17-18, 277-278

Army Air Corps, U.S.
 Army field in San Diego used by the Navy for glide bombing and dive bombing practice in the mid-1920s, 84-86; stunt team called the Three Musketeers flew Curtiss Hawks in the National Air Races of 1927 at Spokane, Washington, 100-103; mock aerial combat against Navy planes in the mid and late 1920s, 107-110; development center at Wright Field, 172-173, 175-176, 187, 189-191, 193-194; development of the North American BC-1/AT-6 trainer in the 1930s, 186-188; testing of the North American NA-21 bomber in the 1930s, 188-190; development of the P-36/P-40 fighter in the 1930s, 190-191; testing of the B-17 bomber at Wright Field in the late 1930s, 193-194

Army Air Service, U.S.
Various interactions with Tomlinson and his aircraft in the 1920s, 43, 55-56, 61, 63-64, 70-71

B-17 Flying Fortress
Army Air Corps bomber tested at Wright Field in the late 1930s, including a fatal crash, 193-194

BC-1
Army Air Corps trainer (later AT-6) developed by North American Aviation in the mid-1930s, 186-188

Barnstorming
Tomlinson flew a Curtiss Jenny in the 1920s to bring in income, 51, 73-74, 77-78, 282

Baugh, Lieutenant Commander Harry V., USN (USNA, 1916)
While assigned to the aircraft carrier Langley (CV-1) in the mid-1920s, set up a practice landing field ashore in Coronado, California, 90

Berlin Airlift
U.S. role in delivering food and fuel to blockaded Berlin in 1948-9, 258-261

Bernelli, Vince
Aircraft engineer who developed a flying wing in the 1930s, 147-149

Boeing Aircraft Company
Development of the Boeing 307 Stratoliner in the 1930s, 165-166, 194-197; development and testing of the B-17 bomber in the late 1930s, 193-194, 201-202

Bombing
Lieutenant Commander Frank Wead initiated glide bombing and dive bombing with Fighting Squadron Two in the mid-1920s, 84-88; FB-5s from the aircraft carrier Langley (CV-1) made a successful dive-bombing attack during a war game in the mid-1920s, 93-94

Buckmaster, Rear Admiral Elliott, USN (USNA, 1912)
Commanded the Naval Air Primary Training Command in Kansas in 1942, 216-217

Bureau of Aeronautics
As Chief of the bureau in 1935, Rear Admiral Ernest J. King was not receptive to Tomlinson's pitch for instrument training for naval aviators, 184-186; concern about aviation training in 1942, 216; interaction with commercial airlines at the beginning of World War II, 226-227; conducted a board to test the unsuitable RY transport plane during World War II, 230-231; deputy bureau chief, Rear Admiral Frank Wagner, rationalized the use of unsafe aviators during World War II, 250

Chapline, George F. (USNA, 1916)
   Former naval aviator who was with Wright Aeronautical in the late 1930s, 202-203

Collisions
   While flying a VE-7 out of North Island in the early 1920s, Tomlinson had a mid-air collision that resulted in the death of the pilot of the other aircraft, 37-40

Condor
   Curtiss-built commercial airliner that was unpopular with pilots in the early 1930s, 144-146

Constellation
   Four-engine transport aircraft developed by Lockheed in the late 1930s and early 1940s, 202-204

Convoying
   The mine training ship Dubuque (PG-17) performed convoy duty off the East Coast in 1918, 13-15

Cook, Ensign Mark R., USNRF
   Had an excellent reputation as a flight instructor at Pensacola in 1920, 26-28

Coronado, California
   Tomlinson landed a Navy Jenny on a street in Coronado in the early 1920s after the engine failed, 35-36

Courts-Martial
   Tomlinson was acquitted in a court-martial in the early 1920s after his engine quit while flying a Navy Jenny, 36-37; Tomlinson was acquitted in a court-martial in the early 1920s after he was involved in a midair collision that resulted in the death of the pilot of the other aircraft, 40-42

Crose, Captain William M., USN (USNA, 1888)
   As skipper of the Naval Training Station at Hampton Roads, got Tomlinson involved in aviation in 1918, 16-17, 276-277

Cuddihy, Lieutenant George T., USN (USNA, 1918)
   Went through flight training in 1920 and had a real enjoyment of flying, 31; maintained a friendship with Tomlinson during the 1920s, 44, 51; killed in an airplane crash after relieving Tomlinson at Anacostia in 1929, 126-127

Curtiss Aeroplane Division
   Development of the Army Air Corps P-36/P-40 fighter in the 1930s, 190-191; testing of the SBC Helldiver in the 1930s, 191-192

Cyclops, USS
This Navy collier was the subject of a search in the Caribbean after she disappeared in March 1918, 16

DC-1
Douglas-built commercial airliner developed in the 1930s for Transcontinental and Western Air, 143, 150-158, 163-164, 168-170, 172

DC-2
Douglas-built commercial airliner that had a stiff-legged landing gear, 196

DC-3
Douglas-built commercial airliner that Tomlinson flew in the 1930s, 166; had a stiff-legged landing gear, 196

DC-4
Douglas-built commercial airliner that the airlines initially turned down in the 1930s as being unsuitable, 199-200

Daugherty, Earl
Pioneer civilian aviator who was one of the top pilots around Long Beach and Los Angeles, California, in the 1920s, 44-49, 52-53, 114, 282; died in the crash of a J-5 Laird in 1929, 128-130

Davis, Lieutenant (junior grade) William V., Jr., USN (USNA, 1924)
Served as a member of the Three Seahawks, the Navy's first formation acrobatics team, in 1928, 103-106, 110; success in mock aerial combat against Army fighters in 1928, 108-110; at the National Air Races in Los Angeles in 1928, 113-118

Depew, Ensign G. G., USNRF
Served as operations officer for flights out of the naval air station at Hampton Roads in 1918, 19, 22

Disciplinary Action
Tomlinson was acquitted in a court-martial in the early 1920s after the engine quit in the Navy Jenny he was flying, 36-37

Dive Bombing
Lieutenant Commander Frank Wead initiated glide bombing and dive bombing with Fighting Squadron Two in the mid-1920s, 84-88; FB-5s from the aircraft carrier Langley (CV-1) made a successful dive-bombing attack during a war game in the mid-1920s, 93-94

Dolson, Lieutenant Charles H., USNR
Former commercial airline pilot who served as operations officer for Naval Air Transport Squadrons Pacific in World War II, 222-223

Doolittle, James H.
Led the Three Musketeers, an Army Air Corps stunt team that flew Curtiss Hawks in the National Air Races of 1927 at Spokane, Washington, 100-103

Douglas Aircraft Company
Development of the DC-1 airliner in the early 1930s, 149-158; the airlines initially turned down the DC-4 in the 1930s as being unsuitable, 199-200

Douglas, Donald W.
Involvement in the development of the DC-1 airliner in the early 1930s, 151, 155-156

Dubuque, USS (PG-17)
Former gunboat that tended nets in the Atlantic during World War I, 12; training ship at the Naval Academy in World War I, 12-13; characteristics, 13-15; convoy duty off the East Coast in 1918, 13-15; search for the missing collier Cyclops in the Caribbean in 1918, 16, overbearing skipper in 1917, 275-276

Engineering Plants
Inadequate Scotch boilers and triple-expansion engines in the mine training ship Dubuque (PG-17) in World War I, 14-15, 275

Erdmann, Captain William L., USN (USNA, 1924)
Proved difficult for Tomlinson to deal with when Erdmann was assigned as a wing commander for evacuation of wounded personnel in the Pacific in 1945, 246-251

F-5L
Tomlinson used the plane for stunt flying in the early 1920s, 34

FB-2
Boeing fighter flown by Fighting Squadron Two during bombing experiments in the mid-1920s, 86

FB-5
Boeing fighter flown by Fighting Squadron Two during bombing experiments in the mid-1920s, 93; FB-5s from the aircraft carrier Langley (CV-1) made a successful dive-bombing attack during a war game in the mid-1920s, 93-94; flying characteristics, 94-95; Rear Admiral Joseph M. Reeves pulled the FB-5s off the Langley in early 1927 because of Tomlinson's complaints about their safety, 95-96; Lieutenant Jackson Tate designed a VF-2 squadron insignia with some errors in it, 97-98; operated from the Saratoga (CV-3) with Marine Corps pilots in the late 1920s but came to grief, 98-99; equipped with flotation gear in the summer of 1927, 99-100; put in storage, 103

F2B
   Boeing-built fighter that was used by the Three Seahawks, the Navy's first formation acrobatics team, in 1928, 103-106; superior performance against Army PW-9 fighters in 1928, 106-110; flew inverted through the Pali on Oahu, Hawaii, 110; at the National Air Races in Los Angeles in 1928, 113-118

F6C Hawk
   Curtiss-built fighter used by the VF-2 for early glide bombing and dive bombing experiments in the mid-1920s, 85-86

F8C Helldiver
   The wings came off this Curtiss fighter when it was tested at Anacostia in the late 1920s, 123-124

Fighting Squadron Two (VF-2)/Fighting Squadron Six (VF-6)
   As commanding officer in the mid-1920s, Lieutenant Commander Frank Wead asked for Tomlinson to be assigned to the squadron, 82-83; beginning of glide bombing and dive bombing in the mid-1920s, 84-88; Tomlinson kept his personal Jenny in the squadron hangar, 88-89; operations from the aircraft carrier Langley (CV-1) in the mid-1920s, 90-95; FB-5s from the Langley made a successful dive-bombing attack during a war game in the mid-1920s, 93-94; Rear Admiral Joseph M. Reeves pulled the FB-5s off the Langley in early 1927 because of Tomlinson's complaints about their safety, 95-96; Lieutenant Jackson Tate designed a squadron insignia with some errors in it, 97-98; in 1928 members of the squadron began the Navy's first formation acrobatics team, the Three Seahawks, 103-106; superior performance against Army PW-9 fighters during mock aerial combat in 1928, 106-110; put on an impressive show at the dedication of Lindbergh Field at San Diego in 1928, 111-113; at the National Air Races in Los Angeles in 1928, 113-118

Fire
   A Navy PN-11 patrol plane caught fire during testing at Anacostia in the late 1920s, 124-126; fire in an Army P-36 being tested in the 1930s, 190-191

Fitness Reports
   As deputy chief of staff to CinCPac in 1945, Rear Admiral Forrest P. Sherman tried to get Tomlinson to soften an unfavorable fitness report on Captain William L. Erdmann, 249-250

Fleetster
   Consolidated-built aircraft that Tomlinson flew in difficult weather in the 1930s, 159-162

Fokker D. VII
   Former German airplane that the U.S. Army Air Service flew in the early 1920s, 70-71

Food
> Rear Admiral John W. Reeves initiated an unsuccessful effort in 1945 to equip Naval Air Transport Service planes to serve warmed-up frozen meals, 251-252

Ford Tri-Motor
> Commercial aircraft that Tomlinson flew through sub-zero weather in 1929, 131-132

Frye, William John
> Airline executive who ran the Aero Corporation in the 1920s, 140; with Transcontinental and Western Air in the early 1930s he was involved in the evaluation and acquisition of aircraft for the company, 143-145; management of the airline, 158, 163-164, 176, 194-195, 198-204; fired by Howard Hughes, 257

Funafuti, Ellice Islands
> A Pan American plane crashed at Funafuti in World War II, 237-239

Gamma
> Northrop-built commercial aircraft developed in the 1930s, 173-183

Gannon, Lieutenant Commander Sinclair, USN (USNA, 1900)
> As assistant to the commandant at the Naval Academy in 1915, prevented Tomlinson from having an airplane on the grounds, 273

Gates, Artemus L.
> Assistant Secretary of the Navy for Air to whom Tomlinson complained about the use of Mars flying boats in Naval Air Transport Squadrons Pacific in World War II, 239-241

Gatley, Colonel George G., USA
> Old-time Army officer who was stationed at Camp Lewis, Washington, in the early 1920s, 62

Gavin, Lieutenant Arthur, USN
> Headed the assembly and repair section at the North Island Naval Air Station in the early 1920s, 37

German Navy
> The Norfolk Naval Air Station sent flying boats out on patrols over the Atlantic in 1918, looking for German U-boats, 17-18, 277-278

Germany
> Aviation developments in the late 1930s, 205-209

Gorton, Lieutenant Adolphus W., USN
> Served as a landing signal officer in the aircraft carrier Langley (CV-1) in the mid-1920s, 91-92

Great Falls (Montana) Air Force Base
  Site of instrument training in the late 1940s for Military Air Transport Service pilots, 261-262

Guam, Marianas Islands
  Base for air evacuation of wounded personnel during World War II, 245-250

HS-2L
  Flying boat that the Navy used for antisubmarine patrols over the Atlantic in 1918, 18; training flights out of Hampton Roads in 1918, 21-23; Tomlinson used the plane for stunt flying in the early 1920s, 34

Halsey, Lieutenant William F., Jr., USN (USNA, 1904)
  Put Tomlinson on report for being out of uniform as a Naval Academy midshipman in the 1910s, 278-279

Hamilton, Captain Walter A., USNR
  Role with Transcontinental and Western Air prior to World War II, 202, 204; as part of Naval Air Transport Squadrons Pacific organization in 1945 he was involved in the overhaul of R5Ds, 255

Hawaii
  Army and Navy fighter planes tangled near Oahu during mock aerial combat in the 1920s, 105-110

Hearn, Major James A., USAF
  Mistakenly reported enemy attacks on his squadron's aircraft while flying in the Berlin Airlift in 1948-49, 259-260

Hewitt, Lieutenant Lambert (junior grade), USNRF
  Naval aviator who maintained a friendship with Tomlinson during the 1920s, 44, 51

Hoffman, Lieutenant Harry D., USN (USNA, 1918)
  USS Oklahoma (BB-37) turret officer who had the ship's rifle team in the 1920s, 61-63

Holcome, Lieutenant Benjamin R. Holcome, USN (USNA, 1916)
  As an assistant detail officer in the mid-1920s, arranged for Tomlinson to get back into naval aviation, 80

Hughes, Admiral Charles F., USN (USNA, 1888)
  As Chief of Naval Operations in 1929, he turned down Tomlinson's request to attend the funeral of friend Earl Daugherty, 130

Hughes, Howard R.
  Aircraft magnate who gained control of Transcontinental and Western Air in the 1930s, 200-201; hesitation on acquiring the Lockheed Constellation, 202-204; fired Jack Frye as head of the company, 257

Ingalls, David S.
   Commanded John Rodgers Naval Air Station in Hawaii during World War II, 232

Instrument Flying
   Tomlinson pioneered Navy instrument flying in 1925 by installing a needle-ball gyro in a Curtiss Jenny, 32-33; experiments with instruments in commercial aircraft by Transcontinental and Western Air in the 1930s, 166-167; value in bad weather in the 1930s, 176-183; in 1935 Tomlinson made a pitch to Rear Admiral Ernest King about instrument training for naval aviators, 185-185; instrument training in the late 1940s for Military Air Transport Service pilots, 261-262

JN (Curtiss Jenny)
   Tomlinson pioneered Navy instrument flying in 1925 by installing a needle-ball gyro in a Jenny, 32-33; Tomlinson flew his personal Jenny for a variety of purposes in the 1920s, 32-33, 43-49, 51-70, 88-89, 118-121; Tomlinson landed a Navy Jenny on a street in Coronado, California, in the early 1920s after the engine failed, 35-36; use for barnstorming, 51, 73-74, 77-78; spare parts available in College Park, Maryland, 79; first cross-country trip in 1925, 80-83; Tomlinson kept his personal Jenny in the Fighting Squadron Two hangar in the mid-1920s, 88-89; Tomlinson cracked up his Jenny when flying into Batavia, New York, in 1928, 118-121

JRM Mars
   Large flying boat transport that was inconvenient for Pacific operations during World War II, 239-241

   See also PB2M-1R Mars

Ju-99
   German four-engine transport plane that Tomlinson flew in 1938, 206-208

Keys, C. M.
   Airline official who was involved in various predecessors of TWA in the 1920s and 1930s, 138, 140, 144-145

Kindelberger, J. H.
   Aircraft engineer who was with Douglas and later North American in the 1930s, 151, 184, 186, 189, 192

King, Rear Admiral Ernest J., USN (USNA, 1901)
   As Chief of the Bureau of Aeronautics in 1935, was not receptive to Tomlinson's pitch for instrument training for naval aviators, 184-186

Kuter, Major General Laurence S., USAF (USMA, 1927)
   In the late 1940s, as commander of the Military Air Transport Service, was insistent on instrument training for pilots, 261-262

Landing Signal Officers
  Role on board the aircraft carrier Langley (CV-1) in the mid-1920s, 91-93

Langley, USS (CV-1)
  Difficulties in landing planes aboard in the mid-1920s, 90-95; FB-5s from the ship made a successful dive-bombing attack during a war game in the mid-1920s, 93-94; members of the Three Seahawks performed during the ship's visit to San Francisco in 1928, 105-106; as commanding officer in 1928, Captain John Towers tolerated Tomlinson's aerial antics--up to a point, 109-110

Lexington, USS (CV-2)
  Took Fighting Squadron Two aboard as the ship began fleet operations in 1928, 111

Lindbergh, Charles A.
  Courted Ambassador Dwight Morrow's daughter in Mexico in 1929, 133-134; was friendly with Jack Maddux of Maddux Airlines around 1930, 137; involvement with Transcontinental and Western Air in the 1930s, 145, 152-153, 234; inspected German aircraft facilities in 1938, 206-207; flew as a fighter pilot in World War II, 232-234

Lindbergh Field, San Diego
  The Three Seahawks, a Navy formation acrobatics team, put on a show at the dedication of this airport in 1928, 111-112

Lockheed Aircraft Corporation
  Development of the Constellation transport plane in the late 1930s and early 1940s, 202-204

Long Island Sound
  Use of the mine training ship Dubuque (PG-17) in an unsuccessful attempt to put antisubmarine nets across Long Island Sound in 1917, 12

Los Angeles, California
  The local airport, Mines Field, was the site of the National Air Races in 1928, 113-118

MB-3
  Boeing-built Army fighter that defeated Navy TS fighters in mock combat in the mid-1920s, 106-107

MacArthur, General Douglas, USA (USMA, 1903)
  As Commander Southwest Pacific Force in 1943, complained about the service from Navy air transport squadrons, 235-237

Maddux Airlines
  John L. Maddux served as president of Maddux Airlines in

the late 1920s, 116; airline was poorly organized and disciplined, 127-128; Tomlinson joined as vice president in 1929, 130-131; flying ventures to Mexico in 1929, 132-136; merger with Transcontinental Air Transport in 1930, 137-138

Maddux, John L.
Served as president of Maddux Airlines (later Transcontinental and Western Air) in the late 1920s, 116, 130-131, 132, 138, 146

Maintenance
Discussions in the summer of 1945 concerning overhaul of R5Ds, 254-255

Marine Corps, U.S.
Marine aviators flew the dangerous FB-5 fighter from the aircraft carrier Saratoga (CV-3) in the late 1920s, 98-99; a Marine pilot crashed his Curtiss Hawk during the National Air Races at Spokane, Washington, in 1927, 100-101

Medical Problems
Tomlinson had trouble passing an aviation physical in 1920 because of heart and vision conditions, 24-25; Tomlinson broke his ankle during a barroom fight in the early 1920s, 50-51; reinjured ankle in aircraft accident, 66; Tomlinson broke a leg in 1914 while climbing around Bancroft Hall at the Naval Academy, 272-273

Mexico
Maddux Airlines had various flying ventures to this country in 1929, 132-136

Military Air Transport Service
After the merger of the wartime Army and Navy components, this service had a large role in the late 1940s, including the Berlin Airlift, 257-263; training of pilots in instrument flying, 260-263

Mines Field, Los Angeles, California
Airport that served as the site of the National Air Races in 1928, 113-118

Mitscher, Lieutenant Commander Marc A., USN (USNA, 1910)
While at Anacostia in the early 1920s, went to a civilian air show in Pennsylvania, 76-77, 80

Moffett, Rear Admiral William A., USN (USNA, 1890)
As chief of the Bureau of Aeronautics in 1928, arranged for Tomlinson to become a test pilot, 117-118

Morrow, Dwight
As U.S. ambassador to Mexico in 1929, interceded with the Mexican government on behalf of Maddux Airlines, 133-134

Muhlenberg, Major Henry K., USA (USMA, 1908)
   Army aviator stationed at Sand Point, Seattle, in the early 1920s, 63-64, 70

Murray, Lieutenant Commander George D., USN (USNA, 1911)
   As executive officer of the naval air station at San Diego in 1921, downgraded Tomlinson's assignment because of a reputation for stunt flying, 33

N-9
   Aircraft used for pilot training at Pensacola in the early 1920s, 26-28

N2S Kaydet
   Stearman-built trainer used for Naval Reserve aviation training in the early 1940s, 214, 218-219

NA-21
   North American-built bomber tested for the Army Air Corps in the 1930s, 188-190

National Air Races
   James Doolittle was among the fliers at the races in Spokane, Washington, in 1927, 100; performance by the Three Seahawks, Navy formation acrobatics team at the National Air Races in Los Angeles in 1928, 113-118

Naval Academy, U.S., Annapolis, Maryland
   Classroom instruction in the 1910s, 4; summer cruise to the West Coast in 1915, 11; use of the training ship Dubuque (PG-17) for midshipmen during World War I, 12-13; post-graduation duty assignments for the class of 1918 were made alphabetically, 12, 20; while on the faculty in the mid-1920s, Tomlinson steered a number of midshipmen toward careers in aviation, 75-76, 79; Lieutenant William Halsey put Tomlinson on report for being out of uniform as a Naval Academy midshipman in the 1910s, 278-279; summer cruise in the battleship Ohio (BB-12) in 1915, 273, 279-280

Naval Air Transport Squadrons Pacific (NATSPac)
   Reorganization in 1943 from Navy to civilian format, 220-222; complement of aircraft, 223; command and control facilities, 224; drew pilots from commercial airlines, 225-228; unsuitability of the RY for transport work, 228-231; Tomlinson's role in inspecting various parts of the command, 235-239, 241-242; difficulties in operating flying boats versus land planes, 239-244; difficulties with Captain William Erdmann in connection with evacuation of wounded personnel, 246-250; unsuccessful effort in 1945 to equip the planes to serve warmed-up frozen meals, 251-252

Naval Reserve
   Aviation training in the vicinity of Kansas City, Missouri, in the late 1930s and early 1940s, 210

Navigation
Primitive air navigation capabilities when Tomlinson made a flight up the West Coast in a Curtiss Jenny in the early 1920s, 53-61

Nimitz, Admiral Chester W., USN (USNA, 1905)
As Commander in Chief Pacific Fleet in World War II, kept track of the operations of the Naval Air Transport Squadrons Pacific, 221-222, 224, 228, 230, 237, 239, 248-249

Norfolk Naval Air Station
Site of training for pilots and enlisted crew members in 1918, 17-18, 21-23, 277-278

North American Aviation
Aircraft manufacturer for whom Tomlinson worked as a test pilot in the 1930s, 184, 186-187; development of the BC-1/AT-6/SNJ trainer in the 1930s, 186-188; testing of the NA-21 bomber in the 1930s, 188-190

North Island Naval Air Station, Coronado, California
Operations in 1921-22, 33-43; Tomlinson landed a Navy Jenny on a street in Coronado, California, in the early 1920s after the engine failed, 35-36; in the early 1920s Tomlinson was flying a VE-7 when he had a mid-air collision that resulted in the death of the pilot of the other aircraft, 37-40; conducted a training program for land-plane operations, 42-43; site of practice field for aviators attached to the aircraft carrier Langley (CV-1) in the mid-1920s, 90

Northrop Corporation
Development of various commercial aircraft in the 1930s, 154-155

Nowland, Major General Bob E., USAF
Commanded the Continental Division of the Military Air Transport Service in the late 1940s during instrument training for pilots, 260-261

OX-5
Curtiss aircraft engine that caused problems during operations in the 1920s, 45-47, 54-58, 61, 63-67

O2U Corsair
Vought observation plane that Tomlinson tested at Anacostia in the late 1920s, 122-123

Ohio, USS (BB-12)
During a Naval Academy midshipman cruise in 1915 was the first battleship to go through the Panama Canal, 273, 279-280

Oklahoma, USS (BB-37)
Tomlinson flew his personal Curtiss Jenny while serving as one of the battleship's deck officers in the early 1920s, 43-70; difficulties steaming in formation with other battleships in the early 1920s, 49-50, 281-282; went to Bremerton, Washington, for overhaul in the 1920s, 51-52, 64-66

Olathe (Kansas) Naval Air Station
Construction and operation in the early 1940s, 212-213, 216, 218-219

P-36
Army Air Corps fighter developed and tested in the 1930s, 190-191

PBM Mariner
Martin-built flying boat used as a transport in Pacific operations in World War II, 236-237

PB2M-1R Mars
Martin-built flying boat that proved a poor performer in Pacific transport operations in World War II, 241-243

See also JRM Mars

PB2Y Coronado
Consolidated-built flying boat used as a transport in Pacific operations in World War II, 240, 243

PN-11
Naval Aircraft Factory patrol plane that caught fire during testing at Anacostia in the late 1920s, 124-126

PW-9
Army Air Corps fighter that lost to Navy F2Bs in mock aerial combat in 1928, 106-110

Panama
Site of a barroom fight among naval officers in the early 1920s, 50-51; in 1915 the USS Ohio (BB-12) was the first battleship to go through the Panama Canal, 279-280

Pan American Airways
Support of Naval Air Transport Squadrons Pacific during World War II, 236-239; Pan American plane crashed at Funafuti in World War II, 237-239

Pensacola Naval Air Station
Site of training for pilots in 1920-21, 26-31

Pihl, Lieutenant Commander Paul E., USN (USNA, 1921)
Served as U.S. naval air attaché in Berlin in the late 1930s, 206, 208

Post, Wiley
Self-promoting aviator who made high-altitude flights in the 1930s, 172-173

Pownall, Rear Admiral Charles A., USN (USNA, 1910)
As Commander Air Force Pacific Fleet in World War II, asked Naval Air Transport Squadrons Pacific for support in evacuating wounded personnel, 245-246

Puget Sound Navy, Bremerton, Washington
Overhauled the battleship Oklahoma (BB-37) in the early 1920s, 51-52, 64-66

R5D Skymaster
Navy transport aircraft developed by Douglas as the DC-4, 199-200; operation by Naval Air Transport Squadrons Pacific in World War II, 223-226, 243-244; unsuccessful effort in 1945 to equip the planes to serve warmed-up frozen meals, 251-252; overhauls of, 254-255

RY Liberator
Consolidated-built Navy transport version of the B-24 and PB4Y was not well suited for its role, 228-231

Radford, Rear Admiral Arthur W., USN (USNA, 1916)
Role as head of naval aviation training early in World War II, 214-215, 218; service in the Pacific during the war, 247

Ramsey, Rear Admiral Dewitt C., USN (USNA, 1912)
As Chief of the Bureau of Aeronautics during World War II, conducted a board to test the unsuitable RY transport plane, 230-231; involved in discussions in the summer of 1945 concerning overhaul of R5Ds, 254-255

Reeves, Rear Admiral John W., Jr., USN (USNA, 1911)
As Commander Naval Air Transport Service in 1945, conducted an investigation when a wing commander caused problems on Guam, 248-249; initiated an unsuccessful effort in 1945 to equip NATS planes to serve warmed-up frozen meals, 251-252

Reeves, Rear Admiral Joseph M., USN (USNA, 1894)
While serving as Commander Aircraft Squadrons Battle Fleet in the mid-1920s, gave permission for Tomlinson to store his personal plane, a Curtiss Jenny, in the Fighting Squadron Two hangar, 88-89; commanded the carrier force during a battle problem in the mid-1920s, 93-94; pulled the FB-5s off the Langley in early 1927 because of Tomlinson's complaints about their safety, 95-96

Rhine-Main Air Force Base, Frankfurt, Germany
Role in support of the Berlin Airlift in 1948-49, 258-261

Richter, Paul E.
Served as an executive for various airlines in the 1920s and 1930s, 140, 155, 183

Robbins, Richard W.
Served as president of Transcontinental and Western Air in the early 1930s, 140-142, 148, 158

Rodgers, Calbraith P.
Civilian aviator who made exhibition flights around the United States in the early years of the 20th century, 6-7

Rogers, Captain Ford O., USMC
Commanded a Marine Corps flight team that experienced a crash during the 1927 National Air Races at Spokane, Washington, 100-101

Russell, Midshipman James S., USN (USNA, 1926)
As a Naval Academy midshipman in the mid-1920s he developed an interest in aviation that provided the direction for his future career, 75

SBC Helldiver
Curtiss-built Navy dive-bomber tested in the 1930s, 191-192

SNJ Texan
Navy trainer initially developed as the BC-1/AT-6 by North American Aviation in the 1930s, 186-188

Safety
Rear Admiral Joseph M. Reeves pulled the FB-5s off the Langley in early 1927 because of Tomlinson's complaints about their safety, 95-96; Tomlinson inaugurated airway traffic control for TAT-Maddux Airlines around 1930 so commercial pilots would fly in safe weather, 138-139

San Diego, California
See North Island Naval Air Station, Coronado, California

Sand Point, Seattle, Washington
Site of a U.S. Army Air Service facility in the early 1920s, 63-64

San Francisco, California
In 1928, the Navy's first formation acrobatics team, the Three Seahawks, put on a spectacular show in the city's downtown area, 105-106

Saratoga, USS (CV-3)
Aircraft carrier from which Marine aviators flew the dangerous FB-5 fighter in the late 1920s, 98-99

Schildhauer, Commander Clarence R., USNR
Naval Air Transport Service staff officer who made an inspection trip to the Pacific during World War II, 244

Sherman, Rear Admiral Forrest P., USN (USNA, 1918)
  As deputy chief of staff to CinCPac in 1945, tried to get Tomlinson to soften an unfavorable fitness report on Captain William L. Erdmann, 249-250; died in 1951, 250-251

Smith, Commodore Donald F., USN (USNA, 1921)
  Commanded Air Transport Squadrons Pacific early in World War II, 220, 224; later commanded the entire Naval Air Transport Service, 230-231, 234

Spokane, Washington
  The Three Musketeers, an Army Air Corps stunt team, flew Curtiss Hawks in the National Air Races of 1927 at Spokane, 100-103

Sprague, Lieutenant Clifton A. F., USN (USNA, 1918)
  Went through aviation training at Pensacola in 1920-21, 19, 26

Sprague, Lieutenant Thomas L., USN (USNA, 1918)
  Went through aviation training at Pensacola in 1920-21, 19, 26

Storrs, Lieutenant (junior grade) Aaron P. III, USN (USNA, 1923)
  Served as a member of the Three Seahawks, the Navy's first formation acrobatics team, in 1928, 103-106, 110; success in mock aerial combat against Army fighters in 1928, 108-110; at the National Air Races in Los Angeles in 1928, 113-118

Stratoliner (Boeing 307
  Commercial airliner developed in the mid-1930s, 165-166, 194-197, 201-202

TS
  A Naval Aircraft Factory-built fighter that performed poorly in mock combat against Army planes in the mid-1920s, 106-107

Tate, Lieutenant Jackson R., USN
  While serving in Fighting Squadron Two in the mid-1920s, designed a squadron insignia with some errors in it, 97-98

Texas, USS (BB-35)
  Difficult for other battleships to steam in formation with the Texas in the early 1920s when she burned coal and they burned oil, 49-50, 281-282

Thornburg, Lieutenant Commander Jack W., USNR
  Transport pilot assigned to run a service of evacuating wounded personnel from Guam in 1945, 246-247

Three Musketeers
   Army Air Corps stunt team that flew Curtiss Hawks in the National Air Races of 1927 at Spokane, Washington, 100-103

Three Seahawks
   Navy flight demonstration team, led by Tomlinson, that began performing in 1928, 103-106, 110; at the National Air Races in Los Angeles in 1928, 113-118

Tomlinson, Captain Daniel W. IV, USN (Ret.) (USNA, 1918)
   Ancestors of, 1-4, 7, 9; parents of, 3-4, 8-9, 95, 119-120, 263; as a Naval Academy midshipman, 1914-17, 4, 10-11, 271-275, 278-279; interest in kites and aviation as a boy and young man, 5-7, 10-11, 273-274; boyhood pranks, 8-9; began flying Navy planes at Norfolk in 1918, 17-18, 21-23. 277-278; received pilot training at Pensacola in 1920-21, 26-31; duty as San Diego Naval Air Station, 1921-22, 33-43; served in the battleship Oklahoma, 1922-23, 49-52; wives of, 52, 70, 73, 76, 189-190, 192-193, 234, 265-270; duty at the Naval Academy, 1923-25, 72-79; children of, 73, 264, 267; assigned to Fighting Squadron Two, 1925-28, 82-118; served as a test pilot at Anacostia Naval Air Station, 1928-29, 122-127; worked in the commercial aircraft industry and as a test pilot from 1929 until the advent of World War II, 130-204; visit to Europe in 1938, 205-210; role in Naval Reserve aviation training in the late 1930s and early 1940s, 209-219; commanded Naval Air Transport Squadrons Pacific, 1943-45, 220-255; post-retirement activities, 256-257, 263-270; recall to active duty in 1948 for service with the Military Air Transport Service, 257-263

Towers, Vice Admiral John H., USN (USNA, 1906)
   As commanding officer of the aircraft carrier Langley (CV-1) in 1928, he tolerated Tomlinson's aerial antics--up to a point, 109-110; concern about training while serving as Chief of the Bureau of Aeronautics in 1942, 216; interaction with commercial airlines at the beginning of World War II, 226-227; as Deputy Commander in Chief Pacific late in the war, 240; discussion in 1945 about overhaul facilities for R5Ds, 254-255

Townsend, Ensign Guy Duker, USN (USNA, 1918
   Unhappy service in the mine training ship Dubuque (PG-17) during World War I, 12, 14-15, 275

Train, Rear Admiral Charles Jackson, USN (USNA, 1865)
   Tomlinson's great uncle who visited the family and talked about his experiences, 7; his widow Grace looked after Tomlinson in Washington, D.C., in the 1910s, 9-10

Training
   Norfolk Naval Air Station was the site of training for pilots and enlisted crew members in 1918, 17; pilot training for regular Navy officers at Pensacola in

1920-21, 26-31; in the early 1920s the North Island Naval Air Station conducted a training program for land-plane operations, 42-43; in 1935 Tomlinson made a pitch to Rear Admiral Ernest King about instrument training for naval aviators, 185-185; Naval Reserve aviation training in the vicinity of Kansas City, Missouri, in the late 1930s and early 1940s, 210; instrument training in the late 1940s for Military Air Transport Service pilots, 261-262

Transcontinental Air Transport
Merged with Maddux Airlines in 1929, 138; merged with Western Air Express in 1930, 139-140

Transcontinental and Western Air
Airline formed by merger in 1930, 139-140; various flights in the early 1930s, 141; aircraft acquisition in the mid-1930s, 142-150; work with Douglas on the development of the DC-1 in the 1930s, 143, 150-158; obtained the Boeing 307 Stratoliner after initial hesitation, 165-166, 194-197; equipped Northrop Gamma for operation in the stratosphere, 173-174; Howard Hughes gained control of the company, 200-204; supplied pilots for Navy service during World War II, 226-228

Transport Squadron Two (VR-2)
Role in Naval Air Transport Squadrons Pacific operations during World War II, 235-236, 240

Transport Squadron Ten (VR-10)
Role in Naval Air Transport Squadrons Pacific operations during World War II, 254

Transport Squadron 11 (VR-11)
Role in Naval Air Transport Squadrons Pacific operations during World War II, 224-225

Tunner, Major General William H., USAF (USMA, 1928)
Commanded the Berlin Airlift in 1948-49, 258-261

Twining, Lieutenant Robert B., USN (USNA, 1920)
Had to go through a hassle with Navy doctors to get cleared for aviation training in 1920, 23-24; washed out of flight training at Pensacola, 29

VE-7
Plane in which Tomlinson was flying out of San Diego in the early 1920s when he had a collision that resulted in the death of the pilot of the other aircraft, 37-40; used by Fighting Squadron Two for glide bombing and dive bombing in the mid-1920s, 84-85

VF-2
See Fighting Squadron Two (VF-2)

VR-2
See Transport Squadron Two (VR-2)

VR-10
   See Transport Squadron Ten (VR-10)

VR-11
   See Transport Squadron 11 (VR-11)

Wadsworth, James W., Jr.
   U.S. senator who went to the Navy Department after Tomlinson's father showed him a letter about problems with Navy FB-5 fighter planes in 1927, 95-96

Wagner, Rear Admiral Frank D., USN (USNA, 1915)
   Served as commanding officer of Fighting Squadron Two during operations from the aircraft carrier Langley (CV-1) in the mid-1920s, 91; as deputy chief of the Bureau of Aeronautics in World War II rationalized the use of unsafe aviators, 250

War Games
   FB-5 fighter planes from the aircraft carrier Langley (CV-1) made a successful dive-bombing attack during a war game in the mid-1920s, 93-94

Wead, Lieutenant Commander Frank W., USN (USNA, 1916)
   As commanding officer of Fighting Squadron Two in the mid-1920s asked for Tomlinson in his squadron, 82-83; began experimenting with glide bombing and dive bombing while commanding VF-2, 84-88; left the squadron after breaking his neck in an accident, 91

Weather
   Importance in aviation of being able to fly through clouds and fog, 31-32, 56; Tomlinson flew a Ford tri-motor through sub-zero weather in 1929, 131-132; Tomlinson inaugurated airway traffic control for TAT-Maddux Airlines around 1930, 138-139; difficult conditions that Tomlinson flew through in the 1930s, 159-171, 176-183; the "jet stream" was not really acknowledged until after World War II, 174-175; Air Force planes encountered St. Elmo's fire during the Berlin Airlift in 1948-49, 259-260

Wheeler Field, Oahu, Hawaii
   Army Air Corps base that was involved in mock combat between Army and Navy fighters in 1928, 106-110

Williams, Lieutenant (junior grade) Alford J., USN
   While stationed at Anacostia in the early 1920s, went to a civilian air show in Pennsylvania, 76-77; made an unauthorized landing at the Naval Academy in a VE-7 in the mid-1920s, 79

Wilson, Commander Eugene E., USN (USNA, 1908)
   As chief of staff in Aircraft Battle Squadrons, in 1928 designated the Three Seahawks to perform formation acrobatics at San Francisco and San Diego, 105-106, 112

World War I
Use of the mine training ship *Dubuque* (PG-17) in an unsuccessful attempt to put antisubmarine nets across Long Island Sound in 1917, 12; use of the *Dubuque* for East Coast convoy duty in 1918, 13-15

Wright, Burdette S.
As president of Curtiss Aeroplane Division in the 1930s was involved in various aircraft development projects, 146, 190

Wright Field, Dayton, Ohio
Site of the Army Air Corps development center in the 1930s, provided information on flying in the stratosphere, 172-173; testing of BC-1 trainer, 187; testing of NA-21 and P-36; 189-191; testing of B-17, 193-194

www.ingramcontent.com/pod-product-compliance
Lightning Source LLC
Chambersburg PA
CBHW080617170426
43209CB00007B/1450